ASIAN DEFENCE REVIEW 2014-2015

Edited by

Air Marshal

Vinod Patney

SYSM PVSM AVSM VrC (Retd)

KNOWLEDGE WORLD

KW Publishers Pvt Ltd

New Delhi

in association with

Centre for Air Power Studies

New Delhi

The Centre for Air Power Studies is an independent, non-profit, academic research institution established in 2002 under a registered Trust to undertake and promote policy-related research, study and discussion on the trends and developments in defence and military issues, especially air power and the aerospace arena, for civil and military purposes. Its publications seek to expand and deepen the understanding of defence, military power, air power and aerospace issues without necessarily reflecting the views of any institution or individuals except those of the authors.

Vinod Patney
Director General
Centre for Air Power Studies
P-284, Arjan Path
Subroto Park
New Delhi 110010

Tele: (91-11) 25699131

E-mail: capsnetdroff@gmail.com
website: www.capsindia.org

ISBN 978-93-83649-64-8

Published in India by Kalpana Shukla

KNOWLEDGE WORLD
KW Publishers Pvt Ltd
4676/21, First Floor, Ansari Road, Daryaganj, New Delhi 110002
✆ +91 11 23263498 / 43528107 ✉ knowledgeworld@vsnl.net • www.kwpub.com

2011 FPBA BEST PUBLISHERS AWARD (ENGLISH)

Printed and bound in India

Contents

Contributors

Dr **Manpreet Sethi** is a Senior Fellow at the Centre for Air Power Studies, New Delhi.

Dr **Sitakanta Mishra** is a Research Fellow at the Centre for Air Power Studies, New Delhi.

Dr **Shalini Chawla** is a Senior Fellow at the Centre for Air Power Studies, New Delhi.

Ms **Chandra Rekha** is an Associate Fellow at the Centre for Air Power Studies, New Delhi.

Ms **Sana Hashmi** is an Associate Fellow at the Centre for Air Power Studies, New Delhi.

Ms **Debalina Ghoshal** is an Associate Fellow at the Centre for Air Power Studies, New Delhi.

Wg Cdr **M K Sharma** is a Research Fellow at the Centre for Air Power Studies, New Delhi.

Mr **Dilipraj E** is an Associate Fellow at the Centre for Air Power Studies, New Delhi.

Wg Cdr **Nishant Gupta** is a Research Fellow at the Centre for Air Power Studies, New Delhi.

Gp Capt **Mondar Bandopadhyay** is a Senior Fellow at the Centre for Air Power Studies, New Delhi.

1

China's Nuclear Power Programme: Status, Prospects and Challenges

Manpreet Sethi

Introduction

Energy, in the form of electricity, is the biggest driver of economic growth in modern times. It is widely accepted that electricity has a direct connect with the economic well-being of a nation and per capita energy consumption is an accepted parameter for rating nations on the Human Development Index (HDI). Therefore, it is hardly surprising that energy, and the ability of a nation to access it from reliable, secure, sustainable, and safe sources tops national priorities everywhere. Energy poverty is considered a handicap for any nation and particularly so for one that is aspiring for fast track economic growth and social development.

China, which has witnessed an average double digit economic growth for well over two decades, understands this reality better than most nations. Former Chinese Premier Jiang Zemin, said rather graphically in a speech at a meeting with energy experts attending a forum on "Reflections on Energy Issues in China", "Energy is the food of industry and the lifeblood of the national economy."[1] Indeed, China's rapid socio-economic transformation, which is today being studied as a model of economic growth unprecedented in history, has been enabled by a phenomenal growth in its electricity production and consumption. In fact, it is mind boggling to see some of the facts that dot China's growth in electricity generation.

This paper examines the role of nuclear energy in the electricity mix of China. After a brief summary of the phenomenal growth in the electricity generation capacity of the country over the last three decades, the paper identifies the major drivers for its nuclear power programme as well as the manner in which the programme has developed to reach a point where 25 reactors are operational today even if the share of nuclear electricity in the total electricity mix is still at a low 2 percent. Yet, it is seen as a fuel of great future potential. The paper maps out the ambitious plans for nuclear expansion, as well as the desire of China to emerge as a major exporter of nuclear reactors, technology and equipment in the coming decade. Of course, this is unlikely to be a smooth ride. The paper concludes by identifying the challenges and making an assessment of the ability of China to reach the high targets that it has set for itself.

China's Electricity Growth Story

From a total electricity production base of only 282 billion kWh (kilo watt hours) in 1979, China is today the largest electricity producer at 4,604 billion kWh or approximately 1,250 GW (Giga Watt), (compared to India's 835 billion kWh or roughly 200 GW). Electricity production has grown at an average annual rate of nearly 10.8 percent over the last decade, with the increase of installed generation capacity touching a phenomenal 19 percent in the last two years. This has amounted to adding about 80-90 GW production every year. Interestingly, the electricity addition to China in one year is the total production of many smaller developed countries such as the UK!

The World Bank recognises China's electricity development as one of the lynchpins for its poverty alleviation efforts over the last 30 years. It has estimated that during this period, China provided electricity to 400 million people. Per capita electricity consumption is believed to have increased from 260 kWh in 1978[2] to 3,510 kWh in 2012[3]. And yet China's per capita electricity consumption is nowhere near the Organisation of Economic Cooperation and Development (OECD) average of 8,000 kWh.

In fact, the country faces a wide gap in its electricity demand and supply. Despite rapid and significant additions and a relative economic slowdown, the projected annual electricity demand is still pitted at 6.7 percent. This is obviously the result of the fact that China is the second biggest economy in the world. Further, the economic growth is anchored in industrial production, especially of the kind of manufacturing that is electricity dependent. Compared to a situation where 20 percent of the industry needs were serviced by electricity in 2000, this figure today stands at 28 percent. Meanwhile, rapid urbanisation has also contributed to the increase in electricity demand since the urban middle class has requirements for infrastructure and domestic consumption that hinge on electricity availability.

In order to meet the needs of its economic growth, premised on industrial production and causing urbanisation, China turned to the rapid addition of thermal power plants through the 1980s and 1990s to provide low cost electricity. However, this has exposed the country to two new and interrelated challenges. The first relates to energy security since China's dependence on external fuel resources has substantively increased from the happy situation in the 1960s when the country was largely self-sufficient in energy. The present energy vulnerability poses a threat to the nation's economic security, and, consequently, has become a driver for national security strategies. As Jiang Zemin pointed out in his speech in 2008, "Given that assurance of a steady supply of energy is a strategic issue confronting our country's development, we must accord energy an important place in our country's overall development strategy and focus on it unequivocally."[4] Evidence of the gravity that was attached to this view can be seen in the decision of January 2010 when China established a National Energy Commission (NEC), directed by none less than Premier Wen Jiabao. And amongst the many measures that he sought to set in place to redress the situation has been directing the NEC to work on improving the country's energy strategy by creating national energy development plans, reviewing energy security, and coordinating international cooperation to put in place a network of sources to keep China supplied with the necessary energy sources.

The second challenge to the quick economic growth and the need to rapidly power it with fossil fuel resources is the price which China is today having to pay in the form of environmental and health mitigation costs owing to the high air pollution and environmental degradation that has occurred in the process. China realises the folly of this since it is estimated by the World Bank to cause an economic loss of nearly 6.5 percent to its Gross Domestic Product (GDP).[5] Having a high economic growth but frittering away its benefits in paying for health and environmental alleviation does not make for a sound policy. Not surprisingly, therefore, the focus from at least the late 1990s has been on intensifying the search for, and exploitation of, clean and reliable energy sources.

It is in this context that China has turned to nuclear power in a big way, besides wind and solar. In the new millennium, China embarked on the world's most ambitious nuclear power programme which envisages increasing the share of nuclear electricity from a lowly 2 percent today to 11 percent by 2040. A 2012 White Paper on Energy Policy mentions nuclear power in the context of "raising the proportion of clean, low-carbon fossil energy and non-fossil energy in the energy mix". Of course, it must be mentioned that China has the world's largest renewable energy programme too. It aims to double and triple its hydro, wind and solar generated electricity in just the next five years. In fact, the country seems to be pursuing all electricity sources with equal focus and vigour, keeping the big picture of its energy requirement in view.

In this context, it is of significance that Beijing has reiterated its nuclear plans even in the wake of the incident at Fukushima which cast a shadow over the future of nuclear power across nations. Some countries in Europe have declared a nuclear phase-out. But China, after a slight pause for undertaking a safety assessment of its plants, has announced staying the course. New nuclear plants have been approved in 2015 and the construction of 25 of the earlier plants is progressing simultaneously. The country plans to spend $370 billion between 2015-25 and triple the nuclear capacity from the current about 20 GW to 58 GW by 2020.[6] Why is China continuing its focus on nuclear power? The following section identifies the rationale for the country's nuclear programme.

Drivers of China's Nuclear Energy Ambitions

Rising Energy Demand

China averaged an economic growth rate of 9.6 percent during 1980-2010. Industrialisation, and the resultant urbanisation that saw the migration of more than 200 million people from the rural to the urban areas over 30 years, and which continues unabated, keeps China in a situation where energy demand continues to outstrip supply despite the huge addition to the country's overall electricity production. Installed generating capacity increased 10.06 percent to 962 Giga Watt electric (GWe) in 2010 and by a further 90.0 GWe in 2011.[7] President Zemin well recognised that a phenomenal increase in electricity was inevitable when he stated in his speech in 2008 that the "development course of developed countries indicates that the energy consumption of a country during the early and middle stages of industrialization typically experiences a period of rapid growth…It is during the late stage of industrialization or the post-industrial phase that energy consumption goes down."[8] China is yet many years away from reaching that stage. The central drivers of its energy demand continue to be its increasing population, growth in the manufacturing industry (despite a relative slowdown owing to global recession), infrastructure requirements, and a rising middle class that is consuming and demanding more and more electricity.

China first began to experience an electricity deficit in the 1980s with the opening of the economy to market oriented reforms. As industrial manufacturing and infrastructure development picked up pace, electricity demand grew at a staggering monthly rate of 15 percent.[9] In order to meet the electricity demand as rapidly as it could, China built coal-fired plants at a hasty pace. Consequently, the proportion of coal in total energy consumption had increased to 76.2 percent in 1990.[10] The availability of cheap electricity certainly enabled industrial production to sustain the economic growth. But it also quickly raised China's position to the second biggest carbon dioxide emitting nation in the world.

Rising Environmental Problems

Focussed purely on economic growth upto the 2000s, China cared little for the environmental crisis that it was creating for itself and others, or for the long-term implications that this would have on its economy by draining its growth statistics in environmental and health mitigation costs. During this period, China resented international pressure on making any changes in its development strategy and considered climate change and pollution as concerns crafted by the Western developed nations to slow/deny growth to the developing countries.

However, by the dawn of the new millennium, China had begun to realise that it was as much a victim of the climate change that it had also contributed to. A need was then felt to take measures that would reduce Greenhouse Gas (GHG) emissions. These were then articulated in the 11th national Five-Year Plan (2005-10), primarily at two levels. One, by increasing the focus on energy conservation and energy efficiency; second, by mandating the shutdown of coal-fired power plants. The 11th Plan, for instance, introduced a self-imposed national target of a 20 percent reduction in energy intensity by 2010. It identified 50 GWe of small and more than 20-year-old coal-fired plants and ordered their demolition, a target that was achieved ahead of schedule in 2009. Another 11 GWe of coal plants was phased out in 2010.[11] Accordingly, the contribution of coal to the total energy production came down from 76.2 percent to 68 percent by 2010. More recently, steel production has been lowered as one way of reducing electricity demand and thereby reducing the pressure on the environment. Forty three percent of the world's steel-making capacity resides in China and a quarter of that is located in Hebei province. It is a matter of little surprise then that seven of the top ten most polluted Chinese cities are in this province. Further, in order to make up for the generation capacity that would be lost due to the shutting down of plants, the emphasis shifted to building more renewable and nuclear plants.

Rising Economic Implications

Besides the environmental cost of use of coal, the economic implication of this has been evident in the logistics problem of transporting coal from where it is mined in the northeast to where it is required in the coastal southeast. According to the International Atomic Energy Agency (IAEA), 48 percent of the railway capacity, 50 percent of the waterway capacity and 25 percent of the highway capacity are locked up in transporting coal.[12]

This heavy reliance on coal which translated into the existence of about 500 coal-fired plants, has not only has brought the problem of air pollution with 40 percent of China suffering from acid rain, but also resulted in an economic loss of 3-7 percent of GDP.[13] Deteriorating health as a result of environmental degradation imposes an additional economic burden on the state due to loss of labour and productive work hours as a result of sickness. According to a 2007 World Bank report entitled, "The Cost of Pollution in China: Economic Estimates of Physical Damage", the total cost of air and water pollution damage to China's economy is a loss of 5.8 percent of the GDP annually.[14] It has also been estimated that 750,000 people die in China of pollution related illness every year.[15]

With realisation and acknowledgement of this reality that was a drag on the Chinese economy, the focus shifted to nuclear power (and renewable energy) in a big way in order to replace the lost electrical output from phasing out of old and inefficient coal plants by an environment friendly source. This partially explains the pick-up in China's nuclear energy development from 2000 onwards compared to the relatively slow pace in the 1980s and 1990s. According to the mid to long-term plans of the National Development and Reform Commission (NDRC) for the period 2005-20, China's low carbon electricity resources would include hydro power at the top at 300 GW, and nuclear at second position at 60 GW, ahead of wind power at 30 GW, biomass at 5.5 GW and solar power at 1.8 GW.[16]

Fig 1: China's Energy Mix, 2015

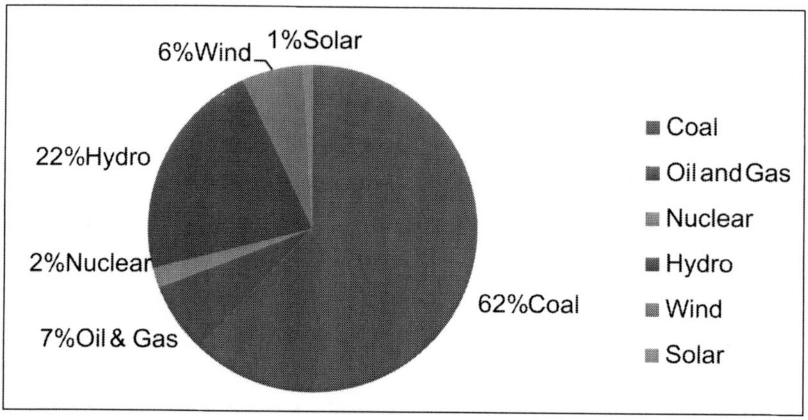

According to an IAEA study undertaken in the early 1990s on a comparative assessment of different energy sources, GHG emissions from the entire upstream and downstream activities involved in electricity generation for a nuclear power plant are nearly 40-100 times lower than for other fossil fuel chains. In fact, GHG emissions from the nuclear power chain are mainly due to use of fossil fuels in the extraction, processing and enrichment of uranium as well as the production of steel and cement used in the construction of reactors.[17]

It is not surprising, therefore, that China has included nuclear power in a large scale utilisation to decarbonise its electricity sector in order to maintain a sustainable economic growth. In fact, by doing so, China will find itself better equipped to meet binding GHG cutback targets compared to other nations. As pointed out by CJ Yang based on his study of the differences in the political and industrial structures of China and the USA, "If China decides to decarbonize its electricity with nuclear power, the US would not be able to match China's pace in reducing GHG emissions."[18]

To sum up, in the words of former Premier Jiang Zemin, China faces the "urgent task of blazing a new and distinctively Chinese trail in energy development in order to achieve its strategic goal of modernization at the lowest possible cost to its energy resources and the environment."[19] In January 2010, whilst at the helm of the National Energy Commission, Chinese Premier Wen Jiabao had admitted that China's growth had been "unbalanced, uncoordinated and unsustainable."[20]

Approach to Nuclear Power

The Early Years

Though China had exploded its nuclear weapon in 1964 and became a nuclear weapon state under the nuclear Non-Proliferation Treaty (NPT), it turned to peaceful use of nuclear energy nearly two decades later. Compared to the other major powers exploiting nuclear fission for generating electricity, China is, therefore, a late entrant. The first nuclear plant at Qinshan (Zheijang province), which was of 300 Mega Watt electric (MWe) and domestically designed, was connected to the grid for electricity production only in December 1991. Two nuclear plants of 900 MWe capacity each, imported from France, were the next to follow at Daya Bay (Guangdong province) in 1994.

As has been stated earlier, the pace of the Chinese nuclear reactor construction really picked up only in the 2000s. And, it is to the credit of the famed Chinese determination that once China had decided to move on from the objective of "moderately develop nuclear power" as outlined in the 9th Five-Year Plan (1996-2000) to "actively promote nuclear energy" in the 11th Plan (2006-10), it put its official machinery and resources into achieving it. Indeed, a number of reactors were constructed between 2000 and 2010 and China today has 24 operational nuclear plants contributing about 2 percent to the country's total electricity production. With eyes set on achieving targets as high as 58 GWe (from the present level of 20 GWe) by 2020 and 200 GWe by 2030, the country today has 25 reactors, the maximum number ever to be simultaneously constructed.[21] Considering that in 2009 China had a 10 GWe nuclear production which had doubled by 2013, the targets that the county has set for itself appear attainable. This is supported by the fact that China has today developed its own Pressurised Heavy Water Reactor

(PWR) design of a 1,000 MWe plant (which it also intends to export), has expanded uranium exploration and mining, including in other countries, and has the full fuel cycle capability.

An interesting feature of China's nuclear programme is the exploitation of different technologies and generations of reactors from France, the USA, Russia and Canada. Instead of standardising on one type of reactor technology (such as light water reactors in the case of the USA and pressurised heavy water reactors in the case of India), China adopted a strategy of importing whatever technology it could from whichever country was willing to offer it on good terms. By following such a strategy of purchasing the best available technology, China circumvented the need to wait for its own technology to mature, and thus, could quickly expand the share of nuclear energy in its energy basket.

The experience of each type of technology has then been used to "adapt, change and finally build their own" domestically designed, second generation nuclear reactors—the Comprehensive Nuclear Power (CNP)-1000 and the Chinese Pressurised Reactor (CPR)-1000.[22] Many of these are planned to be constructed in the coming years. However, the State Council Research Office (SCRO) did caution the Chinese government through a report in 2010 that the country should not build too many of the second generation reactors given that they have a life term of nearly 50-70 years and would be in operation only in the 2060s when the rest of the world would have moved to Generation IV reactors. The SCRO, therefore, recommended restraining the construction of this generation of reactors to what has already been planned, which itself amounts to a total of 57 GWe if all of them were to be constructed and become operational, and to graduate instead to a newer level of technology. That China is moving in this direction is evident from the fact that it is engaged in designing a Generation III+ reactor with France, and also with the USA.

It has mostly been decided that the future reactors in China would be the Generation III AP 1000 of Westinghouse. In October 2009, two Chinese firms, the State Nuclear Power Technological Corporation (SNPTC) and China National Nuclear Corporation (CNNC) entered into an agreement with Westinghouse to co-develop and refine the AP 1000 design for large scale domestic construction. Since China is looking at building nearly two dozen of these in the coming years, it would be able to enjoy cost efficiency that comes with mass production of this nature. Indeed, this is being sold as the positive dimension of this large scale expansion that would undercut the criticism of the high cost of nuclear reactor construction. Building a number of identical nuclear power plants would bring the benefit of economies of scale for a number of related ancillary industries, thereby, adding to the overall economic growth and job opportunities in the country.

What has Changed after Fukushima?

In the wake of Fukushima, China announced a temporary suspension of approval for new nuclear power projects as it carried out a safety assessment of all its reactors – those in operation and those under construction. A national inspection group comprising the National Energy Administration (NEA), the National Nuclear Safety Administration and the China Earthquake Administration was instituted for the purpose. A series of Research and Development (R&D) projects was launched by the NEA in February 2012 to improve plant safety-related technology and emergency preparedness in the event of an extreme disaster beyond design basis. The dictum for now appears to be "steady development with safety". In May 2012, a new safety plan was issued and put out for public comments. Further, in October 2012, speaking on the occasion of the release of a White Paper on Energy Policy, Premier Jinping revoked the suspension, and reiterated the ambitious nuclear plans. He, however, laid the utmost emphasis on safety, insisting that the new reactors comply with the new-generation safety standards. As per China's 12th Five-Year Plan, $ 13 billion will be spent on improving nuclear safety at the operating and under construction nuclear reactors. So, in theory, China appears to be staying the course on its nuclear plans.

However, for nuclear energy to retain its position in the energy mix of nations, even in China and India where there is a clear logic for it, it has become extremely important for the nuclear establishments to win public confidence in the safety of nuclear reactors. The need for this is evident in China too which has traditionally been closed to the idea of engaging with the public on this issue. In fact, China has had a nuclear power programme planned and executed by the state. While this is not very different from the manner in which nuclear programmes have been managed in countries such as France and India, where the role of private industry is limited, there are two points of difference. One, since the Chinese Constitution does not allow private land ownership, land acquisition issues for construction of nuclear power plants have not been very contentious in China. Secondly, legal challenges to nuclear projects, as have been common in the USA, are not possible in China since there is no judicial independence. As put by a scholar, "The Chinese government considers its economic plans equivalent to law… The Chinese national plan is far more forceful than the government plans in Western democracies."[23]

Owing to these factors, China's nuclear power growth has had a relatively smooth run over the last decade and a half. The government has sold the plants as a viable solution to meeting the rising electricity demand in a reliable and environmentally friendly manner. But post Fukushima, as public concerns on plant safety have grown, the need for the government to become more sensitive to the public mood has also increased. This has brought in a new dimension to nuclear decision-making in China. Indeed, public protests on setting up new nuclear plants have hit China too. This was starkly brought out when the plan to build a $ 6 billion uranium processing plant in Guangdong province had to be cancelled in July 2013 in deference to public protests over health and environmental fears. This was attributed to "breakdown of trust, post Fukushima, in official assurances of public safety".[24] Not too surprisingly, however, the overall impact on the numbers of nuclear reactors planned before and after Fukushima has largely been the same as is evident from the chart below.

Fig 2: Nuclear Power Reactors in China

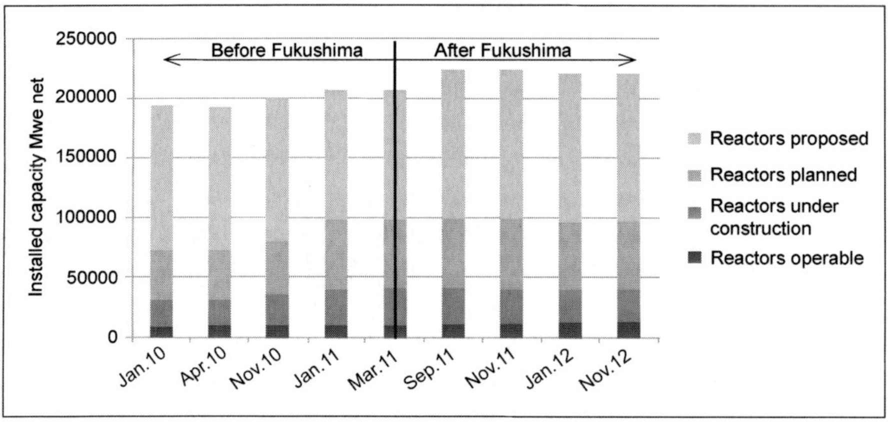

Source: http://www.mining.com, January 29, 2013.

The outlook in China is clear that it needs nuclear energy to meet the rapidly increasing electricity demand to power the industrial production and economic growth of the country in an environmentally sustainable manner. Indeed, China realises the centrality of electricity generated from environmentally friendly sources, in order to keep up an economy that relies on energy intensive manufacturing. A large proportion of industries in China such as metallurgy, chemical engineering and building materials involve high energy consumption. These industries, in fact, account for 47.9 percent of total energy consumption in all industries.[25]

But, the access to modern amenities has also awakened the substantive Chinese middle class to its right to a more participative decision-making that takes cognisance of its concerns and fears. According to one view, "As middle class Chinese realise that their voices are being suppressed, that their access to information is being blocked, and that their space for social action is being unduly confined, increased political dissent may take shape."[26]

Fukushima, in this context, has emerged as a rallying platform to make this demand with somewhat greater stridency. Therefore, today's China is compelled to meet its energy requirements while respecting public sentiment. How will this happen? The next section examines the challenges that the nuclear power programme is likely to face.

Challenges for China's Nuclear Programme

Like in every other country exploiting nuclear power for electricity generation, the people in China too expressed concerns about nuclear safety after the nuclear incident at Fukushima in 2011. Public disquiet has resulted in a dilemma for the world's second biggest economy. As it has economically and politically integrated itself with the rest of the world and seen the quality of life in the Western hemisphere, its increasingly connected citizens have also developed an awareness of a sense of relative deprivation, which especially affects the youth. Inequalities have always been a part of society and people have lived with them. But the problem arises, as has been the case in every revolution in history, when the deprived become increasingly conscious of their unequal situation and desirous of change. Jasjit Singh, one of India's leading national security strategists, had once noted, "Human expectations inevitably keep growing with human progress... But if expectations start rising at a rate far exceeding the rate at which achievement and satisfaction of those expectations rise, social turbulence starts to increase."[27]

The leadership of the Communist Party of China (CPC) is particularly fearful of social instability that could threaten economic development and the Party's political legitimacy. Ever since taking power in 2012, Premier Xi Jinping has repeatedly announced that maintaining social stability would be his topmost priority. He believes that "winning or losing public support is an issue that concerns the CPC's survival or extinction"[28].Warning his Party's elites that they have "grown too lazy, too insulated from the people and lived too lavishly"[29], he has encouraged sobriety in public behaviour by the affluent and seemingly taken steps to address the much resented problem of corruption. Given the authoritarian nature of the state, China has been known to enforce order by controlling information and guiding the perceptions of the people in accordance with Party formulations. The state propaganda machinery has managed this by colouring all state activity with "Chinese characteristics." As Jasjit Singh writes, "It is under such stratagem that China managed its double-digit growth and phenomenal rise for more than two decades, while maintaining politically authoritarian governance."[30] But, rapidly altered expectations are not that easy to control in modern times with the Information and Communication Technology (ICT) revolution. Hence, the challenge before China is huge. Despite the many controls,

Chinese citizens have been known to have deployed smart phones and used the social media to organise protest campaigns. In fact, Chinese official estimates suggest that 100,000 mass incidents (which according to China is any protest involving more than 100 participants) occur every year. Interestingly, China's official budget for 2012 accounts for $ 109 billion for military spending and $ 114 billion for police and public security.[31]

In fact, meeting popular expectations brings the focus on the need for China to balance four competing objectives – sustained and high economic growth to redress poverty; increasing electricity access to the population to ensure continued economic growth and, consequently, improving the standard of living; increasing electricity production from environmentally sustainable energy sources; and, lastly, managing the more aware and aspirational Chinese middle class as it gets used to better standards of living and demands even better social services and environmental protection. This is a tall order for any nation, but when it is posed to the most populous country in the world, the challenges get magnified manifold.

Nuclear power has been conceived of as one way of addressing China's energy poverty by keeping a low carbon economy. But, the information and communication revolution has magnified public apprehensions post-Fukushima. A traditionally closed nuclear decision-making has to handle this issue sensitively through better communication and newer skills. *The Global Times*, a Chinese tabloid owned by the *People's Daily*, the state run newspaper, blamed an "opaque and unreasonable decision-making process" for the cancellation of the project and called on local governments to "establish a system that fosters consultations between officials and the public".[32] Until now, these entities have worked in a closed manner in decision-making and operations. But in the changed environment after Fukushima, the only way to win back public support for nuclear energy will have to include a far greater interaction with the people to explain to them the reasons for the selection of a particular site, the basics of the reactor technology, the redundancies built into operations, etc. Will the changing social dynamics of China, which ironically has been triggered by betterment of the economic status of the masses and access to electricity that runs the ICT, have political repercussions? This is a question difficult to answer at this moment but it is a situation to watch out for.

In fact, the question to ask is whether China can change this attitude without changing its closed political system? Or will it be able to exploit its "unique blend of centralization and decentralization that has sustained growth for a historically unprecedented 30 years"?[33] As explained by a former chief economic adviser to the Government of India, China follows a system in which the overall guidance on the broad directions of growth is provided by the Party. But then it is left to every level of the government and Party, as also in every state and province, to experiment on how best to achieve the objective. Their ability to achieve the growth objective then becomes the measure of their performance and they are rewarded accordingly "through promotion and economic opportunities."[34] Local leaders adopt their strategies to bridge national priorities with local interests. They strengthen formal incentives and create informal ones. During the course of the research for this paper, an article that explains this process in the context of how China has complied with energy efficiency mandates appeared most relevant for the nuclear domain as well.[35] As the authors highlight, the local officials were able to "convert national energy saving policies from a conservation-oriented and restrained development framework into local growth models aimed at creating expanded production, improving enterprise competitiveness, ensuring stable employment and addressing growing regulatory demands at the local level."[36] In the case of nuclear power too, it is possible that the local administrations in the province became far more proactive in engaging the public on the need and safety aspects of nuclear power. In this, a government that runs on Party cadres might be able to provide a far more penetrated network to reach out to the public to assuage its concerns. But, this is an area where further academic research is possible.

Meanwhile, two points of focus are evident on the basis of which Beijing is trying to build public support for its nuclear expansion plans. The first of these is to sell nuclear energy as a necessary solution to the problem of environmental pollution. At a recent Party Congress, the leaders seriously deliberated on the problem of chronic smog over several industrial cities of China and agreed to declare a "war on pollution"[37]. The nuclear programme is seen as part of the solution to this problem. Secondly, the export of domestic reactors, technology and equipment is also being used to validate national nuclear plans.

China has articulated plans to emerge as a major nuclear supplier in the coming years. It already has three customers in Argentina, Romania and Pakistan. The last in fact has been a long time taker of Chinese nuclear products (including nuclear weapons materials and designs) and already has Chinese supplied nuclear reactors operational and plans for several more despite being in violation of the guidelines of the Nuclear Suppliers Group (NSG) which does not approve of nuclear commerce with non-NPT states. China will be supplying a large portion of the financing and technical expertise for its nuclear reactor supplies to all the three countries. As of now, the UK is the only Western client of China and its contract to build and operate a nuclear reactor here is co-shouldered with Electricite de France.

However, in order to bag a bigger piece of the pie of international nuclear commerce, China has to overcome two significant challenges. The first of these relates to the lack of technological confidence in the reactors that it is selling. The indigenous Generation III reactors that China has on the market have been certified by its own regulatory authority only in 2014 and there is no such reactor operating in China as of now. It would take at least another five years for such a plant to come up and become operational in China to instill confidence in others. While China has adapted this from the technologies that it received from Westinghouse GE, it has the licence to sell it as its own. Given that China's nuclear reactors have little experience with international level stringent regulatory requirements, the confidence of countries importing these reactors, even if the price that China is offering is competitive, is relatively low as the memory of Fukushima is high. Reports such as the one put out by French nuclear regulators suggesting that "Chinese officials were understaffed and unprepared for the size of their nuclear programme" further undermine the confidence in its nuclear industry.[38] Issues continue to be raised on the safety and regulatory practices of China given that there is a veil of opacity on many of these issues.

The second problem afflicting China's exports is more internal, arising as it does from the presence of a number of state owned nuclear companies. The currently operational 24 nuclear reactors in China are under the ownership of either the SNPTC, CNNC, China Power Investment Corporation (CPIC) or China General Nuclear Power Corporation (CGNPC). Many of these also have individual bilateral arrangements with foreign nuclear industries such as Areva or Westinghouse for nuclear technology transfers or for research and development of the next generation of reactors. This leads to a conflict of interest as different Chinese firms plan to market separate versions that compete with each other. Realising this problem, the Chinese leadership has undertaken a reorganisation of the domestic nuclear sector in recent times. One example of this is the merger of the SNPTC with the CPIC to form a new company called the State Power Investment Group (SPIG). This would be merging the capability of the SNPTC to build Generation III reactors with the licensing authority of the CPIC to construct and operate reactors, thereby making SPIG a one stop shop for buying, building and operating nuclear power plants. More such restructuring may be on the anvil.

Conclusion

Just about four years after Fukushima, on February 27, 2015, the Ministry of Environmental Protection approved the construction of two new nuclear reactors in China. These will be the AP 1000 third generation reactors built by Westinghouse. News is also in that the provinces of Hunan and Hebei have been lobbying with the central government for permission for the start of construction of inland reactors, a decision that the country had suspended in the wake of Fukushima. As it appears then, the country is keen to realise the nuclear aims that it has set for itself. As stated by one analyst, "China has a sense of urgency that is not felt elsewhere, and for good reason. Its cities are choked in smog, and aside from needing more electricity to power its growing economy, it also needs to find cleaner sources of power and shut down some coal plants."[39]

Continued buoyant economic growth in China over the last three decades has been enabled by a huge jump in electricity production. This has, in turn, ignited an insatiable thirst for more electricity to drive industrialisation, urbanisation and prosperity – processes that are perceived to be part of socio-economic development. As a result of this, concerns about energy security, environmental protection and climate change have coalesced in the Chinese consciousness over the last 15 years. While the country well understands the importance of sustained economic growth to realise its socio-economic transformation to a middle income nation, it is also keen to stay this course through a low carbon route so as to avoid repeating the mistakes it made in the early years of its rapid economic growth. In order to achieve this objective, China is focussing on a broad spectrum of measures ranging from improving energy efficiency to mastering carbon capture and storage technologies to increasing the share of non-fossil fuels in its total energy mix.

It is from this menu of options that China is exploiting that this paper has studied the case of nuclear power as one of the ingredients for the transformation of its energy system. But as is evident, its nuclear power programme plays a role beyond fulfilling the need for electricity. Popular sentiment on nuclear power after Fukushima has emerged as a manifestation of the dilemmas that China faces, and will face, as its population gains access to electricity and begins to exploit it in all aspects of life.

Deeper penetration of ICT in society through greater access to electricity has not only brought benign socio-economic transformation but has also posed political challenges of new types. As pointed out by a young Indian economist, China is "moving to a new stage, one in which costs and public reaction matter".[40] Chinese leaders can no longer afford to be focussed on fast growth alone. They are compelled by China's new reality to be more concerned about anger over inflation and threats to social stability. For example, as Sharma points out, Beijing recently "banned billboards advertising luxury goods, not to restrain spending but to avoid stirring up resentment. Whereas Deng Xiaoping proclaimed that 'it's glorious to be rich', his successors are making sure no one gets too rich."[41]

The ruling party cannot afford issues that stoke popular revolt given that resentment on economic inequality is sub-surface in the current stage of China's socio-economic transformation. "Dying for Development" is the phrase that a recent issue of the journal *China Quarterly*, used to explain the dilemma for China. It wrote, "The Chinese state and many of its citizens are dying for development in the sense that they yearn for it, but also in the sense that they suffer from its side effects."[42] Industrialisation and urbanisation (both demanding huge electricity generation capacities) are vital for poverty alleviation but the manner in which this electricity is generated and the use to which it is put has implications for the environment and the health of the citizens. Therefore, striking a balance between sustainability and development poses a live challenge for modern China. The implications of how it resolves this will go beyond the mere economic to much deeper issues such as the emergence of citizens' initiatives, public activism, state-society relations, social justice, etc. New faultlines are evident and the Chinese leadership is well aware of this.

Ironically, while China has grown stronger in its military might and has a more assertive foreign policy today, its leaders appear more insecure at home and fearful of domestic challenges. Therefore, maintaining economic growth is critical for maintaining stability at home and retaining the legitimacy of the Party. The handling of the nuclear issue will be worth monitoring in this context. The nuclear establishment and the government will have to be more receptive to public views on the matter and undertake more proactive engagement. Otherwise, if the state attempts to steamroll opposition to new nuclear sites, nuclear energy may well end up 'powering' more than just economic growth and social transformation in China.

Indeed, China appears to be in a race with itself to reach the stiff nuclear energy targets that it has set. While the country's turn to clean, low carbon fuels would be of great benefit for not just its own citizens but also for global warming, it is of equally critical importance that the goal is pursued keeping utmost focus on nuclear safety. Stringent and effective regulatory mechanisms are imperative. Because any one mistake by the nuclear industry anywhere would have a serious impact on nuclear programmes worldwide. Therefore, in a sense, China's nuclear power programme is also carrying on its shoulders not just the dreams of its own people but also the future of the nuclear industry worldwide.

Notes

1. Speech as reproduced in Jiang Zemin, *Research on Energy Issues in China*, trans by Central Translation Bureau, Beijing (Burlington, MA, USA: Elsevier Academic Press, 2008), p.4.
2. Sang Dongli, "Nuclear Energy Development in China", in Xu Yi-chong, ed., *Nuclear Energy Development in Asia: Problems and Prospects* (New York: Palgrave Macmillan, 2011), p. 56.
3. World Nuclear Association, "Nuclear Power in China", http://www.world-nuclear.org, March 2015.
4. Zemin, n.1, p. 3.
5. "Costs of China's Air Pollution and Cost to Greatly Reduce the Problem", http://www.thenextbigfuture.com, March 18, 2015.
6. "China will Spend $370 Billion Building Nuclear Reactors over the Next Decade", http://www.thenextbigfuture.com, March 2015.
7. Ibid.
8. Zemin, n.1, p. 10.
9. Wei Zhihong, "China's Challenging Fast Track", *IAEA Bulletin*, vol.46, no.1, 2004.
10. Zemin, n.1, p. 23.
11. World Nuclear Association, "Nuclear Power in China", http://www.world-nuclear.org, March 2015.
12. As cited in Chris Meyer, "China and Nuclear Energy: Solving an Energy Crisis – Part 4", *Energize*, March 2011, p. 18.
13. Zhihong, n. 9.
14. Xu Yi-chong, "Nuclear Energy in Asia: An Overview", in Yi-chong, ed., n.2, p. 6.
15. Ibid., p. 6. Of course, not all these deaths are due to air pollution. Rather, modernisation, industrialisation and urbanisation have happened in China with a sole focus on economic growth, and the scant regard for the environment has led to pollution of all kinds, including of water and food. Exposure to heavy metals from industries, excessive use of chemicals in agriculture and addition of noxious substances during food production have led to "cancer villages" and "diseases of transition" caused by this uneven transition from poverty to affluence. For more, see Special Section on "Dying for Development", *China Quarterly*, no. 214, June 2013.
16. As cited in Chi-Jen Yang, "A Comparison of the Nuclear Options for Greenhouse Gas Mitigation in China and in the United States", *Energy Policy*, vol. 39, 2011, p. 3027
17. For more on this see, HR Hans and K Arshad, "Comparing Energy Options – Progress Report on the Inter-Agency Decades Project, *International Atomic Energy Agency Bulletin*, vol. 40, no.1, 1998, pp 2-7.
18. Yang, n. 16, p. 3028.
19. Zemin, n.1, p. 25.
20. Ruchir Sharma, *Breakout Nations: In Pursuit of the Next Economic Miracle* (London: Penguin Books Ltd., 2012), p. 17.
21. "Nuclear Energy in China: Views and Prospects from the OECD Nuclear Energy Agency's Perspective", in *China in Focus: Lessons and Challenges* (Paris: OECD, 2012) as available at http://www.oecd.org/china, p. 115.
22. Ibid., p. 116.
23. Yang, n. 16, p.3027.
24. Charlie Zhu, "Public Trust Crisis Threatens China's Nuclear Power Ambitions', *Reuters*, July 18, 2013.
25. Zemin, n.1, p. 74.
26. Cheng Li and Ryan McElveen, "Can Xi's Governing Strategy Succeed?", *Current History*, September 2013, p. 208.

27. Jasjit Singh, "Revolution in Human Affairs", *Cadmus*, vol. 1, no.2, April 2011, p. 118.
28. As cited in "China Protest Forcing Nuclear Retreat Shows People Power", *Bloomberg News*, July 15, 2013.
29. Minxin Pei, "The Here and Mao", *Indian Express*, October 19, 2013.
30. Singh, n. 27, p. 119.
31. Li and McElveen, n. 26, p. 209.
32. Ibid.
33. Arvind Virmani, "A Right to Growth", *Indian Express*, October 21, 2013
34. Ibid.
35. Genia Kostka and William Hobbs, "Local Energy Efficiency Policy Implementation in China: Bridging the Gap between National Priorities and Local Interests", *China Quarterly*, vol. 211, September 2012, pp. 765-785.
36. Ibid., p. 784.
37. Shannon Tiezzi, "Why China Will Go All-in on Nuclear Power", *The Diplomat*, October 8, 2014
38. Keith Johnson, "Nuclear Renaissance, Redux", *Foreign Policy*, March 23, 2015
39. Nick Cunnigham, "China Moves Forward with New Nuclear Reactors", http://www.thenextbigfuture.com, March 2, 2015
40. Sharma, n. 20, p. 17
41. Ibid., p. 25
42. Yi-chong, n. 14, p. 245.

2

Zero Justifiable Gains: Lessons from Cold War TNW Discourse

Sitakanta Mishra

The concept, evolution, and significance of Tactical Nuclear Weapons (TNWs) remained contested both during the Cold War and in the post-Cold War era. This is evident from the fact that TNWs have not been employed even in situations where their use was seriously considered; and despite the end of the Cold War, they continue to be integral to the nuclear strategy of the North Atlantic Treaty Organisation (NATO) and Russia. The future role of these weapons is a matter of speculation, but the choice for development and deployment of TNWs by both the superpowers was "a major decision not reached lightly" and "continues to be a point of concern to this day."[1] Given the "high level military ambivalence about the utility of nuclear weapons in a tactical role"[2] during the Cold War, the *raison d'être* of Pakistan's strategy needs serious introspection since neither India nor Pakistan's nuclear postures are based on those of the Cold War. Revisiting the Cold War perspectives on TNWs would help in drawing inferences for the South Asian nuclear discourse though the geo-political contexts are completely dissimilar.

An attempt is made here to critically examine the issues and complexities underlying the Cold War rivalry involving TNWs; the historical context in which TNWs were considered; the synergy between conventional forces and TNWs (the boundary between nuclear and conventional force application); the command and control intricacies; the deterrence role (the stability-instability paradigm); and the issue of 'secrecy and security'. Besides, a brief description, in consideration of the definitional confusion on the concept of TNWs, is attempted to highlight the difficulties in categorising them. The aim is to extrapolate the complexities involving TNWs during the Cold War to the South Asian nuclear discourse in vogue, and the likely implications for deterrence stability in the region.

TNWs' Nomenclature

The Stockholm International Peace Research Institute (SIPRI) Research Report (No. 10, 1995) finds that the "writing on the nuclear weapon complex of the former Soviet Union is a classic case of trying to shoot at a moving target".[3] This assertion may be appropriate for the TNWs' discourse as a whole as no exact formulation or definition of TNWs is available. At the end of the 1960s, when the former USSR and USA began the Strategic Arms Limitation Talks (SALT), they had to come up with some way of delineating TNWs within their diverse nuclear arsenals.[4] A functional definition was arrived at only towards the end of the 1980s after a series of bilateral treaties (especially the Intermediate and Short-Range Nuclear Forces Treaty, signed in December 1987) for the limitation, reduction and banning of certain types of nuclear weapons.[5]

Along with various terminologies – non-strategic, battlefield, theatre, or sub-strategic – TNWs come in a great array of varieties; some are more easily distinguishable from strategic nuclear weapons than others. Owing to several criteria employed – range, yield, target, national ownership, delivery vehicle, capability, etc. – to define them, the discourse has remained contested. Both superpowers are known to have settled for the attribute of 'range' (the ability to reach each other's territory) as the main criterion for defining them. However, using the exclusion method, one may define TNWs as *de facto* nuclear weapons which are not covered by existing treaties.[6]

Usually, TNWs range from 0.1 kilotons (equivalent to 110 conventional bombs) to 10-15 kilotons, and upwards to 1 megaton.[7] Their actual size is smaller allowing for different delivery systems applied to more discreet targets.[8] They are being developed with yields as low as tens of tons and are 1,000 times cleaner than current nuclear weapons. The other meaning of 'tactical' relates to *function* – the manner in which the employment of such weapon affects the course of events on the battlefield. The intended utility of such weapons is to maximise target damage, minimise collateral damage, and not make it too difficult for friendly forces to traverse the damaged territory in a future advance.[9] Therefore, TNWs are nuclear weapons with low-yield and limited range for use against military targets on the battlefield.

NATO's strategy of TNWs had evolved during the 1950s and 1960s largely to offset the perceived conventional forces disadvantage against the Soviet Army and its allies. They are, therefore, considered as a "subclass of military assets" intended to reduce the adversary's military confidence and increase the allies' reassurance that they would not be the object of an attack.[10] During the Cold War, they were developed by the two super powers in mass quantities, including the air-delivered gravity bombs.[11] Considering the kind of nuclear weapons of higher yield developed in the subsequent decades, one may consider the bombs dropped on Japan as low-yield (below 20 kilotons) "tactical" weapons. On the other hand, many would also argue that "a nuclear detonation is a strategic event" regardless of the *yield* or the delivery means.[12] In fact, it is the *effect* and consequence that define the class of a weapon. Though "a 20 kiloton yield is arithmetically smaller than a one megaton yield, the destructive firepower of the smaller nuclear weapon remains far above the conventional threshold."[13]

For that matter, can any nuclear weapon be considered "tactical" or theatre-level, especially taking into account the immense political and strategic pressure that would inevitably follow its detonation? Many would argue that a TNW detonation is politically and militarily a 'strategic' event, regardless of the yield or the delivery means. Certainly, TNWs have the inherent potential for rapid and dramatic destruction, shock, and death, regardless of whether they yield one megaton or 20 kilotons. Therefore, distinguishing between "strategic" and "tactical" is more or less academic,[14] and the entire class of TNWs runs into a *doctrinal malaise.*[15]

Moreover, the word "tactical" denotes "an undeniably close link between nuclear weapons and a nation's conventional military capabilities" and highlights the notion that nuclear war can be fought and won, which has been proved to be illusory.[16] The Cold War experience underlines the fact that a 'limited war' may not remain limited once TNWs are used as the difference between "strategic" and "tactical" is considered semantic. The Liddell Hart advocacy of "logic control of war" may have been easier, and more applicable in the past due to the limitations of military technology than in the nuclear age. Though the use of TNWs is viewed to strengthen both 'deterrence through denial' and 'deterrence through punishment', "there is an air of unreality about the whole effort to limit nuclear war".[17] Even Brodie, Blackett, and Hart, later on, found the idea of 'limited war' to be complicating. According to Henry Kissinger, the more the pressures built up against any use of nuclear weapons, the greater the gap among deterrence policy, military capability and psychological readiness.[18] Therefore, during the late 1950s and early 1960s, Western strategic planners were known to have doubted the efficiency of TNW employment which resulted in the concept of "flexible response" and the build-up of conventional arms.[19]

Contrarily, many others view that the use of TNWs is advantageous and the dangers of limited use of nuclear weapons has been exaggerated. Kenneth Waltz is of the opinion that "early use of very small warheads may stop escalation. Defensive deployment, if it should fail to dissuade, would bring small nuclear weapons into use before the physical, political and psychological environments have deteriorated. The chances of de-escalation are high if the use of nuclear weapons is carefully planned and their use is limited to the battlefield."[20] Probably on this basis, according to Kenneth Waltz, "after the Soviet intervention in December 1979, American officials had considered using nuclear weapons in the Middle East, if need be. At various times, some American strategic planners have thought of reasons for making limited counter-force strikes – firing a few missiles at the Soviet Union—to show their determination."[21] The views of US Gens Earle G. Wheeler and George Brown of the USA "emerging from a nuclear war with a 'relative advantage' over the Soviet Union by targeting its 'war recovery capabilities' are well known. US Presidential Directive 59, signed by President Carter in July 1980, had contemplated fighting a limited nuclear war, perhaps a prolonged one, if deterrence should fail."[22] Similarly, some Soviet military leaders were known to have publicly emphasised the utility of nuclear weapons to win wars.

The Global Inventory

During the 1970s, the US stockpile of TNWs ranged around 7,000 to 8,000, and by the 1980s, there were 100 storage sites in at least seven European countries.[23] The figures increased phenomenally in the years ahead. The UK was the first country in NATO to receive US nuclear weapons on its soil in 1954. Other NATO members including Belgium, France, Germany, Greece, Italy, the Netherlands and Turkey were added to the list in the subsequent decades. In 1971, there were around 7,300 US nuclear warheads, for both missiles and free-fall bombs, across the European NATO area, excluding France.[24] However, a gradual decline of the stockpile, with a reduction of over 1,000 warheads, occurred in 1980, and by 1991, the number of warheads deployed across NATO member countries was around 2,500, with a variable yield between 0.3-170 kt.[25]

The Soviet Union, on the other hand, had 23 storage sites in Eastern Europe, holding a total of 370 to 1,070 TNWs.[26] Significant increase in the inventory of delivery systems in Europe during the 1960s can be marked. The Soviet Union had given its East European allies reason to believe that they would be provided nuclear weapons in war-time. The Polish and Czechoslovak commands were trained for that purpose.

According to the estimate of the director of the US Central Intelligence Agency, by January 1979, the Warsaw Pact theatre nuclear force comprised aircraft, missile launchers and artillery totalling 2,640, 1,160 and 288 respectively. This included Soviet and East European forces in the non-Soviet Warsaw Pact (NSWP) countries (East Germany, Poland, Czechoslovakia, Hungary, Romania, and Bulgaria) and Soviet forces in the Baltic, Belorussian, Carpathian, Leningrad, Odessa, Kiev, North Caucasus, and Transcaucasus Military Districts of the USSR.[27] The Soviet Navy was also equipped with nuclear-capable weapon systems for use in theatre warfare. All operational submarines were carrying at least two nuclear torpedoes and at least half of the missiles aboard Soviet cruise-missile submarines were equipped with nuclear warheads.[28] According to another estimate, the number of TNWs deployed within the Soviet Union was around 15,000 as of early 1991.[29] Particularly, since the late 1960s, the tactical nuclear forces of the Soviet Union had experienced important changes in both size and capabilities.

However, the greatest irony is that no TNWs have been employed even in situations where their use was seriously considered by both the superpowers – most notably during the Korean and Vietnam Wars, and, to a lesser extent, in Chechnya. Therefore, the notion that TNWs are "usable" is contested; however, this is not sufficient to rule out their potential use in the future. As long as they continue to exist and nations remain intent to acquire them, conditions may arise where the decision to use them would be made. So, it is imperative to derive perspectives by understanding the nuances and issue areas underplaying the Cold War rivalry involving TNWs, which may help provide a direction for today's discourse.

Issue Area I: Conventional-Nuclear Boundary

Perhaps, keeping in mind the idea of sub-strategic or tactical nuclear weapons, Oppenheimer once hoped that the "battle would be brought back to the battlefield". Gen Omar Bradley speculated that "the atom bomb in its tactical aspect may well contribute towards a stable equilibrium of forces since it tends to strengthen the defensive army".[30] Therefore, the major calculation behind NATO's decision to adopt a strategy of TNW deployment was to counter-balance a perceived conventional forces disadvantage against the Soviet Army and its allies. "NATO conventional forces were generally deemed insufficient to defend against a Soviet attack. The presence of tactical nuclear weapons served both as a line of defence and as a deterrent based on the notion that a conventional Soviet attack would necessarily lead to the use of TNWs," which would then greatly heighten the risks of a general nuclear war.[31] In fact, the West abandoned its quest for matching Warsaw Pacts, conventional forces, and placed nuclear weapons in Europe.

The first NATO strategy document of 1949 recognised the role of TNWs by integrating them to a plan of forward defence and strategic bombing. In the National Security Council Paper 68 (1950), American strategists concluded that there was no alternative to achieving a "preponderance of power" to back the strategy of containment. Therefore, Truman accepted the notion that to achieve preponderance, NATO would require maximum use of the US advantage in nuclear weapons of all ranges and yields. This suggests that the perceived conventional inferiority of NATO culminated in a nuclear posture which was "loud, stubborn and explicit."[32]

On the Soviet front, the age-old belief was that the balance had to be a perfect "correlation of forces".[33] Lenin's idea of "quantity has a quality all its own" seems to have guided Soviet strategy for a "vast quantity of less sophisticated weapons to maximise firepower and speed."[34] Along with TNWs, the Warsaw Pact maintained its conventional force superiority in numbers. The "Soviet General Staff seems to have concluded in the late 1970s that their most effective option against NATO would be conventional but extremely rapid deep operational manoeuvre groups..."[35] The Soviet view was that a tactical nuclear exchange could only slow down this offensive as well as carry the risk of a total nuclear war. However, the Soviet doctrine had always stressed on military operations in a chemical or nuclear environment. In the later part of the 1980s, nuclear weapons had emerged as a major consideration in Warsaw Pact staff training.[36] Documents that were recovered after the German unification reveal that towards the late 1980s, the Soviets believed that victory was possible with massive initial use of TNWs. All this suggests that the military strategy of the Warsaw Pact in the early stage of the Cold War was focussed on maintaining conventional superiority, but gradually shifted towards a strategy mainly based on TNWs.

Though the US and NATO on many occasions threatened to use TNWs, initially, there were doubts about reliance on them. By 1957, particularly after the Sagebrush Exercise, the US Army had concluded that "TNWs did not favour defense".[37] Then came the realisation of the risk interest in the "massive retaliation" strategy, that led consequently to the strategy of "flexible response" in search of a wide range of available options prior to the nuclear one. This emphasised the notion that nuclear weapons are "weapons of last resort". However, to counter Soviet conventional superiority, the US initiated the Revolution in Military Affairs (RMA) implemented through the CDI (Conventional Defence Improvement), CMF (Conceptual Military Framework), and FOFA (non-nuclear Follow on Force Attack) to adapt the latest military technology to European battlefield conditions.

NATO's adoption of RMA had a great impact on the strategic vision of the Warsaw Pact. During the late 1980s, therefore, TNWs suddenly reappeared as a major, if not primary, consideration in the Warsaw Pact's strategy. According to some literature, the Western adoption of RMA produced a new willingness in the Warsaw Pact (especially the Group of Soviet Forces in Germany) to be prepared to go nuclear from the beginning of any conflict.[38] "When NATO placed nuclear weapons in Europe directly in front of the assumed axes of the Soviet advance, the Soviet high command was known to have wrestled with the dilemma of what would happen if Western commanders were to really fire TNWs in desperation. As a result, Soviet commanders worked out their own plans for first-use of TNWs, for massive use and retaliation."[39]

This highlights two important trends: (1) at the beginning, NATO's perceived conventional force inferiority guided it to emphasise a strategy based on TNWs; (2) towards the end, technological inferiority against NATO's RMA forced the Warsaw Pact to reconsider use of TNWs at the beginning of any conflict. However, all these options led to the same dead end of escalation, strategic retaliation, and catastrophe.[40]

Therefore, the intricate issue comprises the boundary between conventional and nuclear forces. As evident, the conventional forces status of both sides was a major factor in the evolution of the Cold War TNW discourse. This is also evident from the Treaty on Conventional Forces in Europe (November 1990) that marked the end of the Cold War nuclear strategy, which greatly reduced the future dangers of a surprise conventional attack. It introduced many Confidence-Building Measures (CBMs), eliminating many threatening offensive combat assets.

Issue Area II: Command and Control

The second issue area is the custody or command and control structure which was a complex and demanding enterprise for both sides. Normally, command and control systems depend upon the size and composition of the arsenals and the characteristics of available delivery systems. With a growing number of arsenals, diverse delivery systems, and varied areas of operation, the complexity of the command and control system increases.[41] Therefore, the chances of failure of command and control, thereby misappropriation or inadvertent use, increase.

In the Cold War environment, "war was not expected to be linear"; operations were expected to be fluid and combat units would find themselves fighting without the security of friendly units around.[42] This needed an ability or system where commanders at all levels could act quickly, decisively and independently of the higher command authority. For that matter, the *Soviet command structure was normally centralised,* which negated the needed decentralised structure to fight a non-linear war. "There was no equivalent ferment within the Warsaw Pact where nuclear weapons were retained under the direct control of KGB detachments". There was no debate in the alliance either though the Soviets had assured their allies that they would give them nuclear weapons during war-time. Only Czechoslovakia and Poland requested for special training in 1983.[43]

The NATO command and control structure was based on "limited pre-delegation of nuclear release" for certain forward deployed and vulnerable posts which seems to have been allowed at the end of the 1950s.[44] But this policy was reversed by McNamara's insistence on centralised control during the 1960s. The US also began to apply great efforts to ensure that the securely coded Permissive Action Link (PAL) systems were fitted into all the devices to restrict unauthorised or inadvertent use.

The day-to-day maintenance, storage and security of TNWs was the responsibility of the United States Air Force (USAF) Munitions Support Squadrons (MUNSS), each comprising around 100 personnel. In times of crisis, if directed to do so by the US president's National Command Authority (NCA), following a NATO request for their employment, the MUNSS would hand the weapons over to the national air forces of Germany, Belgium, Italy and the Netherlands for use on those countries' aircraft, to be delivered against NATO nominated targets.[45] In the event of NATO requiring the weapons' use, this would "in theory require a host nation agreement."[46] In a war-time situation, after being directed to do so by the NCA following NATO's request, the local American commander of the nuclear weapons would hand over the control to the local air force and the local air force would deliver them. In this pursuit, the "Belgian, German, Italian and Dutch pilots and ground crews were trained to handle nuclear weapons. Though the weapons are American-made and supplied and under MUNSS custody, on a day-to-day basis, American personnel are based at those air bases. The weapon's storage bunkers are operated by the Americans and they maintain overall control over the weapons".[47] At the political level, these weapons remained under the control not of America, but NATO and were considered NATO's nuclear weapons.

As an integral part of the command and control structure, the communication network is vital. Even as late as 1987, NATO had "failed to develop a comprehensive system integrating conventional and nuclear C3 … that would tie together major headquarters, responsible political officials, and the relevant military commanders down to at least the divisional level".[48] Similarly, the command and control structure in the Warsaw Pact was unlikely to have been any more efficient, except for more standardisation.[49]

Issue Area III: Deterrence Role

The third issue area is the deterrence utility of TNWs. Particularly, the forward-based ground TNWs were seen as enhancing deterrence through their "use-it-or-lose-it" quality.[50] The Healey-Schroder Report in May 1969 considered guidelines for the employment of TNWs within the 'flexible response' framework. It suggested that "NATO's objective in initiating the use of nuclear weapons would be political – the purpose would be to confront the aggressor with the risks of escalation if he continued, with the aim of convincing him to stop his attack. Moreover, the initial use of nuclear weapons would be 'limited' and 'selective' and would be designed to control the risk of escalation, minimize collateral damage and facilitate continuous political control."[51] The report clearly visualised NATO TNWs as having *a political signalling function rather than being designed to assure a battlefield victory*.

Initially, NATO viewed TNWs as contributing towards a stable equilibrium of forces, since they strengthen the defensive army. But after the Sagebrush Exercise in 1957, the US Army had concluded that TNWs did not favour defence. NATO exercises made clear that Germany would be devastated through the effects of the blast and fallout following even limited employment of nuclear weapons.[52] There were also differing opinions regarding the demonstrative use of TNWs, especially for deterrence purposes, in the event of hostility: the UK wanted a round fired at sea; West Germany wanted a round fired high in the sky by an air defence missile; whereas, the US declined to adopt a demonstrative-use bandwagon seeing it as a sign of weakness rather than a demonstration of strength.[53]

The Soviet leaders, on the other hand, considered TNWs as weapons of mass destruction and "incitement to escalation which could not be used precisely against military targets separate from the civilian population". Soviet experts, therefore, judged that "the high attrition rates resulting from nuclear exchanges would require even larger conventional forces as replacements and reserves."[54] In fact, the growth of TNWs with NATO did not cause the Soviet General Staff to abandon their underlying belief that only a ruthless military offensive could secure victory for the USSR. They were constantly planning on the assumption that "early nuclear strikes of intermediate range missiles and tactical weapons, combined with mass conventional air attacks and armoured offensives, would cancel out NATO TNWs and shatter alliance cohesion".[55]

However, the fundamental question is of how the different classes and deployments of TNWs affect the psychology and politics of friends and enemies. Both the superpowers had viewed TNWs as "a subclass of military assets intended to reduce adversary military confidence and increase friends' reassurance that they would not be the object of attack".[56]

Issue Area IV: Stabilising or Destabilising?

Undoubtedly, TNWs contributed to the Cold War security dilemma but they were "not in themselves a major cause of instability".[57] They improved the correlation of forces from the NATO perspective and did not lend themselves to "bolt from the blue scenarios" because they were emboldened in conventional forces.[58] According to Richard Weitz, by 1960, Kissinger and other analysts had noted the failure of the Services to develop a coherent doctrine for TNWs. Rather, there were fundamental disagreements within NATO over them; in fact, the problems with NATO's strategy resulted from the Soviet nuclear build-up.[59]

The Soviets began to introduce their own TNWs in the belief that TNWs added to the overall East-West correlation of forces, whose imbalance in their favour could exert pressure, threat, and even blackmail.[60] However, they still saw them as weapons of mass destruction and likely sources of escalation to all-out exchanges. The United States, on the other hand, saw TNWs as "a cheap and readily available means of enhancing US regional military power" in possible wars. They were considered "the ultimate deterrent to aggression" and also a "symbol of US commitment to the defence of its allies".[61]

On the issue of strategic stability, Aleksei Fenenko concludes that the old definition of strategic stability based upon mutual assured destruction no longer applied. The new weapons [TNWs] were making it much easier to cross the nuclear threshold to achieve more limited objectives, which could bring about the end of enemy resistance.[62] Though Kennedy and McNamara "evinced willingness to push for higher conventional alliance spending in the interests of strategic stability," TNWs remained a part of NATO's strategy of 'flexible response' until the end of the Cold War.[63] They also served a political function in terms of ensuring a stable link between the US and its allies.

Issue Area V: Secrecy and Security

The last issue area is ensuring the secrecy and security of TNWs. It is frequently claimed that the security of TNWs is somehow worse than that of strategic nuclear weapons.[64] As far as their storage is concerned, normally, TNWs were "collocated with strategic weapons in major nuclear weapons storage facilities that contain multiple bunkers."[65] This was the case with both the superpowers. However, the major concern was the security of warheads during transport, forward deployment, and unauthorised use.

On many occasions, both superpowers had come close to unauthorised or unexpected firing in fast moving unanticipated, unplanned and unrehearsed situations. During the Cuban missile crisis, the US did not know that the Soviet submarines that were depth-charged had nuclear tipped torpedoes aboard and had conditional authorisation for their use. Further, at the height of the Cuban missile crisis, on October 27, 1962, a US U-2 reconnaissance aircraft from Alaska accidentally strayed into Soviet air space over the Chukotski Peninsula and radioed for assistance. A USAF-102 armed with a nuclear air-to-air missile, was scrambled from Alaska and headed towards the Bering Sea, while Soviet MiGs took off to intercept the U-2. Fortunately, it managed to exit Soviet air space without shots being fired.[66]

There was the difficulty of detection of TNWs even with the most intense local surveillance. According to the latest revelations, Soviet TNWs remained in Cuba undetected despite Khrushchev's assurance of having removed all the weapons. The security and safety of those undetectable systems became a major cause of concern in the post-Soviet era. Witness the dangers of scattered, poorly guarded TNW storage sites in different parts of the Central Asian Republics after the disintegration of the Soviet Union. These were the "loose nukes" exposed to theft, illegal sale or forcible seizure.[67] Also, there was the risk of misuse of TNWs owing to the provision of pre-delegation of nuclear release for forward-deployed positions; that was the reason why McNamara insisted on centralised control of TNWs.[68]

Extrapolating to the South Asian Context

"Those who cannot learn from history are doomed to repeat it," rightly said George Santayana. Arguably, "The Cold War and South Asian nuclear standoffs present dilemmas associated with tactical nuclear weapons that are different primarily in degree rather than in kind. …Whether they are called tactical, battlefield, or short-range nuclear weapons, the dilemmas they pose apply to all nuclear rivals."[69] Is Pakistan learning the right lesson?

Perceptibly, the motivation behind Pakistan's pursuit of TNWs against the conventionally superior India stems from NATO's perceived military inferiority against the Soviet Union. But Pakistan must observe keenly the reasons for which the US withdrew most of its TNWs from Europe in 1991. Certainly, the US goal was to deter any conventional attack by the Soviet Union on Western Europe. It also wanted to avoid any escalation of the conflict to a full-fledged nuclear war between the two superpowers. TNWs were "proved to be useless militarily as nuclear use at the tactical level would lead to a strategic response and an uncontrollable escalation. Pakistan, however, has embraced this discarded strategy...."[70] The understanding in the Pakistani side probably is that its "actions at the tactical or operational level have no strategic implications and a limited nuclear war will not escalate into a full-fledged nuclear war."

Introspection on the Pakistani calculation behind TNWs would reveal that "Pakistan is not seeking to exploit the military utility of TNWs"; rather it aims "to reclaim the space that India maintains exists for a conventional war even in the presence of nuclear weapons."[71] The misperception on which Pakistan is basing its TNWs strategy is that their use would not be seen as sufficiently provocative by India, and the international community would stop it from continuing its conventional campaign or undertaking nuclear retaliation. Therefore, in the Pakistani perception, the TNW is a deterrent at best, and a war termination weapon at worst, but does Pakistan make any justifiable gains? First, according to Rajesh Basrur, "The Pakistani threat to initiate the use of TNWs will be self-deterred. ... The nuclear detonations that occur – even if limited

– will be either within Pakistan's territory or so close to it that the fallout will likely affect its own population."[72] The Cold War rivals are geographically thousands of miles apart, unlike the South Asian rivals where the missile flight time comprises less than seven minutes from one side to the other which, in turn, increases the risk of misperception and unintended escalation, as both sides are introducing dual-use delivery vectors that "make it difficult to discriminate between incoming nuclear and conventional attacks".[73]

Second, TNWs carry the risk of preemptive strikes. During the Cold War, the Soviet Union keenly monitored all the nuclear sites, approximately 20, by sophisticated technical systems or human means in West Germany and there was a strong temptation to destroy the weapons before they were launched. Pakistan's lack of 'strategic depth' and the short flight time between India and Pakistan exacerbate this tension as the decision-making time for leaders during a crisis is extremely short. The real lessons from the Cold War, therefore. is not to develop, and rely on, TNWs for deterrence stability but to reduce reliance on them through transparency measures, using diplomacy to alleviate an arms race.[74]

Third, the safety and security of TNWs is of utmost importance as their deployments require delegation of arming and launching authority to the local commanders. This increases the chances of their misappropriation or unauthorised use. Also, the risk of inadvertent escalation heightens during a conventional conflict by a nuclear-armed unit which might feel it necessary to use the weapons in order to avoid defeat. More importantly, "Restraint regimes for tactical or battlefield nuclear weapons are very difficult to construct. Washington and Moscow have not been willing or able to tackle negotiated constraints on TNWs."[75]

In addition, "dispersed storage and movement under field conditions, as launchers must move from hide to hide to avoid being easily targeted by the enemy, increases the risk of accidents..."[76] This necessitates the involvement of a large number of personnel who need to be cleared, periodically screened, and monitored for reliability. According to Shaun Gregory, "As many as 70,000 people in Pakistan reportedly have access to, or knowledge of, some element of the Pakistani nuclear weapons production, storage, maintenance, and deployment cycle, from those involved in the manufacture of fissile material, through those engaging in nuclear weapons design, assembly and maintenance, to those who transport and safeguard the weapons in storage and would deploy the weapons in crises. That number will also rise steadily as the size of the nuclear arsenal grows."[77] Above all, "the danger posed by Pakistan's growing nuclear arsenal, especially short-range systems, is amplified by Pakistan's growing weaknesses in governance, persistent internal instability, and the potential for clashes with India."[78] Therefore, "TNWs bring in a higher level of instability and a much lower level of deterrence."[79]

Fourth, contrary to Pakistan's understanding that "actions at the tactical or operational level have no strategic implications, and a limited nuclear war will not escalate into a full-fledged nuclear war," India adheres to a straightforward nuclear posture – deterrence by punishment, where 'strategic' or 'tactical' is irrelevant.[80] Therefore, TNWs have little utility in the South Asian context; especially, no major advantages seem to accrue from them to Pakistan.

Fifth, according to unclassified US Army weapons effects manuals, TNWs are not effective against mobile or armoured forces. For example, "a one kiloton nuclear device would have to detonate within a 90 meter radius of a tank to inflict even moderate damage on that vehicle and the prompt radiation from such a weapon is far more lethal to the crew of a tank than the blast effect, incapacitating crew members within a 360 meter radius. However, such a blast would not kill that many tanks or even incapacitate that many crew members in a deployed armor battalion maneuvering in battle."[81] David O. Smith points out a few more difficulties involved with TNWs as experienced by the Cold War rivals, such as: they complicate command, control and communications; nuclear release authority for tactical targets is difficult to obtain; they are difficult to secure when deployed and require scarce manpower; nuclear launch units must be withdrawn from battle to ensure their survivability. More interestingly, Smith considers use of TNWs as "not decisive" on the basis of NATO understanding. NATO "studies have concluded time and again that a two-sided exchange of battlefield nuclear weapons would quickly destroy both sides' forward combat forces, after which they (Warsaw Pact) would win the ground battle by bringing forward reserves that NATO could not match".[82] Faced with defeat by an enemy's conventional forces, the other side would either expend TNWs or escalate directly to the strategic level. The ultimate effect of either decision would be the same – a strategic nuclear exchange.[83]

A Critical Assessment

One may argue that the Cold War TNW model is not analogous to the current India-Pakistan scenario as the "geopolitical context is very dissimilar".[84] Nevertheless, past experience would help draw lessons for those who choose the same path, and may help review the current positions of the countries that possess them, to avoid any unforeseen contingency. First, the hardest lesson for Pakistan is that its "nuclear romanticism"[85] based on the idea that TNWs can solve its conventional military imbalance with India, only promises "lowering the nuclear threshold and guaranteeing a larger nuclear exchange."[86]

Secondly, India must not be tempted at any point to respond to Pakistan's misadventure in terms of tactical assets. India has not yet formally acknowledged the utility of TNWs; however, many refer to its short range platforms and are of the view that they can easily be modified to carry nuclear warheads. This is unlikely, but before India embraces a culture of TNWs, "a major change in thinking in both the military and civilian senior leadership in New Delhi and in its doctrinal posture must occur."[87]

David O. Smith presumes three unsettling developments if the development, refinement, and deployment of TNWs continue apace in South Asia. (1) the development and deployment of new systems will precede the development of doctrines for their employment; (2) India will match (and perhaps even exceed) whatever numbers of weapons Pakistan eventually builds; and (3) the numbers of deployable weapons may be limited only by the fissile material production capacity on both sides rather than the number perceived to be needed for deterrence.[88] A few strategic thinkers in India advocate TNWs for India so as to not raise the nuclear ante to full-scale retaliation in case of a Pakistani first strike. However, Gurmeet Kanwal views this as "a dangerous argument and would completely degrade the potential not only of India's nuclear deterrence but also of India's conventional superiority."[89]

It is unlikely that India will adopt a tit-for-tat policy in response to Pakistan's TNW programme sooner or later. It is also unlikely that India will resort to a doctrinal revision in haste. During the 16th Lok Sabha election in 2014, the Bharatiya Janata Party (BJP) made a pledge in its election manifesto for an "independent strategic nuclear programme" to "revise and update" India's nuclear doctrine, that resurfaced the debate on the change and continuity of India's 'no-first-use' posture. One may argue that a revision of India's nuclear doctrine is long overdue. Western scholars view India's current doctrine as being similar to the US doctrine of massive retaliation during the 1950s. As a logical evolution, India would look for a doctrine which can provide "flexible response" options "allowing policy makers every possibility in a crisis – pre-emptive strike, counter-force and counter-retaliation."[90] But this is easier said than done. In fact, India's current nuclear posture provides many advantages; equating the BJP's nuclear test decision in 1998 with its urge to revise the doctrine would be misleading. Rather, what India is likely to do in the foreseeable future is signalling to Pakistan in concrete terms that it would play the nuclear game according to its own rules. In the business of deterring Pakistan, India will decide the Pakistani threshold on its own terms, undeterred by the TNWs and red-lines drawn by its retired military generals – signalling zero justifiable gains out of the TNW strategy.

Notes

1. William F. Burns, "Tactical Nuclear Weapons and NATO: An Introductory Reminiscence", in Tom Nichols, Douglas Stuart and Jeffrey D. McCausland, eds., *Tactical Nuclear Weapons and NATO* (US Army War College, April 2012).
2. David O. Smith, "The US Experience with Tactical Nuclear Weapons: Lessons for South Asia", http://www.stimson.org/images/uploads/research-pdfs/David_Smith_Tactical_Nuclear_Weapons.pdf, p. 7.
3. SIPRI, "The Soviet Nuclear Weapon Legacy", *SIPRI Research Report No. 10* (Oxford University Press, 1995), p. 1.
4. Alexander Pikayev, "Nonstrategic Nuclear Weapons", in Alexei Arbatov and Vladimir Dvorkin, eds., *Nuclear Proliferation: New Technologies, Weapons, Treaties* (Moscow: Carnegie Moscow Center, 2009), pp. 104-105.
5. Alexander Pikayev, "Tactical Nuclear Weapons," icnnd.org/Documents/Pikayev_Tactical_Nuclear_Weapons.doc
6. George Lewis and Andrea Gabbitas, "What Should be Done About Tactical Nuclear Weapons?", *Occasional Paper,* The Atlantic Council, March 1999, pp. 1-4.
7. Brian Alexander and Alistair Millar, *Tactical Nuclear Weapons: Emergent Threats in an Evolving Security Environment*, vii (2003); William Potter et al., *Tactical Nuclear Weapons: Options for Control* (Geneva: United Nations Institute for Disarmament Research, 2000).
8. Robert P. Chatham, "Tactical Nuclear Weapons: Lawful Use in the Aftermath of the ICJ Opinion", *The Reporter*, Summer 2010, p. 42.
9. Nichols, et. al., eds., n.1, p. xv.
10. North Atlantic Treaty Organisation, Security Council Simulation at Yale XXXV, http://scsy.yira.org/wp-content/uploads/2012/09/NATO.pdf
11. John T. Cappello, "Tactical Nuclear Weapons: Debunking the Mythology", *INSS Occasional Paper 46*, August 2002, www.dtic.mil/cgi-bin/GetTRDoc?AD=ADA435014, p. 3.
12. Ibid.
13. Ibid., p. 5.
14. Richard Weitz, "The Historical Context" in Nichols, et. al., eds., n.1, p. 4.
15. John T. Cappello, Gwendolyn M. Hall, and Stephen P. Lambert, "Tactical Nuclear Weapons: Debunking the Mythology", *INSS Occasional Paper 46*, August 2002, p. 3
16. Gurmeet Kanwal, "Does India Need Tactical Nuclear Weapons?", http://www.idsa-india.org/an-may-03.html
17. Sudha Raman, *Nuclear Strategy: The Doctrine of Just War* (New Delhi: Manas, 2006), p. 31.
18. Henry Kissinger, "Conventional War: Limited or Nuclear?: A Reappraisal", *Daedalus*, vol.89, no. 4, 1960.
19. Kanti Bajpai, "The Military Utility of Nuclear Weapons and the Case for Disarmament", paper presented at the Pugwash Conference, School of International Studies, Jawaharlal Nehru University, New Delhi, March 25-27, 2001.
20. Kenneth Waltz, "The Spread of Nuclear Weapons: More May Better," *Adelphi Papers*, no. 171 (London: International Institute for Strategic Studies, 1981).
21. Ibid., p. 28.
22. Ibid., pp. 28-29.
23. Nichols, et. al., eds., n. 1.
24. Thomas Withington, "The Tactical Nuclear Weapons Game", Swiss Federal Institute of Technology Zurich, *ISN Security Watch*, August 12, 2008.
25. Ibid.
26. Director of the Central Intelligence Agency, "Warsaw Pact Forces Opposite NATO", January 31, 1979, http://www.foia.cia.gov/sites/default/files/document_conversions/89801/

DOC_0000278530.pdf, p. 45.
27. Ibid., p. 41.
28. Ibid., p. 45.
29. "Where the Weapons are", *Bulletin of the Atomic Scientists*, vo. 47, no. 9, November 1991, pp. 48-49.
30. Nichols, et. al., eds., n. 1, p. 17.
31. Alexander and Millar, n. 7.
32. Paul Schulte, "Tactical Nuclear Weapons in NATO and Beyond: A Historical and Thematic Examination", in Nichols, et. al., eds., n. 1, p. 18.
33. Wilbur E. Gray, "The World War that Never Was: NATO vs. The Warsaw Pact," http://www.alternatewars.com/WW3/the_war_that_never_was.htm
34. Ibid.
35. "Pakistan, NATO, and Tactical Nuclear Weapons: Two of a Kind?", https://shashankjoshi.wordpress.com/2012/10/17/pakistan-nato-and-tactical-nuclear-weapons-two-of-a-kind/
36. Ibid.
37. Weitz, n. 14, p. 5.
38. Gray, n. 33.
39. Nichols, et. al., eds., n. 1.
40. Ibid., p. ix.
41. Zia Mian, "A Nuclear Tiger by the Tail: Some Problems of Command and Control in South Asia", PU/CEES Report No. 328, June 2001, http://www.princeton.edu/sgs/publications/articles/report328.pdf, p.3.
42. Gray, n. 33.
43. Schulte, n. 32, p. 49.
44. Ibid., p. 40.
45. Withington, n. 24
46. "The Tactical Nuclear Weapons Game", http://www.isn.ethz.ch/Digital-Library/Articles/Detail/?id=89456
47. Ibid.
48. Catherine McArdle Kelleher, "NATO Nuclear Operations" in Ashton B. Carter, John D. Steinbrenner, and Charles A. Zraket, eds., *Managing Nuclear Operations* (Washington, DC: The Brookings Institution, 1987), p. 460.
49. Schulte, n. 32, p. 34.
50. Weitz, n.14, p. 5.
51 Jane E. Stromseth, *The Origins of Flexible Response: Nato's Debate over Strategy in the 1960s* (Palgrave Macmillan, June 1988), p. 184.
52. Nichols, et. al., eds., n.1.
53. Burns, n. 1, p. xvi.
54. Nichols, et. al., eds., n. 1.
55. Schulte, n. 32, p. 31.
56. Weitz, , n. 14, p. 3.
57. Ibid., p. 9.
58. Nichols, et. al., eds., n. 1.
59. Weitz, n. 14, pp. 5-6.
60. Ibid.
61. Simon Lunn, "The Role and Place of Tactical Nuclear Weapons—A NATO Perspective", in Nichols, et. al., eds., n. 1, p. 235.
62. Aleksei Fenenko, "Problematikaiadernoistabil'nosti vsovremennoizarubezhnoipolitologii,"*Me zhdunarodnyeprotsessy*, no. 6, 2004.

63. Schulte, n. 32, p. 39.
64. Joshua Handler, "The 1991-1992 PNIs and the Elimination, Storage, and Security of Tactical Nuclear Weapons", in Alexander and Millar, n. 7, p. 39.
65. Alexander and Millar, n. 7.
66. Schulte, n. 32, pp. 37-38.
67. Kelleher, n. 48, p. 449.
68. Alexander and Millar, n. 7.
69. Michael Krepon, Ziad Haider, and Charles Thornton, "Are Tactical Nuclear Weapons Needed in South Asia?", http://www.stimson.org/images/uploads/research-pdfs/ESCCONTROLCHAPTER6.pdf, pp. 137, 147.
70. Saira Bano, "Pakistan is Learning the Wrong Lesson: Tactical Nuclear Weapons in South Asia", *International Policy Digest*, December 27, 2014.
71. Manpreet Sethi, "Responding to Pakistan's Tactical Nuclear Weapons: A Strategy for India", *IPCS Debate*, Article No. #4263, January 18, 2014.
72. Rajesh Basrur, "South Asia: Tactical Nuclear Weapons and Strategic Risk", *RSIS Commentaries*, no. 65/2011, April 27, 2011.
73. Mark Fitzpatrick, "Cold War Lessons for South Asia Nuclear Arms Race", www.iiss.org, September 12, 2013.
74. Bano, n. 70.
75. Krepon, et al., n. 69, p. 121.
76. Gurmeet Kanwal, "Pakistan: Is Hatf-9 Inherently Destabilising?", http://www.eurasiareview.com/11112013-pakistan-hatf-9-inherently-destabilising-analysis/
77. Shaun Gregory, "Terrorist Tactics in Pakistan Threaten Nuclear Safety", *CTC Journal*, June 2011, vol. 4, issue 6, p. 5.
78. Jeffrey D. McCausland, "Pakistan's Tactical Nuclear Weapons: Operational Myths and Realities", http://www.stimson.org/images/uploads/research-pdfs/McCausland.pdf
79. Amit Gupta, "India, Pakistan and Tactical Nuclear Weapons: Irrelevance for South Asia", http://www.ipcs.org/article/india/ipcs-debate-india-pakistan-and-tactical-nuclear-weapons-irrelevance-for-4239.html
80. Bano, n. 70.
81. US Army Field Manual 101-31-3, Nuclear Weapon Employment Effects Data: Planning Staff Officers, (Washington DC: Department of the Army, 1977), Appendix E. Quoted in Smith, n. 2, p. 24.
82. Smith, n. 2, p. 27.
83. Ibid.
84. Statement made by Lt Gen Kidwai (Retd), during a presentation on October 25, 2006, at Washington, DC. Quoted in Smith, n. 2, p. 4.
85. The term nuclear romanticism was coined by Richard Weitz to describe the "delusional thinking" among the Soviet military high command that nuclear weapons would allow for a decisive victory over NATO. Weitz, , n. 14.
86. Smith, n. 2, p. 43.
87. Ibid.
88. Ibid., p. 3
89. Kanwal, n. 16
90. Ajai Shukla, "Come Out of the Nuclear Closet", http://www.business-standard.com/article/opinion/ajai-shukla-come-out-of-the-nuclear- closet-114041400866_1.html

3

Growth of Extremism in Pakistan

Shalini Chawla

Pakistan has been in existence now for more than six decades but the state has not been able to define its identity till date. The identity crisis in the state has invariably strengthened its threat perceptions. Pakistan has been a nation of contradictions; it has shared an ambiguous relationship with Islam; tried to embrace Western notions of modernity, and, at the same time, tried to retain its orthodox Islamic identity; has an overpowering and ambitious army which has ruled the nation for more than 30 years directly, and for nearly an equal period with a civilian façade, but has still struggled periodically to go back to the democratic order controlled by the fractured political leadership; and has suffered a deep national identity crisis. Lack of identity has encouraged the rise of ethnicity and pluralism within the Pakistani society. Born as a result of the demand for a separate Muslim homeland, it eventually stood as the saviour of Islam and, in the process, the military led state adopted policies based on religion which have had severe repercussions for the state. Religion has been used in Pakistan for objectives ranging from nation building to strategic security.

Pakistan has shared a varying relationship with Islam and presently is experiencing Islamist extremism in the most violent form. The Peshawar attack on December 16, 2014, which killed 135 innocent children was indeed one of the most horrifying acts of terror ever witnessed in Pakistan. More than the numbers, the brutality of the act generated immense outrage among the masses. Pakistan has become a breeding ground for terrorism, with the extremist elements in the country now on a much stronger footing than ever before, posing a threat to very existence of the state. Pakistan's involvement in the war on terror post 9/11, has further facilitated the growth of the terrorist network not only on the frontier boundaries of Pakistan, but also in the heart of the state where the extremist elements have managed to penetrate even the army headquarters—the most secure place in Pakistan—and various air force and naval bases. Liberal thinking finds its survival extremely challenging which is exemplified by the assassinations of Punjab Governor Salman Taseer, who tried to oppose the blasphemy law, and *Asia Times* journalist Salman Shahzad, who tried to disclose the links between the terrorists and the military. The question that needs to be addressed is: did Pakistan fall prey to extremism as a result of its involvement in the war on terror? The answer is clearly 'no'. Pakistan today, is actually facing the blowback of its own policies which it has believed in, and pursued, in the last five decades. Its reliance on terrorism as a foreign policy tool is indeed responsible for its drift into extremism. This paper attempts to study Pakistan's journey towards the present state of extremism, which the Pakistani leadership is unable to control, posing the most alarming challenge to the stability of the country.

Background

Pakistan was born as a demand for a separate homeland for Muslims as the All India Muslim League led by Muhammad Ali Jinnah strongly argued that Muslims had a special identity which would not be able to survive in a Hindu dominated society, thus, a separate homeland for Muslims was the only solution. But, Jinnah's dream was quite different from what Pakistan actually transformed into. There was lack of consensus over Pakistan's ideological and territorial contours, as Ayesha Jalal has rightly pointed out:

> Jinnah's resort to religion was not on an ideology to which he was ever committed or even a device to use against rival communities; it was simply a way of giving a semblance of unity and solidarity to his divided Muslim constituents. Jinnah needed a demand that was specifically ambiguous and imprecise to command general support, something specifically Muslim though unspecific in every other respect.[1]

Jinnah in his famous speech before the Constituent Assembly on August 11, 1947, outlined his secular vision:

> You are free; you are free to go to your temples, you are free to go to your mosques or to any other place of worship in this state of Pakistan. You may belong to any religion or caste or creed–that has nothing to do with the business of the state….We are starting with this fundamental principle that we are all citizens and equal citizens of one state…In the course of time, Hindus would cease to be Hindus and Muslims would cease to be Muslims, not in the religious sense, because that is the personal faith of each individual, but in the political sense as citizens of the state.[2]

Jinnah's dream was a secular state where the Muslim culture and social norms could be promoted. Jinnah's vision was the outcome of a different set of circumstances where, on the post-colonial movement, he visualised an arrangement for the Indian Muslims who could be free in an independent state. But, over the decades, Pakistan drifted away from Jinnah's spirit. Pakistan never inherited a uniform vision and there were contesting ideas, thus, the birth of the nation itself suffered a lack of consensus and clarity on the issue of Islam. In the following years, Pakistan did not have the benefit of a committed and visionary leadership. The state was driven differently by different regimes following different objectives. Jinnah passed away on October 11, 1948, and this was indeed a deadly blow to the spirit of Pakistan, and hardly anyone would disagree that his death altered the course of history.

Many of Pakistan's political elites were uncertain about the role of Islam in defining the nation's constitutional foundations.[3] It took the policy-makers close to a decade to formalise the Constitution of Pakistan into one which dissolved Jinnah's spirit of secular Islam.

This confusion about the interpretation of Islam had severe political, social, economic, educational and even military ramifications. The persistent confusion and lack of consensus gave the political and military leadership enough space to exploit the factor of religion to serve their own interests. After independence, the most daunting task for the Pakistani leadership was to secure Pakistan from internal and external threats. Internally, Pakistan was fragmented and the two wings, West Pakistan and East Pakistan, which differed ethnically, culturally and economically, were separated by thousands of miles of Indian territory. Alongwith the issue of East Pakistan, Pakistan also experienced insurgency in Baluchistan in the 1940s itself. The Northwest Frontier Province (NWFP) also was opposed to the idea of being a part of the Pakistani state. Added to these internal vulnerabilities was the perceived threat from India, which Pakistanis suspected had hegemonic ambitions, and had been unfair in providing Pakistan its due share of resources inherited from British India. Hostility against India was the leading factor which obviously got exaggerated with Pakistan's internal struggles.

The Beginning of the Ideological Drift and Pakistan's Wars for Kashmir

The factor of religion became the most critical one in Pakistan's strategic security.

The need to control Jammu and Kashmir (J&K) and incorporate it into Pakistan was felt very strongly in Pakistan ever since the British declaration of India's partition. The prime reasons for Pakistan's quest for J&K were economic and strategic. The first was that Pakistan felt that with J&K state as an integral part of India, Pakistan's security would be jeopardised.[4] The major fear was that India could establish its military forces anywhere within a few miles of the 200-km-long vital road and rail route between

Lahore and Rawalpindi. Geographically, most of West Punjab's prominent cities lie close to J&K's western border. Considering that the Punjabi elites dominated Pakistan's decision-making, this factor of vulnerability weighed heavily on their minds. The second factor was economic and psychological. Kashmir going to India could seriously impact Pakistan's economy which was based mainly on canal irrigated agriculture. West Punjab particularly depended for its agriculture on the rivers flowing from Jammu and Kashmir.[5] Given the security and economic concerns, Kashmir was seen as necassary and not just desirable for Pakistan. But this in no way denies the fact that the issue of religion was important for the Pakistanis, shaping their attitude towards Kashmir. Pakistan's demand for Kashmir was also due to the frustration of the political leaders who felt cheated with a "moth-eaten" Pakistan which came into their share. Thus, the desire to expand the boundaries and have a Muslim majority state added to the geo-economic concerns in Pakistan.

Pakistan launched the first war for Kashmir in 1947-48 in the name of a "tribal revolt". The Pakistan Army, with the consent of the political leadership, incited the tribesmen and the retired and serving army officers in the name of *jihad*, to raid and seize Kashmir. Islam was leveraged at the very inception of the state itself to respond to the Indian threat. The government in Pakistan called on religious scholars to issue supportive *fatwas* (religious decrees).[6] The importance of the 1947-48 aggression was that it laid the basic guidelines for future aggressions by Pakistan. This was the beginning of the use of religion to forward the state polices and also conduct covert operations backed by the full-fledged support of the military.

Internally, Jinnah's dream of a pluralistic society was being challenged and in the early 1950s there were street protests calling for the Ahmedis to be declared non-Muslims.[7] The protests were orchestrated in part to destabilise the ruling polity, and the resignation of Pakistan's first Foreign Minister, Sir Zafarullah Khan, an Ahmadi, was demanded.[8] In 1974, Ahmadis were officially declared non-Muslims through a constitutional amendment. On similar lines, in 1965, during the first indirect presidential elections held under Ayub Khan, opposition was raised against Fatima Jinnah, sister of Mohammad Ali Jinnah, from contesting for power and a *fatwa* was issued to say that Islam did not allow a female head of state.[9] Thus, religion became an important factor for the political groups to lead in the power struggle. Unequal rights on the basis of sect and gender became prevalent.

On the external front, the Pakistan Army's covert activities expanded in Jammu and Kashmir after the 1962 India-China War. A close study of the covert activities indicates that the factor of religion started to gain momentum in the 1960s. Pakistan's covert activities in Kashmir were now gradually moving towards using religion as a driving force to gain support for the disintegration of India.

Another development in the late 1950s and 1960s was Pakistan's entry into a Cold War alliance with the United States. Pakistan entered into military agreements with the US and started to receive massive amounts of military aid. The US alliance provided Pakistan with high technology weaponry for its army, air force and navy. This added to its aggressive instincts to acquire Kashmir. The military establishment and rule were further strengthened in Pakistan with the US assistance, and it gave the military greater confidence to carry on its covert war in Kashmir.

In the 1950s, Pakistan's covert operations in Kashmir Valley did not yield results and were adding to the frustration and impatience in Pakistan, even leading to the military officers' plotting the Rawalpindi conspiracy against the civilian government. In 1964, Pakistan developed a strategy that came to be known as *Operations Gibraltar* and *Grand Slam*, that comprise a landmark in the history of both nations. Although, the initial reasons for wanting to annex Kashmir had ceased to exist, the first factor of insecurity, due to the presence of the Indian Army on the western border, was solved as a result of the ceasefire agreement in 1949. The second factor, regarding the waters of rivers originating from Kashmir was also solved with the Indus Water Treaty, signed in 1960, through the good offices of the World Bank during Ayub Khan's regime.

Operation Gibralter was a covert operation but it gained little success as Pakistani preparations were not in place and it did not get the expected support from the Kashmiris. Soon after the launching of Operation Gibraltar, on August 10, a body called the Revolutionary Council was in place in Kashmir, calling on the people to join hands in the revolt against the illegitimate occupants of the Valley – India.[10] Pakistan's failure in 1965 to achieve its objectives aggravated its reliance on religion to attain its objectives in Kashmir. In the late 1960s, a new set of *jihadis* emerged, deriving their inspiration from left wing anti-imperialist struggles. The Pakistani military and political leadership were more and more convinced about the indispensability of covert warfare in their religiously driven strategies towards Jammu and Kashmir. This new outfit was named 'Al Fatah' and it received clear instructions from Pakistan to launch intense attacks on government offices, banks, etc in Jammu and Kashmir. The outfit believed in using more aggressive means as compared to its earlier counterpart to attain its objective of creating unrest and terror in the Valley. Defeat in 1965, of its aggression, only added to Pakistan's leaning toward Islamic ideology.[11]

1971: Dismemberment of Pakistan

In the late 1950s and early 1960s, Pakistan witnessed a rising image of the military in the eyes of the people. Gen Ayub's era, in fact, marked the beginning of military control in the political and civil systems of Pakistan. This was important as it eventually led to the splitting up of Pakistan. Ayub's successor Gen Yahya Khan, talked about the Islamic identity of Pakistan and kept defence at the top of its agenda. Yahya Khan, utilised the intelligence agencies to motivate the Islamic parties to work against the two major political parties, the Awami League and Pakistan Peoples Party (PPP). These parties were accused of being unIslamic. The military regime had close ties with the Jamaat-e-Islami and also encouraged the mushrooming of other Islamic groups. [12]

In the 1960s, the military's role expanded and also, political and ethnic tensions increased. The two wings of Pakistan, the West and the East, were undoubtedly very different. The common factors between the two wings were *Islam* and *fear of India.* The central leadership could have utilised these for integration and to build goodwill between the two parts. The political parties and leadership struggled with their own weaknesses and failed to rise above provincialism, and exploited religion for power politics.[13] Islam lost meaning as a unifying factor, as the socio-economic factor had a significant contribution in increasing alienation in the Eastern wing.

Shortly after partition, Mountbatten had predicted that East Pakistan would break away from Pakistan within a quarter of a century.[14] The Bengalis may have been Muslims but they had a distinct identity of their own – they had a different culture and language which they respected. Unfortunately, the West Pakistanis never valued or respected this identity of East Pakistan and what was more painful for the East was the discriminating attitude of the Punjabis who considered themselves to be a superior class. The tensions in the Eastern Wing resulted in an insurgency and Pakistan's third war with India. Like the previous wars in 1947-48 and 1965, religion was used as the factor of motivation. During the war, Lt. Gen. Tikka Khan, drawing from Sir Mohammed Iqbal, exhorted the troops: "Allah, exalts the *mujahid* whether he lives or dies. He is a *ghazi* (crusader) if he lives, and a *shaheed* (martyr) if he dies. The *mujahid* seeks Allah's grace. He does not covet wealth and property."[15]

Even Yahya Khan, the commander-in-chief and President of Pakistan, boosted the soldiers by saying that they (Pakistan Army) were fighting the anti-Islamic *kafir* army and were upholding the highest traditions of *mujahideen* – soldiers of Islam.[16]

What was most critical was the evolution Pakistan's grand strategy after the 1971 War. The grand strategy incorporated two important objectives which decided the future course of action for the Pakistani leadership. First, to expand territory eastward (take Kashmir). This implied a rise in covert activities in J&K and added emphasis on radical

Islam in the name of *jihad*. Thus, terrorism came to be adopted as a foreign policy tool. Second, to expand control westward (to gain leverage in Kabul). This implied creating strategic depth in Afghanistan and also facilitating Pakistan friendly governance.

Global Rise of Islamic Ideology in the 1970s and 1980s

The 1970s and 1980s witnessed the reemergence of Islam as a potent global force starting with the spread of Saudi Wahhabi ideology. The Iranian revolution had shattered the secular basis of nationalist thinking and expectations of modernisation and development theories. The revolution drew attention towards the significant changes that were taking place in many Muslim countries across the globe in the 1970s. Ironically, the revival of Islamic ideology was most prominent in the societies which were modern or in the process of modernisation, with a well-trained, Western oriented, secular elite, for example, countries like Egypt, Lebanon, Tunisia, Turkey and Algeria. In Egypt and Malaysia, the resurgence of Islam was manifested in the people's lives, the conventional religious beliefs and also the state politics. Religion came much more into practice and was reflected in the form of daily prayers, fasting and the way people dressed. Spiritualism was emphasised with the revitalisation of Sufi Islamic ideology. Muslim rulers laid stress on Islamic identity to gain legitimacy, and Islamic organisations and symbols assumed paramount importance for the state.

Bhutto's turning towards Islam has to be studied in the context of developments worldwide. He turned towards Islam to counter his Islamic critics and also to strengthen ties with the oil-rich nations of the Arabian Gulf. Thus, Islam in the 1970s and 1980s was used as a source of protest and opposition and also to legitimise the seizure of power. Ironically, the same Islamic ideology was used by Zia to overthrow Bhutto.

Bhutto's Islamic Socialism

The idea of an Islamic Pakistan was pronounced by Bhutto and then subsequently nurtured and developed by Zia, who used religion aggressively for controlling the state. Bhutto took forward the idea of *Islamic Socialism* and, thus, enforced Islam as a major factor in statecraft. Stephen Cohen points out, "If the Pakistan movement and the first twenty-five years of the history of Pakistan can be characterized as a struggle to turn Indian Muslims into Pakistanis, the years since 1972 have been an extension of the process; a struggle to turn Pakistanis into good Muslims."[17] Bhutto's Islamic Socialism was considered insincere – it was seen as more to establish the non-Indian identity of Pakistan.[18] Zia put the state at the service of Islam and took steps to inculcate Islamic practices within the state by banning alcohol and gambling, and declaring Friday as a non-working day.

In 1976, Bhutto had appointed Zia-ul-Haq as the new army chief and allocated him the responsibility to Islamise the Pakistan Army. It was during this period that "*Jihad*" was included in the motto of the Pakistan Army, apart from "*Iman*" and "*Taqwa*".

The Quranic Concept of War

Bhutto's active plan for the Islamisation of Pakistan was supported by interpretations of the teachings of the Holy Quran. Although Jinnah believed that Pakistan would be able to become a major power because of it being a Muslim state, there had been no serious strategy based on Islam that the nation followed. Eventually, the Quran was interpreted to develop Pakistan's doctrine and strategy of war through terrorism.

The most comprehensive and precise study on war doctrine and strategy in the context of the Holy Quran has been by Brig S.K. Malik in his book, *The Quranic Concept of War*. According to Brig Malik, "The Holy Quran has given a comprehensive treatment to its concept of war" and "determines all aspects of the use of 'force' in inter-state relations."[19] Brig Malik regards the Quranic philosophy of war as supreme, providing the directions for the initiation, planning and control of war. According to his interpretation, the very "initiation of war is for the Cause of God" and *jihad* is the "most glorious word in the vocabulary of Islam".

Terror, according to the author and a majority of Pakistani military officers, is central to the war strategy. Use of terror as an instrument to impose one's will and decisions on the enemy has been legitimised, citing examples from the Holy Quran and arriving at the conclusion that "when God wishes to impose His will upon his enemies, He chooses to do so by casting terror in their hearts".[20]

The Islamic concept, as derived from the Holy Quran by Brig Malik, relies on the use of terror in the preparatory stages of war in order to assure victory and achieve direct results.[21] Thus, terror has been legitimised in the Islamic ideology which has till today shaped the military strategy of Pakistan. Brig Malik asserts, "Terror struck into the hearts of the enemies is not only a means, it is the end in itself."[22] It is emphasised that *fear* has to be an important part of the preparation of war and it determines that "the test of utmost preparation lies in our capability to instill terror into the hearts of the enemies."[23]

The Quranic interpretation of the conduct of modern war legitimises *jihad* and use of terror. One of the most effective modes of generating terror is through *covert warfare*, thus, creating physical and mental unrest and fear in the enemy territory. Covert warfare, as practised by Pakistan, includes different tactics like guerilla warfare, inciting insurgencies and destruction of buildings, all of which work towards generating terror and insecurity in the minds of Indians and, thus, aim to weaken India's physical and mental capabilities.

Gen Zia's Pursuit of Islamisation

Gen Zia systematically reinforced the *Islamisation of Pakistan* which was propagated by his predecessor, Zulfikar Ali Bhutto. Zia's vision came out very clearly in his words: "Pakistan, which was created in the name of Islam, will continue to survive only if it sticks to Islam. That is why I consider the introduction of the Islamic system as an essential prerequisite for the country."[24]

Zia introduced "Islamic Reforms" in various aspects of the Pakistani society and economy. A number of banking and commercial practices based on Islam were introduced, a dress code in accordance with Islamic norms was enforced, new women's universities were proposed, and strict regulations were laid down on the sale and consumption of alcoholic beverages.[25] Islamic practices in the day to day life of the people were made mandatory by the state. During this period, the Pakistan Army developed close links with the various Islamist groups and religion was increasingly used in strategic thinking. In the process of reinforcing the Islamisation of Pakistan and introducing Islamic reforms, Zia allowed the Tablighi Jamaat (an Islamic missionary society) to operate freely within the army. Zia was also the first army chief and the first politician in Pakistan to attend the Tablighi Jamaat's annual convention at Raiwind.[26]

Bhutto had entrusted Zia with the task of Islamisation of the Pakistan Army when he took over as the army chief. Bhutto considered Zia as the right man to take the Pakistani military to the next stage of its evolution as the guarantor of an anti-India, Islamic ideology.[27] Even as a corps commander, Zia distributed books written by the Jamaat-e-Islami's founder, Maulana Sayyed Abdul Ala Maududi, as rewards for the officers who proved their calibre in various fields in his garrison. Gen Zia-ul-Haq's early steps towards Islamisation of the army are identified by Lt Gen Jahan Dad Khan as deputy martial law administrator and corps commander:

> A devout Muslim, it was a matter of faith with [Zia ul–Haq] to propagate Islam wherever he could. Immediately after his appointment as COAS [chief of army staff], the motto he gave the troops was *Eman* (Faith), *Taqwa* (abstinence), *Jehad Fi Sabeelillah* (war in the way of, or for the sake of, God). He urged all ranks of the army, during his visits to troops as well as in written instructions, to offer their prayers, preferably led by the commanders themselves at various levels. Religious education was included in the training program and mosques and prayer halls were organized in all army units.[28]

In his first speech as chief martial law administrator, Zia described himself as a "Soldier of Islam" and declared his commitment to building a new political, economic and social order based on religion.[29] Adherence to the Islamic practices emerged as a major criterion for selection in the army. According to Zia, a soldier had to be a true Muslim before he could take on the responsibility of defending the Islamic Republic. In the armed forces, the status of religious teachers was raised to the level of commissioned officers. This became a major attraction for qualified individuals from universities and religious institutions.

During Zia's regime, the practice of Islamic tenets increased greatly compared to the times of the earlier political or military regimes in the country. The state was now being run on values interpreted on the basis of religion. The number of mosques increased in the country. The education system was deeply influenced and Islamiat and Pakistan studies became compulsory even for B.A., engineering, medical, commerce and law students.

The Islamist parties and especially groups like the Tablighi Jamaat linked to the Deobandi tradition got greater access to military officials. Zia encouraged the Islamist parties to counter the political forces. They received favourable treatment from the ruling militia and members of the Jamaat-e-Islami were offered senior positions in the important ministries. The judicial system of the state was Islamised and a Shariat Council consisting of *ulema* was established to look into constitutional and legal matters pertaining to the state, which were to be conducted in accordance with Islamic thought.

It was during this process of *Islamisation* that the Afghan War came into the picture and altered the total dynamics of Pakistan's political, military and strategic policies.

The Afghan War in the 1980s

Following the Soviet invasion of Afghanistan, Pakistan became the frontline state for the United States in the fight against Communism. Pakistan had already been a party to the destabilisation of Afghanistan which increased with the Soviet intervention and the reaction to it by the US and Pakistan as its frontline state. Pakistan's threat perception from India had consistently engaged the military and political leadership in Pakistan—worrying about the eastern border, and turmoil in Afghanistan made its western borders also insecure. Gen Arif outlined the three options available to Pakistan at the time of Soviet invasion: "Firstly she could accept the *fait accompli* as she lacked the capacity to challenge the Soviet Union. Secondly, she could provide open and full support to the Afghan freedom struggle, despite the risks involved. And, thirdly, she could give overt political, diplomatic, and humanitarian support to the refugees with covert assistance to the Mujahideen".[30] Pakistan was not in a position to face the Soviet Union alone and was tempted by the American assistance which would serve its diplomatic, economic and defence interests. Pakistan opted for the third option outlined by Gen Arif and entered into a second term alliance with the US. The status of US ally gave the Pakistan military an opportunity to fulfill its dreams for military modernisation. This major strategic development placed Pakistan in a position where it could demand the latest military weapons. Pakistan received an enormous amount of military aid from the US. It also received unlimited funds from Saudi Arabia and the Gulf countries to finance the US weaponry, which Pakistan opted to procure in the 1980s.

Pakistan offered its territory to the Americans and Zia's military regime undertook the responsibility of training the Mujahideen to carry out covert operations to fight the Soviets. The operations directed by the US Central Intelligence Agency (CIA) comprised some of the largest operations planned by the US and shaped a relationship between the CIA and the Pakistani intelligence agency, Inter-Services Intelligence (ISI), as the two worked in coordination for about a decade.

Pakistan's alliance with the US in the 1980s led to the development of the factors given below.

Religion Becomes a Major Driving Force

The US' war in Afghanistan led to the structural and organisational development of the factor of *religion in war*. The soldiers were being trained to fight in a "holy war" in the name of God. The declaration of *jihad* in Afghanistan led to the legitimised structural development of the institutions preparing young fighters. It was reported that over a period of time, over 80,000 volunteers who were trained for the war, came not only from Pakistan and Afghanistan but also other Muslim countries like Sudan, Bangladesh, Algeria and Turkey. The combination of courage, specifically amongst the Afghan fighters, and their strong religious belief, made the Mujahideen formidable warriors.[31] The belief was strengthened that the Mujahideen were fighting a holy war against the unbelievers—the *kafirs*—and "once the *jihad* was declared by their religious leaders, it was the duty of all men to fight, to save their faith, to defend their honour, to protect their independence and to guard their land and families".[32] The battle cry for the Mujahideen was (and is till date) "*Allah o Akbar*"—God is Great—which they shout as they are attacking the enemy camps, bases or personnel.[33] Thus, the fight for religion proliferated.

Pakistan: Training Ground for the Guerrilla Fighters

Ever since the creation of Pakistan, the Pashtuns or the Baluchis have been motivated by the creation of an independent state advocated by the Pashtun regimes in Kabul. This made the leadership in Pakistan worried about the vulnerability of the country and, thus, the possibility of ethnic unrest.

Following the Soviet presence in Afghanistan in December 1979, Lt Gen Akhtar Abdul Rahman, the director general of the ISI, convinced Gen Zia that Pakistan had the capacity to defeat the Soviets in a large-scale guerrilla war. The military leadership agreed to support the guerrilla warfare with arms, ammunition, money, intelligence, training and operational advice. Gen Akhtar, also suggested to Zia that Pakistan should offer the border areas of the NWFP (now Khyber-Pakhtunkhwa—KPK) and Baluchistan as a sanctuary for both the refugees and the guerrillas. The base was essential for the covert forces as without a secure cross-border base, no such campaign could succeed.[34]

Pakistan offered its territory as a secure base for the Mujahideen guerrilla fighters, providing them with arms and ammunition apart from food and shelter, training and intelligence.[35] According to Brig Mohammad Yousaf and Maj Mark Adkin: "The border areas of Pakistan had grown into a vast, sprawling administrative base for the *jihad*. The Mujahideen came there for arms, they came to rest, they came to settle…."[36] Since the US assistance to the Mujahideen started as a covert affair, the ISI Directorate became the channel for not only ensuring the secrecy of the operation but also providing expert advice to, and training, the Mujahideen in guerrilla tactics.

In this process, Zia cultivated a venomous strain of Islamic ideology in Pakistan. The ISI, in partnership with the right wing Islamic parties like the Jamaat-e-Islami and Jamiat-e-Ulema-e-Islam, recruited millions of Afghan refugees in Pakistan and students from the *madrassas* for the fight in Afghanistan as holy fighters. In this process, these Islamic parties developed an extensive network in Pakistan and also became much more influential.[37]

Along with this *jihadi* culture, what was also encouraged was sectarianism which resulted in the killing of thousands in Pakistan. On the external front, the Islamic revolution in Iran in 1979, played a crucial role and the Khomeini regime began exporting its revolutionary message across the Muslim world. Pakistan, invariably became a battle ground for the transplanted war between Iran and Saudi Arabia, which worked towards restricting the spread of Shia influence. [38] Baluchistan became the hub of hundreds of *madrassas* which were basically established to limit the Shia influence into Pakistan. On one side was the Iranian-backed Tehrik-e-Nifaz-e-Fiqh-e-Jafaria and, on the other, were Sunni extremist groups within Pakistan like the Sipah-e-Sahaba, that demanded that Shias (who comprised 15-20 per cent of Pakistan's population) should be declared non-Muslims like the Ahmadis.[39] The Islamisation process during Zia's time gave a totally different dimension to the *jihad* and encouraged a violent *jihadi* culture and also encouraged sectarianism in Pakistan.

Non-Accountability of US Weapons: Tools for Jihad

In the 1980s, the US intelligence services followed a strategy of supplying enormous amounts of arms and ammunition to the Mujahideen leaders and commanders in the field. The weapons pipeline was under the control of the ISI which actually was responsible for deciding the recipients and the quantity of weapons. The ISI retained the majority of the weapons and equipment (reportedly 60 per cent) for its own covert war against India. The weaponry supplied during the Afghan War remained in the region after the war ended. The intelligence agencies faced the problem of concealing their responsibility of distributing arms and the US did not want to be projected as providing direct military aid to the *jihadis*. It has been reported that the "US intelligence services set up bank accounts in Switzerland into which the US and the Saudi governments directed their contributions to the Afghan resistance, which were then used to pay for weapons from a variety of sources. Wealthy individual Saudis and the Iranian government also contributed to the Mujahideen."[40] The Dubai based Pakistani managed Bank of Credit and Commerce International (BCCI) and Pakistan's own Mehran Bank where profits from the narcotics trade were also recycled, stand out in this regard. Initially, the supply of US weapons was a trickle—also the weapons supplied to the Mujahideen were mostly outdated, but as the fighting intensified, the types of weapons supplied improved. Reportedly, Washington provided over two billion dollars of covert assistance to the Afghan War.[41]

Development of the Narcotics Trade

Another important development during this period comprised the narcotics trade which flourished with the CIA's assistance to fund the covert operations. Opium production went up from 200 metric tonnes in 1980 to 1,200 metric tonnes in 1989.[42] Initially, in the 1980s, the narcotics trafficking network was used to support the US-Pak strategy of arming and supplying the Afghan Mujahideen. Eventually, the military in Pakistan developed significant financial interest in the drug trade and this helped in the development of the drug economy in Afghanistan and Pakistan. The drug money was also believed to have been used by the military to support Pakistan's active nuclear programme which was initiated by Bhutto in the early 1970s. Thus, the narcotics trade was initially developed to generate funds for the war against the Soviets and eventually it became one of the major resources for the military to fund its weapon modernisation plans and covert operations in India, not only in Kashmir but also in Punjab.

Rise in Terrorism in the 1980s and 1990s

In the 1980s, religious resurgence, coupled with increasing alienation of the youth for diverse reasons, started to grow in Kashmir, and Pakistan's strategy of covert war through terrorism began to concretise. What was happening in Afghanistan and also simultaneously in Khalistan (with Pakistan's active assistance), had a direct impact in the Kashmir Valley. Thus, in the mid-1980s, disturbances in Kashmir were growing with an unusual amount of Jamaat activity, processions and resentment against the Hindus, and the communal divide had started to be a major disturbing factor. Pakistan continued its covert war and the year 1984 witnessed substantive escalation of violent acts in J&K. In the late 1980s and 1990s, Pakistan became much more active in sponsoring terrorism in J&K. The ISI encouraged young Kashmiris to come to Pakistan for training. The ISI initially trained the secular groups in Kashmir and eventually shifted to training of the groups linked to Pakistan's own Islamic parties.[43]

The weapons used by the terrorists had undergone a change as Pakistan had acquired modern arms in the 1980s to equip the covert fighters in Afghanistan. On one side, Pakistan had equipment for the Afghan Mujahideen which could be easily smuggled into Kashmir, and on the other, Pakistan also acquired modern weapon systems, including F-16s from the US during this period and, thus, felt psychologically stronger to carry on its covert strategy in Kashmir. But the most important factor for the escalation of the covert war in Punjab and J&K was the acquisition of nuclear weapons by Pakistan which it perceived as the security guarantee against a robust Indian military response.

Pakistan's Nuclear Weapons: Shield Against Terrorism

Pakistan accelerated its nuclear programme in the 1980s under Zia. The military regime in Pakistan tried to exploit the India "threat" and acquisition of nuclear capability to gain domestic legitimacy. It was under Zia's rule that Pakistan became a nuclear state and defined a coherent nuclear strategy. By 1987, Pakistan was believed to be able to carry out a full nuclear explosion. By 1992, Pakistan declared officially that it possessed the cores of nuclear weapons, and in 1998, the Pakistani nuclear tests followed India's new posture of a nuclear state.

The acquisition of nuclear capability enhanced Pakistan's capability to wage and escalate the covert war in Kashmir as nuclear weapons were believed to deter India from responding with conventional military retaliation. Policy-makers in Pakistan seem to be convinced that they will be able to carry on, or rather accelerate, their activities in Kashmir by holding out the threat of using nuclear weapons, if required, and this would control India's strategic moves in the Valley. This thought process seems to have grown with Pakistan's "first use policy". Pakistan claimed that it had the capability of the making a nuclear bomb in 1987, and it is noteworthy, that during the late 1980s, the activities in the Valley also witnessed a shift. Terrorist acts increased significantly in numbers and were planned in a more organised manner, making the job of the Indian security forces more difficult.

Pakistan became more vocal about the possession of nuclear weapons in the late 1980s, and then, in the 1990s, in order to create the impression that any radical move from the Indian side might be retaliated against with the *Islamic Bomb.* Pakistan's strategy has been to use the nuclear card for aggressive militancy in Kashmir and, thus, the Pakistan military now had the nuclear umbrella to shield it from the Indian military response. *Jihad* now had the protection of the nuclear bomb for Pakistan. There is a clear correlation between the progress in the acquisition of nuclear weapons and the launch of covert war during the last 25 years.

1990s: Political Tug of War

After Zia's death, Pakistan faced innumerable challenges. The nation had been under military rule for a long period and, thus, getting back to democracy was a challenge, the economic downslide had started to appear, the *jihadi* culture had taken firm roots in the country, the US alliance had just ended, and Pakistan stood isolated internationally. The democratic regimes between 1988 and 1999 were unstable and changed frequently, especially if the agenda of the elected governments challenged the power and functioning of the army. During this period, there were four elections and both Benazir Bhutto and Nawaz Sharif returned to power twice. There were four caretaker governments in between as neither of the elected governments could complete its term.

The ISI became an important centre of power on account of its role in the Afghan War and its involvement with the Americans. Although the fundamentalists and Islamists appeared to have lost in the elections, their influence continued to grow, especially, among the intelligence agencies, military officers and emerging middle class in Pakistan. The ISI also managed to create and sustain the differences between the political parties which hampered the evolution of a mature democratic set-up in Pakistan and contributed to the frequent changes on the political front. The intelligence encouraged and utilised the Islamist parties to counter the political groups which went against the military's interests.

On the external front, there were two developments in this decade. Both these developments comprised a continuation of Pakistan's existing polices. The leadership in Pakistan intensified its terrorist activities on the Indian soil through their proxies and anti-India terrorist organisations became much more active in the Valley and other parts of India. The ISI was now a fully trained and equipped organisation with a ready infrastructure for *jihad* which was now fully diverted towards India to continue Pakistan's strategy of 'bleeding India through a thousand cuts'. By 2002, Pakistan became home for more than two dozen militant groups operating in the neighbourhood and pursuing their agenda which was looked at favourably by the state. The largest among them were the Laskhar-e-Tayyeba (LeT), Jaish-e-Mohammad (JeM), Harkat-ul-Mujahideen (HuM) and Harkat-ul-Jihad-al-Islami (HJuI). All these organisations shared a similar source and pursued similar goals. These organisations had the state's patronage and funds were never a problem. The state's patronage, in fact, helped the *jihadi* organisations to raise funds in public places.

On the western front, Pakistan was keen to create its strategic depth and not have a hostile government. The army and ISI, along with the political leadership, came together to support a new class of warriors – the *Taliban*. In 1994, Afghanistan saw the outbreak of the Taliban, which was composed of the younger generation of Pakistani-Afghans. The Taliban were mainly the Afghans who had grown up in the Pakistani refugee camps and were products of *madrassas* which were encouraged during Zia's time and were funded by the Saudi money. Maulana Fazl-ur-Rahman, the leader of the Jamiat-e-Ulema-e-Islam-F (JUI-F) supported the Taliban and being a close ally of Benazir, played a critical role in facilitating communication between Pakistan and the Taliban.[44] The Pakistani leadership extended full-fledged support to the Taliban and added to their strength from Pakistani *madrassas*. The Taliban began to take over one province after another in Afghanistan, and finally brought the whole of Afghanistan under their control in less than five years.[45]

Musharraf's Coup and US led War on Terror Post 9/11

The military under the leadership of Gen Musharraf assumed control of the state in 1999 and, even though the coup was condemned by most world leaders, it was mostly supported by the Pakistani populace. Pakistan once again witnessed a major strategic development and entered into a third alliance with the US post 9/11. Once again, Pakistan arrived at a critical crossroads. Musharraf attempted to project a path of moderation and publicly announced on January 12, 2002, that Pakistani territory would not be used for (*jihadi*) terrorism. In 2004, he announced his plea for *Enlightened Moderation* which could provide an answer to Pakistan's identity and its relationship with Islam. Defining the enlightened moderation, he said:

> The strategy of enlightened moderation... involve a win-win situation for the whole of the world as well as for the Muslim countries. This is a two-pronged strategy. One prong is to be delivered by the Muslim world itself by shunning militancy and extremism and adopting the path of socioeconomic uplift to achieve its own emancipation. The other prong is meant to be delivered by the West, and the United States in particular, to determinedly resolve with justice all political disputes in which Muslims are engaged and also assist in the socioeconomic betterment of the deprived Muslim world.... The time has come to re-think our position. What we need is a renaissance.... We have to concentrate on human resource development, and the best way for that is through poverty alleviation, greater education, better health and assured social justice.... We have to adopt the path of moderation, a conciliatory approach, a pacific approach, in order to cleanse ourselves of the charge that Islam is a religion of militancy and is averse to modernization, democracy and secularism.[46]

Although Musharraf talked about the moderate, secular path which included rejection of extremism, the actual strategies which the military pursued were certainly not in sync with the announced enlightened moderation. It was more to appease the West and project an image of Pakistan as a moderate Islamic nation which believed in countering extremism and was more focussed on socio-economic development.

The military regime came under immense pressure by the Bush Administration to act against the terrorist organisations, leading Musharraf to issue orders banning some of the key militant outfits, and also for registeration of the *madrassas*. These efforts failed to provide results and the popular consensus has been that the military's flawed approach towards the war on terror has been responsible for the rising extremism and flourishing insurgency on Pakistan's frontier borders, NWFP (now KPK) and Federally Administered Tribal Areas (FATA). These have been troublesome regions even in the most peaceful times and are now engaged in a full-blooded insurgency. Pakistan, for the first time, is facing terrorist attacks within its own territories. The military has a history of waging insurgencies (in the name of *jihad*) since the time of the country's creation in 1947, and, post 9/11, has been compelled to take on a reversal role of counter-insurgency. It has been flagrantly discriminating between various terrorist groups and has not given up on *jihadi* terrorism as a state policy.

A study by Ashley Tellis identifies four different types of terrorist groups implicated in this regard: domestic sectarian groups, anti-Indian terrorist groups, the Taliban and Al Qaeda.[47]

The first set includes the domestic sectarian groups like the Sunni Sipah-e-Sahaba and its offshoot, the Lashkar-e-Jhangvi, and the Shia Tehrik-e-Nifaz-e-Fiqh-e-Jafaria and its offshoot, the Sipah-e-Muhammad. These groups have been engaged in massive sectarian violence activities within Pakistan. Although these groups were initially supported and encouraged by the military, they became a major challenge for the military leadership, posing a serious threat to the domestic order. The global war on terror provided an opportunity to the military leadership to crack down on these elements. The state leadership was selective in suppressing these organisations and the target groups were the ones whose objectives fell out of sync with the military's perception of national interests, and those engaged in the *jihadi* violence within the state rather than in support of the military's external ambitions vis-à-vis India and Afghanistan.[48]

The second set of terrorist groups includes the organisations working in coordination with the Pakistan Army and ISI against India, such as the LeT, JeM, and HuM. These are the terrorist groups which the Pakistan Army has trained, encouraged and financed to carry out the covert war in Jammu and Kashmir and the rest of India since the 1980s. These groups are an extension of Pakistan's military strategy to continue sub-conventional warfare through various means and, thus, received different treatment from Gen Musharraf, as compared to the sectarian groups. These groups are viewed as working to legitimise the struggle for self-determination for the Kashmiri people and, thus, have been excluded from the military's campaign against violence and extremism.[49] These groups have been active not only in J&K but also in other parts of India, creating occasions to spark a war or to precipitate action from India.

The third group of extremist elements comprise the Taliban, who were forced to leave Kabul after the initial success of Operation Enduring Freedom.[50] The Taliban, after their defeat by the Northern Alliance, reverted to their villages in the southern and eastern Afghan provinces, as well as along the border areas on the western side of the Durand Line separating Afghanistan from Pakistan.[51] A significant number of the Taliban leaders, along with the Pakistani Pashtuns, being the prime targets in the global war on terror, took refuge in FATA. Most of the Taliban's fighters were originally mobilised by the ISI from the Gilzai confederation of Pashtuns who dominated southeastern Afghanistan and from other Pashtun tribes belonging to FATA, and, thus, their returning to a relatively secure place, their original homeland, was natural after the Pakistan military decided to join the US in the aggressive military operation against the Taliban.[52] The Taliban have made Pakistan's tribal belt the base for training camps and for conducting action plans in Afghanistan and the Pakistani territory. The Taliban leadership has manoeuvred an independent administrative set-up in FATA and the locals are in no position to oppose them.

From the beginning of 2008, there have been reports of the Taliban extending their conservative extremist norms to the civilians in the region, controlling even their day-to-day lives. Pakistan's former Interior Minister, Aftab Khan Sherpao, whose ancestral village is at the foothills of the tribal region, has very categorically stated that there is a serious risk of "total Talibanization" in the KPK.[53] It is tough to believe that the Taliban are able to regenerate to this extent without the support of the Pakistan military and the intelligence units which has allowed them to flourish and operate in cities like Karachi within Pakistan. Because the Pakistani leadership was so deeply involved in the making of the Taliban, it has undeniably avoided the killing or capturing of the senior Taliban leadership in southern Afghanistan or in FATA. The Taliban have enjoyed the leverage from the Pakistan Army and expanded the *jihadi* terrorist network within Pakistan, resulting in massive suicide bombings and revolts.

The fourth group, Al Qaeda, which also found sanctuary in FATA, received a much more aggressive and firm response from the military.[54] Although Al Qaeda commands some sympathy within the Pakistani society, the 9/11 terrorist attacks in the US were conclusively attributed to this terrorist outfit, and the US embarked on a worldwide campaign against it. Pakistan did extend support to the US by conducting various law enforcement and internal security operations targeting the terrorist financing, and apprehending and rendering terrorist targets for prosecution abroad.[55] The massive military operation resulted in the arrest of around 700 terrorists from Al Qaeda and other extremist organisations. Although the aggressive military operations led to the arrest of numerous Al Qaeda operatives, the top leader, Osama bin Laden, was not touched (till May 2011). The operations forced the militants to disperse further from, and into, Pakistan, as Khyber Pakhtunkhwa, while considered secure for the Taliban, became unsafe for these operatives; also, the cities in Pakistan provided them with a more advanced mode of communication in order to connect them to the extremist network.[56]

In May 2011, Osama bin Laden was killed in an operation undertaken by the US Navy SEALs from the US Special Operations Command. Bin Laden had been living for years in a military compound in Abbottabad, Pakistan, where he was holed up in a two-storey house just 100 yards from a Pakistani military academy. Abbottabad, is located just 50 km from the capital, Islamabad, and is home to three Pakistan Army regiments, and thousands of military personnel. The area is relatively affluent, with several retired military men residing there. Although Gen Kayani has repeatedly claimed that he was unaware of Osama's location, it is tough to believe that Bin Laden was residing in the army compound without the knowledge of the Pakistan military and intelligence officials. Accordingly President Obama's chief counter-terrorism adviser John Brennan, it was "inconceivable that Osama bin Laden did not have a support system in the country that allowed him to remain there for an extended period of time".[57] The end of Bin Laden has marked a major shift in the Pakistan-US relationship. The level of trust between the two allies has been deteriorating, bringing the relationship between the two nations to the lowest level.

After almost a decade of blatant military operations, the Americans appear increasingly frustrated with their results. Not only have the numbers of extremist acts escalated, the terrorist attacks are also much more intense, better planned, and persist with deadly regularity, making it difficult for the American intelligence to detect them. Increasing drone attacks by the US and North Atlantic Treaty Organisation (NATO) forces have increased anti-US sentiments in Pakistan tremendously.

Taliban Insurgency: Emergence of the Tehrik-e-Taliban Pakistan (TTP)

The Taliban insurgency began as early as 2003 when Al Qaeda and the Afghan Taliban fighters were flushed out of Afghanistan by the US armed forces. In 2007, the Tehrik-e-Taliban Pakistan (TTP) emerged as an entity in the context of a series of military operations (that took place post 9/11)—the Pakistani military operations as well as the US Unmanned Aerial Vehicle (UAV) strikes in FATA. Until then, most of the component groups of the TTP were loosely organised, with ties to the Afghan Taliban. The TTP started to professionally organise itself when Abdullah Mehsud of the Afghan Taliban returned to Waziristan from the Guantanamo Bay camp. He blew himself in Pishin, Baluchistan, during a siege by Pakistani forces in 2006.[58] After Abdullah Mehsud's death, Baitullah Mehsud, a leading member of the Afghan Taliban, organised all the groups operating in FATA that professed a similar ideology and knit them into a most dangerous terrorist/ insurgent group called the TTP.[59]

The organisation consists of a number of militant groups (around 20 of them) and is rooted in the tribal belt of Pakistan. The TTP's creation in December 2007 marked a new development arising out of the realisation among the local and foreign militants that a central command was required in order to attain their objectives, and Baitullah Mehsud provided them the unifying force. The prime objectives of the TTP have been: Pakistan must end its cooperation with the US and NATO forces; and the *Sharia* must replace the existing legal system in Pakistan. The TTP has adopted a strictly anti-state and specifically anti-military agenda and has been conveying its message by consistently attacking the government/military offices. In other words, the TTP has organised itself as a true insurgency, ideologically as well as organisationally.

The TTP draws its ideological guidance from Al Qaeda and also provides a safe haven to the Al Qaeda allies in FATA. Given the mutual cooperation between the two organisations, it would not be wrong to state that the TTP is a force multiplier for Al Qaeda.[60] The TTP has launched numerous attacks against US, NATO and Pakistani targets. The organisation regards the Pakistani state as an enemy of Islam for siding with the US. It has adopted an anti-state posture and has claimed responsibility for most of the terrorist attacks, including the assassination of Benazir Bhutto, the bombing at the Mariott Hotel, the attack on the Mehran Naval Base and Karachi airport, and the deadliest of all, the attack on the Peshawar school. The organisation is growing in influence among young and unemployed youth and is using the *Sharia* to promote its political and ideological agendas. There have been also reports suggesting that the Pakistani Taliban have pledged allegiance to the Islamic State of Syria (ISIS) and its leader Abu Bakr al-Baghdadi.[61] These developments are dangerous and would have grave consequences for Pakistan, given the fact that the ISIS has managed to establish its identity as the most brutal and violent force in the competitive world of terrorism. Pakistan certainly has become a natural ground for the ISIS where it is likely to comfortably find allegiance and an operational base.

Conclusion

Presently, Pakistan is facing a broad landscape of militancy. A variety of terrorist groups, with varying agendas operate from Pakistan and share a varied relationship with the state. Some of these organisations like the TTP regard the state as an enemy of Islam for joining hands with the West and killing its own people. On the other side, are the deadly groups like the Jamaat-ud-Dawa (JuD), which are flourishing in the heart of Pakistan and enjoy the state's patronage. For the first time, militancy has managed to penetrate the interiors of Punjab and Sindh, and the Army General Headquarters (GHQ) became one of the terror targets in the recent past. In fact, bases of all the three forces have been attacked, and the air force bases have become frequent targets The impact of the Afghan War has allowed Al Qaeda, the Haqqani network and the Taliban inside Pakistan where they have been expanding their influence. The Pakistan military and ISI have nurtured some of the terrorist organisations which they categorically grade as "strategic assets" and are clearly not willing to act against them. These so-called "friendly"[62] groups, as Ayesha Siddiqua Agha terms them, include: the Good Taliban, LeT, JuD, and JeM. The Haqqani network which has strongholds in the bordering Afghan districts of Paktia and Khost and is involved in the anti-US and anti-NATO operations, has enjoyed state patronage for long. [63] The military has desisted from acting against these groups and has been "selective and partial" in its counter-terrorism approach, which has been the root cause for the lack of success in the war on terror.

The frontiers borders—the FATA and KPK—have become the breeding ground for terrorism and the region presents a conglomeration of various insurgent and terrorist groups to the Pakistani military and NATO forces. Al Qaeda, the Haqqani network and Taliban have established their sanctuaries in these areas. Insurgency in Baluchistan, which became active in 2004, has aggravated much more after the killing of Akbar Bugti in 2007. The Baluch have always suffered a deep sense of alienation from the state and resisted it regularly which the leadership tried to curb with brute military force in the past, starting in the 1940s. Added to this deadly mix of extremist groups is the TTP, which, in a way, is an extension of the Sunni Deobandi militancy and poses a real danger to the state. The Pakistani Taliban have absorbed members of radical Sunni organisations. This has also further exaggerated the problem of Shia-Sunni violence not only in the tribal belt but also in other parts of Pakistan.

Islam has remained extremely critical for Pakistan in its domestic and foreign policy. But the interpretation of Islam has varied under different regimes. Jinnah's vision was that of a secular nation where Muslim culture and norms could be protected and practised freely by the Muslims. Obviously, his vision was shaped under a different set of circumstances, and eventually, as one can see, the state adopted different interpretations of Islam, deviating completely from Jinnah's spirit. Religion, under Zia, found its most extremist expression and Pakistan's ideological posture was reshaped. The underlying problem is that the state has not been able to define its relationship with Islam till date. The Pakistani leadership cannot allow itself to be entangled in contradictions, where it talks about enlightened moderation on one side, and, simultaneously, patronises the terrorist outfits which brainwash the young Pakistani minds to join hands in fighting a holy war in the neighbourhood. Pakistan is facing a deadly *jihadi* blowback of its own long stated policies based on terrorism, threatening the very survival of the state. The leadership in Pakistan needs to seriously reconsider its strategic calculus and refrain from using terrorism legitimised by religion as a foreign policy tool.

Notes

1. Ayesha Jalal, *The State of Martial Rule* (Cambridge: Cambridge University Press, 1990), p. 16.
2. *Quaid-i-Azam Mohammad Ali Jinnah's Speeches as Governor-General of Pakistan1947-48,* (Karachi: Government of Pakistan, 1964).
3. Farzana Shaikh, *Making Sense of Pakistan* (London: Foundation Books, 2009), p. 5.
4. Maj Gen Akbar Khan, *Raiders in Kashmir* (Delhi: Army Publishers, date not available), p.9.

5. Air Cmde Jasjit Singh, *Kargil 1999: Pakistan's Fourth War for Kashmir* (New Delhi: Knowledge World, 1999), p. 2.
6. Ziad Haider, "Ideological Adrift", in Maleeha Lodhi, ed., *Pakistan Beyond the Crisis State* (New Delhi: Rupa Publications, 2011), p. 116.
7. Ahmedis are followers of an alleged 19th century messiah called Mirza Ghulam Ahmed.
8. Haider, n. 6, p. 116.
9. Ibid., p. 117.
10. Brig Z. A Khan (Retd), *The Way it Was* (Karachi: Alibaba, 1988), pp. 155-156, as cited in Owen Bennett Jones, *Pakistan: Eye of the Storm* (New Delhi: Viking, 2002), p. 77.
11. For details, see Praveen Swami, *India, Pakistan and the Secret Jihad: The Covert War in Kashmir: 1947-2004* (London: Routledge, 2007), p. 62.
12. Haider, n. 6, p. 118.
13. Safdar Mehmood, *Pakistan Divided* (New Delhi: Alpha Bravo, 1983), p. 5.
14. Larry Collins and Dominique Lapierre, *Freedom at Midnight* (London: Harper Collins, 1997), p. 159.
15. Quoted in unpublished manuscript, p.217, as cited in Stephen P. Cohen, *The Pakistan Army 1998 Edition* (Karachi: Oxford University Press, 1998), p. 87.
16. Ibid.
17. Ibid., p. 89.
18. See Stephen Cohen, *The Idea of Pakistan* (New York: Oxford University Press, 2005), p. 170.
19. Brig S.K. Malik, *The Quranic Concept of War* (New Delhi: Himalayan Books, 1986), p. 1.
20. Ibid., p. 57.
21. Ibid.
22. Ibid., p. 59.
23. Ibid., p. 144.
24. "General Zia ul-Haq's Address to the Nation on July 5, 1977", quoted in Hasan Askari Rizvi, *The Military and Politics in Pakistan 1947-1986* (Lahore: Progressive Publishers, 1986), pp. 289-93.
25. Cohen, n. 15, p. 91.
26. Cohen, n. 18, p. 113.
27. Husain Haqqani, *Pakistan: Between Mosque and Military (*Lahore: Vanguard Books, 2005), p. 112.
28. Lt Gen. Jahan Dad Khan, *Pakistan Leadership Challenges* (Karachi: Oxford University Press, 1999), p.158); Haqqani, n. 27, p. 113.
29. Haqqani, Ibid., p.127
30. Gen Khalid Mehmood Arif, *Working With Zia: Pakistan Power Politics 1977-1988* (Karachi: Oxford University Press, 1995). p. 314.
31. Brig Mohammad Yousaf and Maj Mark Adkin, *The Bear Trap* (Lahore: Jang Publishers, 1992), p. 32.
32. Ibid., p. 33.
33. Ibid.
34. Ibid., p. 25.
35. Ibid., p. 49.
36. Ibid.
37. Haider, n. 6, p. 122.
38. Ibid., p. 123.
39. Ibid.
40. "India: Arms and Abuses in Indian Punjab and Kashmir", September 1994, vol.6, no.10, at http://www.hrw.org/campaigns/kashmir/1994/index.htm. Accessed on July 20, 1996.

41. Haqqani n. 27, p. 318.
42. T. Raghvan, "The Narcotics Trade in South-West Asia: Geography and Production", *Security Research Review,* at, http://www.bharat-rakshak.com/SRR/Volume14/raghvan.html. Accessed on November 10, 2009.
43. Ahmed Rashid, *Descent into Chaos* (London: Penguin Group, 2008), p. 111.
44. Hassan Abbas, *Pakistan's Drift Into Extremism: Allah, the Army and America's War on Terror* (New York: M.E. Sharpe, 2005), p. 154.
45. Ibid., p. 155.
46. Speech by Gen Musharraf, "OIC Challenge and Response: Enlightened Moderation", June 1, 2004, at http://presidentmusharraf.wordpress.com/2005/01/18/musharraf-oic-enlightened-moderation/. Accessed on June 10, 2010.
47. Ashley J. Tellis, *Pakistan and the War on Terror: Conflicted Goals, Compromised Performance* (Washington DC: Carnegie Endowment, 2008), p. 4.
48. Ibid.
49. Ibid., p. 5.
50. Ibid., p. 6
51. Ibid.
52. Ibid.
53. Jane Perlez, "Ex-Pakistani Official Says Policy on Taliban is Failing", *The New York Times,* January 27, 2008.
54. See Zafar Abbas, "Pakistan Army Confronts Al Qaeda", *BBC News,* January 8, 2004, at http://news.bbc.co.uk/2/hi/south_asia/3378395.stm. Accessed on February 15, 2004.
55. Tellis, n. 47, p. 9.
56. Ibid., p. 10.
57. "Inconceivable that Osama Had no Support System in Pakistan: US", *The Hindu* May 3, 2011,
58. Imtiaz Gul, *The Al Qaeda Connection: The Taliban and Terror in Pakistan's Tribal Areas* (New Delhi: Penguin Books, 2009), p. 51.
59. The TTP was the revival of an older organisation of the same name founded in 1998 in Orakzai Agency.
60. "Tehrik-e-Taliban is a Terror Group", *VOANEWS.com Policy,* July 9, 2010, at http://www.voanews.com/policy/editorials/Tehrik-e-Taliban-Is-A-Terror-Group-102393269.html. Accessed on August 10, 2010
61. John Hall, "The Growing Influence of ISIS Now Reaches Pakistan as Taliban Leaders Pledge Allegiance to Brutal Jihadist Group", *Mail Online,* October, 15, 2014, http://www.dailymail.co.uk/news/article-2793622/the-growing-influence-isis-reaches-pakistan-taliban-leaders-pledge-allegiance-brutal-jihadist-group.html. Accessed on December 20, 2014.
62. Ayesha Siddiqua Agha, "Pakistan's Counterterrorism Strategy: Separating Friends from Enemies", *The Washington Quarterly,* Winter 2011, pp. 149-162.
63. Ibid.

4

Indo-Russian Relations in Contemporary Times: A Realistic Assessment

Chandra Rekha

Introduction

A resurgent Russian foreign policy and the current geo-politics in the wake of the ongoing Ukraine crisis and sanctions imposed by the West have raised concerns about Russia-US relations. Failure to find a common security space between Russia and the US is seen as a major setback in the relationship. Despite efforts by both countries to engage on wider global issues, mutual suspicion and hostilities towards each other have hampered a positive outcome between Washington and Moscow. Ironically, these developments have impacted the international community as well. Ukraine, one of the 'privileged interests' of Russia has become a new geo-political theatre for the West and Russia to establish their influence in the region. Undoubtedly, the geo-political face-off between the two former Cold War adversaries – Russia and the US – will have ramifications on countries that have shared robust partnerships with the two nations.

In this context, a realistic assessment is required in understanding the strategic partnership between India and Russia which are fast emerging as potential global players in the post Cold War era. This is particularly necessary as the current world order has dragged the two countries into a diplomatic dilemma and has given rise to complexities and challenges in bilateral relations. Thus, the turbulence in the contemporary international environment will call for readjustments and reorientation in some areas and also a need to survey the possible aspects to overcome the pitfalls in the relations, if any.

But before assessing the traditional partnership between India and Russia in the contemporary international milieu, let us examine Russia's current international status, its geo-political aspirations, foreign policy priorities and security threats.

Contemporary Geo-politics of Russia

When President Putin took over the reins of Russia in 2000, his immediate challenge was to tackle the domestic crisis as the country had failed to overcome the predicaments that came along with the disintegration of the Soviet Union. The Kremlin continued to fail in its endeavours to overcome the economic crisis, flagging the defence industrial complex and corruption that had marred the country's progress in the new geopolitical system. Moreover, despite Russia adopting a pro-western system and foreign policy, lack of support from the west to absorb Russia in the new world order, agitated the Russian administration. Putin's major task was to realise his vision of repositioning Russia as an influential global entity. Accordingly, the reforms and policies initiated by him assisted in Russia making remarkable progress in its economy, defence as well as its global image. These developments provided the much needed impetus for Russia to pursue rigorous and pragmatic long-term foreign policy objectives. Moscow altered its national security priorities which became distinct with Putin's foreign policy measures and its successes in Chechnya in 1999, the Georgia War in 2008, and the accession of Crimea through a referendum.

The West, alarmed by Russia's resurging international influence, has begun to pursue a policy of 'containment' towards its growing global presence. Russia's foreign policy priorities,mainly concentrated on its economic growth and geo-political interests, to a large extent, coincided with the growing expansionist policies of the US led North Atlantic Treaty Organisation (NATO) in the former Soviet space. The persistent efforts of the West to bring the region under the security umbrella of NATO caused major discomfiture to the Kremlin. For instance,NATO's encroachment on Russia's 'near abroad'through the 'colour revolutions', 'Euromaidan'[1]and threats of proposed placement of anti-ballistic missile systems in Poland and the Czech Republic[2] have added to the Russian threat perception. In fact, the redefinition of NATO's agenda in the former Soviet space compelled Russia to pursue territorial assertiveness in the region. Russia' security concerns and muscle flexing are often defended as acts to keep its former satellite states out of the orbit of US influence.

Russia has also been suspicious of the European Union's (EU) initiatives in the Russian zone of influence. In fact, one of the major factors for the recent Ukraine imbroglio was the postponement of a planned Association Agreement of the EU trade deal in favour of the Russian trade deal which would throw Ukraine back into Russia's grip. With the signing of such a treaty, EU goods could enter Ukraine, free of import duties, which may affect Russian trade. And the finalising of the European trade deal increased Moscow's apprehension that European and American transnational companies could edge out Ukrainian firms linked to Russia, especially in the militaryindustries and high-tech areas generally located in eastern Ukraine.[3] Besides, Ukraine adds to Russia's geo-strategic significance as Ukraine's future as a NATO member would be a major blow to the Russian Eurasian Customs Union.[4]

Failure of 'Reset' Between Russia and the West in the New World Order

One of the arguments presented by the academic community for the current developments in Ukraine is that relations between Russia and the US never really had a 'reset' despite the fact that the two countries made efforts to overcome the strains in the relations. One of the attempts by the West to cajole Russia was by trying to attract Putin towards the West during the initial years of his presidency. Under Putin, the West expected the continuation of the Euro-Atlantic foreign policy that had prevailed during the Yeltsin period. But Putin displayed an autonomous foreign policy that promoted core Russian national interests and priorities. The West made unsuccessful attempts to encircle Russia and constrain its influence through 'colour revolutions', proposed placement of anti-ballistic missiles in the NATO member countries of Poland and the Czech Republic, and the recent Ukraine ethnic mobilisation.[5]The ongoing crisis in Ukraine and the impact of the sanctions on the Russian economy are also seen as attempts by the West to incite an anti-Putin and anti-Russian campaign.[6]

The West's efforts to destabilise Russia's growth were also waylaid by Moscow's success in the Georgian War in 2008, prevention of military intervention in the Syrian crisis and providing asylum to Edward Snowden. The Kremlin described the 'Euromaidan' as a Western-backed coup to fuel the conflict. It has strongly resisted a greater regional role of the trans-Atlantic powers in the region. The Kremlin often justifies its response and counter-measures as only standing up against all the possible scenarios being drawn up by the US-led NATO policies of containment of Russia in its strategic neighbourhood.[7]

US and the International Response

The accession of Crimea, and the Kremlin's support to pro-Russian rebels in eastern Ukraine led to a stringent international response to fence in Moscow's growing influence in the region. By mainly targeting its energy and financial sectors, the uncompromising sanctions have caused long-term damage to the Russian economy as it predominantly depends on the oil markets for its hard currency revenue. The US and Organisation of Petroleum Exporting Countries (OPEC) member nations have pursued an astute strategy by refusing to consider an oil production cut.[8] The sanctions have also put to test Russia's economic endurance as the sharp decline in oil prices as a culmination of weak growth in oil demand and a global supply glut, has maintained pressure on crude prices.[9] A severe drop in crude oil prices has also affected the strength of the ruble.

It is important to note that the decline in the value of the ruble has had a domino effect on several other countries as well, as seen across the Central Asian Republics (CARs) since the region's economy continues to depend on transfers from migrant workers in Russia and also on its imports. As local currencies follow the ruble downward, the costs of imported essentials have risen; this is a reality check for the CARs, reminding them just how much they continue to depend on Russia.[10]

However, the impact of sanctions has not been a one-way affair as President Putin has declared a one-year ban on imports of fruits and vegetables, dairy products and meat from countries that been involved in imposing sanctions on Russia which include the European Union and the US.[11]

3Ds of Russia's Economic Revival Programme

Although the sanctions have impacted the Russian economy, Putin has devised his own economic counter-strategy. Let us have a look at these measures by President Putin to stabilise the value of the country's falling ruble and revive its economic status.

They are:

(a) De-Dollarisation;(b) De-Offshorisation; and (c) Diversification

De-Dollarisation

The de-dollarisation initiative is to devalue the US dollar's position in the international market and to dethrone the 'petrodollar'(the means for settling international trading in oil) by carrying out international trade in oil and gas using the national currency of the trading countries. Moreover, de-dollarisation, if it succeeds, will have a major impact on the value of the US currency in Russia. Alongside Russia, countries like China are intending to weaken the petrodollar by promoting the use of their own national currencies for trading in oil and for other commercial transactions which will come in the form of bilateral currency agreements. For example, the $400 billion natural gas deal between Russia and China is actually a zero dollar agreement. Accordingly, payment for the gas will be settled in the ruble and yuan, thus, avoiding transactions in the US currency.[12]

However, how far the de-dollarisation measure can depreciate the value of the dollar is debatable as the US dollar is the international reserve currency and there is always a demand for it.

De-Offshorisation

De-offshorisation means taxing the profits of foreign companies and the incomes of foreigners. In other words, it means controlling foreign companies to prevent them from having an advantage over domestic enterprises. This can be achieved by introducing taxes that are levied heavily on the foreign company and are easy on domestic enterprises. This measure will help Russia because it prevents entrepreneurs from offshoring their profits thereby causing each penny to be accountable to tax and, thus, preventing the most common form of tax evasion. It will also increase state revenue and, at the same time, the government does not become despotic in levying more tax from its own population. De-offshorisation also means that the gas profits won't be drained away to other countries; instead, a part will be spent within Russia to increase domestic production like food products.

If the de-offshorisation policy is brought into effect, many foreign companies that operate in Russia will find it difficult to cope with the economic measure. For instance, Russia is a hub of the international energy trade and many Western companies, ranging from giants like Exxon Mobile and British Petroleum to small contractors like Halliburton operate in Russia. Exxon Mobil Corp has partnered with Rosneft to explore prospects in the Arctic and Siberia. In addition, Exxon has been pumping oil and natural gas from the Sakhalin Island, which is located off Russia's eastern coast,[13]hence, this measure can create a risky environment for the company in Russia.

Diversification

As for diversification, to avoid a perilous impact on Russia's already struggling economy, Moscow has now sought to diversify its energy and defence markets. For instance, Putin has accelerated the 'Asian Focus' by signing a 30-year agreement worth $400 billion for the purchase and sale of natural gas between the China National Petroleum Corporation and the Russian gas giant Gazprom.

Russia is also tapping into defence markets which are looking for diversification. With the modernisation efforts of the defence sector, it is Russia's only high-tech industry which is internationally competitive.Arms exports and the revenues these exports generate are essential for the Russian defence companies' business and for their ability to develop new weapon systems. In the early 2000s, China and India accounted for up to 80 per cent of Russian arms deliveries on export contracts. With China now capable of indigenous production of much of its military equipment, it has resulted in a decline in Chinese defence orders, while India has been diversifying its defence markets.[14]Knowing Pakistan's urge to upgrade its defence equipment and its need for a reliable defence market,Moscow has began defence cooperation with Pakistan to further enlarge its defence markets.

Additionally, Russia has imposed an embargo on food imports from countries that participated in imposition of sanctions against Moscow. As a result, import substitution from domestic producers and other countries will lessen the impact on Russian consumers. For long, conservatives have been pushing for state-led reindustrialisation, with protection against foreign imports, and spending revenues generated by energy markets on infrastructure and new technology.[15]

It is true that Russia is now looking for viable options to revive its flagging economy due to the impact of the sanctions but one cannot conclude prematurely that the above mentioned economic measures comprise the solution to the crisis as, even if they achieve the desired aim, it will still take a few more years for Russia to overcome the current economic crisis.

Interdependence

Russia is Europe's main energy supplier, accounting for nearly 30 percent of Europe's natural gas and 35 percent of its oil imports. Moscow recently cut off its energy supply to six European countries which include Bulgaria, Greece, Czech Republic, Slovakia, Romania and Croatia, with many more to follow. Gazprom's move to cut gas exports to Europe by 60 percent has plunged the continent into an energy crisis. Russia also stated its plans to shift all its natural gas flows through a proposed link under the Black Sea to Turkey, fully replacing shipments via Ukraine. Hence, Europe will have to develop new infrastructure that will transport gas to the rest of the continent.[16]

Fig 1

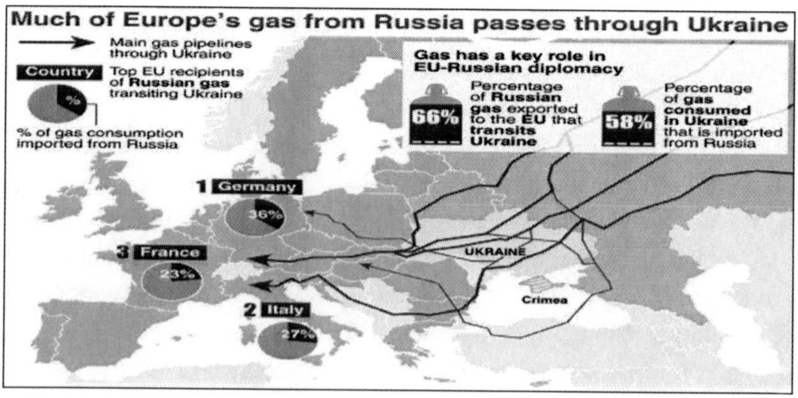

Source: Chatham House, Inogate, IEA

It can be stated that Russia has now smartly brought into play the energy supplies as leverage to counter the stringent measures by the Western alliance. Consequently, the heavy dependence of the EU on Russia for trade and energy markets has led to major repercussions for the European Union's energy security.[17] Not surprisingly, few of the EU countries are reluctant to press harder sanctions on Russia as it is the biggest oil and gas supplier to the region.

Not only is there economic interdependence between the EU and Russia, there is interdependence in production and sale of military equipment also which may cripple the defence engagements between Russia and other Western allies. For instance, one important reason for the French reluctance to cancel the delivery of two Mistrals is that it will thwart French defence markets as competitors may tar the French as unreliable suppliers.[18]Putin's counter-attack on Europe's role in imposition of sanctions has brought to light that Russia too has retaliatory options which should not be ignored.

Putin's move to put pressure on the EU to reconsider its position on the sanctions imposed on Russia has caused concerns regarding dependable energy markets for the European zone. The move is also seen as having negative ramifications on Russia as a reliable gas supplier. Many opine that this will compel Europe to reconsider its dependence for fuel exports on the Russian energy markets in the future.

But, knowing that the European zone is already grappling with its economic crisis since the 2008 global recession, it will have to invest in development of new infrastructure for alternative energy markets and energy supply routes. Therefore, Russia will continue to have a strong hold over the European energy markets for some time.

Russia's Dilemma

While the strategic objectives of Russia remain undeterred despite stringent action by the West and the sanction politics, political scholars have raised several questions about whether Russia is capable of sustaining its economic growth. In addition, the Eurasian Economic Union is designed as an economic alternative to the European Union which, in turn, makes its neighbouring states the centre of Russia's own geo-political landscape. So far, Belarus and Kazakhstan are members of the Customs Union formed in 2010 as a precursor to the Eurasian Economic Union, which is expected to be formed in 2015. Armenia, Kyrgyzstan and Tajikistan are also expected to become members and Russia is hopeful that Ukraine and even Georgia might join. Russia's support to the pro-rebellion region in Eastern Ukraine and accession of Crimea has augmented concerns as it may hamper the ambitious dream project of Putin, the Eurasian Economic Union.[19]

In addition, the 2008 Russia-Georgia conflict revealed large-scale Russian military operational failures that led to the vast military modernisation of Russia through measures taken up by Kremlin for the revival of the defence industrial complex and military capabilities. Besides Russia's defence industrial complex needs funds to keep these mammoth industries functioning. While Russia may have shifted its focus to the 'Asia Pivot' to revive its stumbling economy, its need for foreign scientific and design developments will be affected as a result of constant altercations with Europe and the USA on foreign policy issues and such requirements which will have a major setback.[20] The ongoing crisis over the delivery of the two naval assault ships of the new Mistral class[21] is a case in point.

With all these factors in place, there is an interesting linkage as these developments have in a way shifted the focus in determining India-Russia relations. Bilateral ties between Russia and India are extensive. India and Russia have always rendered unstinting support to each other on major international crises. But with the current developments in the global affairs, a certain degree of uncertainty in the cooperation between the two strategic partners has been predicted. In consequence to these aspects, the following section deals directly with Indo-Russian relations, the issues and the challenges, and future prospects in the strategic partnership.

Let us first look into the synergies in Indo-Russia relations in the new millennium.

Synergies in Indo-Russian Relations in the New Millennium

Both India and Russia have pursued a strategic partnership which has mainly focussed on the growing security threats and challenges to carry forward the vision, aspirations and national goals in the international arena. The premise of the bilateral relations rests on mutual trust, mutual interests and mutual understanding. The reflection of assurance between the two countries was observable on several occasions when Soviet Russia extended its unconditional support to India, as in the 1971 War of Liberation against the Islamabad-Washington-Beijing alliance. The Kremlin vetoed in support of New Delhi in the UN Security Council on the liberation of Goa in 1961, and has consistently endorsed India's concerns over the Kashmir issue, and added value to its relations when it supported India post 1998 Pokhran nuclear tests.

India's Response to Ukraine Crisis

As a response to Russia's role in the Ukraine crisis, India extended its diplomatic support to Russia over the accession of Crimea through a referendum on March 18, 2014. The event put India in a tight spot as it had to carefully calibrate its position on a dispute that triggered concerns over Russia's military intervention in support of a pro-Russian rebellion in Eastern Ukraine,on the one hand, and a West-supported overthrow of a democratically elected government in Ukraine, on the other.[22] Hence, India's support to Russia would have had negative ramifications on the growing proximity with Washington, and taking an active position against Russia and condemning its role in the Crimean crisis,would have harmed New Delhi's strategic relations with its old ally. Nevertheless, India offered virtual support to Moscow when it abstained from voting in the UN General Assembly (UNGA) resolution, drawn up by the United States, which urged nations not to recognise the results[23] of the March referendum of Crimea on March 27, 2014.[24] Abstention from voting by the BRICS member states–India, China, Brazil, and South Africa[25]–displayed the spirit of not isolating Russia. New Delhi also criticised the unilateral sanctions imposed on Russia by the West.

Moreover, the presence of Crimean leader Sergey Aksyonov in Delhi last year and his interactions with Indian businessmen are viewed by some as yet another show of India's solidarity with Russia.

Druzhba-Dosti: A Vision for Strengthening the Indian-Russian Partnership[26]

The mechanism to conduct an annual summit every year between India and Russia is seen as a principle vehicle to advance their strategic partnership in various fields. Not going into the details of all the annual summits that have taken place so far between New Delhi and Moscow, this paper will evaluate the path-breaking agreements that were signed between the two countries at the 15th Annual Summit held in New Delhi last year, 2014. However, before the summit could begin, the international community, especially the US and Ukraine, displayed disapproval over India intending to continue normal relations with Russia despite the international isolation of Russia by the Western alliance. US Deputy Secretary of State Marie Harf, in her briefing on the eve of President Putin's visit to India, commented that "this is not the time to do business as usual with Russia, and we have conveyed this to our partners across the world."[27]

But, the denouement of the 15th annual summit once again reflected the synergy between the two time-tested strategic partners. The conclave laid out the signing of nearly 20 agreements within 24 hours between the two countries, covering various sectors such as defence, nuclear cooperation, energy, trade and industry, infrastructure and Research and Development (R&D).

Russia is poised to play a significant role in ensuring India's energy security through the nuclear energy sector, an important plank in Indo-Russia relations which was further enhanced with Russia agreeing to build 12 new nuclear plants in India. Its step to invest in India's nuclear energy sector has given Russia a monopoly in India's nuclear market by default.[28]

Defence cooperation continues to be of paramount importance for both countries. According to the latest agreement, as part of the joint ventures, Russia will extend its technology and equipment to manufacture 400 Kamov 226T light utility helicopters with Indian partners, including Hindustan Aeronautics Ltd.[29]This helicopter deal, worth $3 billion, has further bolstered Prime Minister Modi's vision of 'Make-in-India'as the partnership will move beyond buyer-seller relations and further strengthen joint-production and research in the defence sector.

Although economic interaction, other than in the defence and energy sectors, between the two traditional partners continues to be a weak link, there was some progress in this area, as, for the first time, agreements have been signed to boost cooperation between the private sectors or between state-run companies and private players.[30] In order to boost the flagging trade and economic relations, agreements have been reached for the supply of rough diamonds in the next three years by Russia to India; fertilisers and pharmaceuticals have also been identified as promising areas for increased cooperation. Both sides have set a target of $30 billion worth trade turnover and $30 billion investment in each other's country by the year 2025. It has been decided to accelerate the functioning of the North-South International Transport Corridor and sign a Free Trade Area and Comprehensive Economic Cooperation agreement with the Eurasian Economic Union for strengthening trade and economic cooperation.[31]

Both countries have also agreed in principle to long-term crude oil exports from Russia to India. The signing of a raft of pacts that would allow India's Essar group to import one million tonnes of crude oil and petroleum products from Russia's major oil giant Rosneft for over a decade was a booster for Russia. A $2 billion potash mining project was also signed which would help Russia to increase the total production of potash to meet both domestic consumption and export demands, including those of India. In addition, India, which owns the largest rough diamond cutting industry in the world and Russia, which controls 25 per cent of world diamond deposits, struck another deal worth $2.1 billion in which nearly 12 Indian diamond companies can import diamonds directly from the Russian diamond mining giant, Alrosa, which controls about 27 per cent of the global diamond trade. Nevertheless, the agreements worth $100 billion signed between the two countries will reinforce the falling value of the Russian ruble,that has declined by about 40 per cent since the international sanctions,and also bankroll the defence industrial complex of Russia.

Additionally, India has benefited immensely from Russian science and technology at the outset of a number of significant accords and annual summit meetings between the two countries. The Indian space research programmes also gain from Russian assistance as it mainly focusses on important lines of activity such as space navigation, lunar exploration and man-controlled space flight programmes. In fact, many Indian experimental and remote sensing satellites were launched with Soviet cooperation. Russia has also agreed to provide India with access to signals from its Global Navigation Satellite System (GLONASS).[32]

Despite many areas of cooperation, there have been hiccups between the two countries in recent times. Although both India and Russia attach a lot of importance to their partnership, clearly, there is a tilt in the foreign policy priorities of both towards building regional and international relations in a polycentric world order. Both countries have pursued a pragmatic foreign policy that aims to achieve their core national interests through diversifying their foreign policy interests. The academic community is now questioning whether the old and time-tested Indo-Russian ties have any relevance for either country today.

While bilateral relations generally remain on a firm footing, the turbulence in the contemporary international environment will call for some readjustments and reorientation in some areas as both countries are pursuing a pragmatic foreign policy to achieve their core national interests through diversification.

Diversification of Indian and Russian Foreign Policy Interests

The China Factor

From India's perspective, China is a potential threat due to its posturing in the border areas, an all-weather friendship with Pakistan and the current compulsions of its assertive inroads into the Indian Ocean region through the "String of Pearls". Even as Beijing repeatedly stresses that its rise is "peaceful," these security concerns do nothing to assuage the apprehensions of New Delhi, which has found it increasingly difficult to deal with China. Hence, it is crucial to evaluate the emerging strategic partnership between Russia and China also.

The contemporary developments, i.e. the Western sanctions and efforts to politically isolate Russia, on the one hand, and China's global ambitions, on the other, have pushed both Moscow and Beijing, and led to an upward trend by further strengthening their bilateral engagements. Both China and Russia have also pledged to develop long-term strategic and military interaction. This has put Indian security under strain.

The growing proximity between the two countries is mainly based on a number of mutually shared strong strategic interests. These include:

- Both countries realise that closer economic cooperation would benefit them both.
- China's demand for energy resources will enhance Russia's energy security as Moscow is in search of geo-political diversification of energy markets apart from the European Union nations.
- China's growing infrastructural development and economic prosperity has, in turn, led to growing energy demands. The Russian energy market is the key to China's energy consumption.
- More importantly, both China and Russia are concerned about the hegemonic position of the US in contemporary international relations.

While Russia sees China as a potential energy market and an ally to counter US hegemony, China is also concerned about the US' 'rebalancing strategy'. This has given way to inevitable competition between the US and China as the former aimed to halt Beijing's global ambitions. The upward trend in US-India relations is viewed by many Chinese scholars as a counter-strategy against China, especially in its maritime interests and security. Given the long-standing relations between India and Russia, even the slightest miscommunication by Russia with regard to its closer cooperation with China will have a major impact on the wider engagements in its bilateral ties.

There are also growing concerns on the strengthening of ties between Russia and China,including joint military drills and closer economic and political ties. In addition, both these countries are prominent players in the Shanghai Cooperation Organisation (SCO). Moreover, both China and Russia have a mutual interest in gaining more control over, and access to, the Central Asian Republics, where they share common worries about the spread of Islamist terrorism in the region and fear the rise of terrorist organisations like the Islamist Movement of Uzbekistan.

More recently, Russia and China signed a 30-year agreement worth $400 billion for the purchase and sale of natural gas between the China National Petroleum Corporation and the Russian gas giant, Gazprom. Deliveries are to begin in 2018, and will see 38 billion cubic metres of gas per year shipped to China at $350 per 1,000 cubic metres.[33]

Fig 3

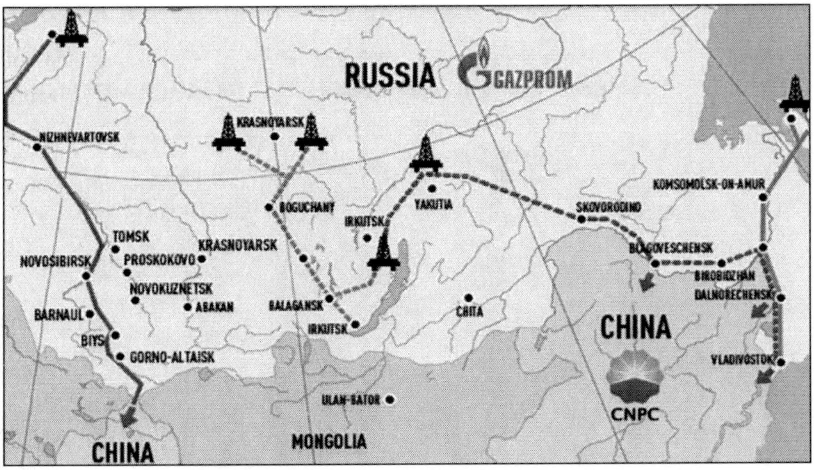

Source: http://www.talkradionews.com/world-news/2014/05/20/russia-china-negotiate-terms-major-natural-gas-deal.html#.VPQdaHyUf1U

However, statements made by Russian officials, scholars, and commentators suggest that Moscow's security concerns stem from three principal external security challenges: the West (especially the US), Islamist fundamentalism, and China.[34] As for recent trends in Sino-Russia relations, given Russia's geo-strategic position and economic situation which is characterised by hostility towards the US, the Kremlin needs a valuable partner for the political and economic modernisation of post-Soviet Russia as well as to counter numerous security problems, which have ranged from the real threat of terrorism to expansionism of NATO in the Russian neighbourhood. Close cooperation with China would bolster Russia's aim of monitoring US and NATO hegemony in world affairs.[35]

But with China becoming aware of its global status in the 21st century and its progress in the international arena,it has only become evident that China has the potential for a 'role reversal' between the two countries as inequality is growing at a pace fast enough to cause discomfiture to Russia, which fears downgrading of its status to that of a junior partner. Hence, the constant fear of 'role reversal' between Beijing and Moscow has made the relations more complex, on the one hand, and substantive, on the other. The two countries are, however, balancing the partnership delicately between strategic convergence and suspicion. For instance, China's growing influence in Central Asia through the SCO, wherein China is planning to reopen the ancient "Silk Road"—and this "New Silk Road" is likely to be longer than the ancient route—has great economic significance. This will further widen Russia's suspicion of China's role in Central Asia as Moscow fears that the People's Republic of China (PRC) may exert geo-political pressure on a weakened Russia. Such worries are already being voiced in Moscow.[36]

Fig 4: Silk Road Economic Belt and Maritime Silk Road in the Making

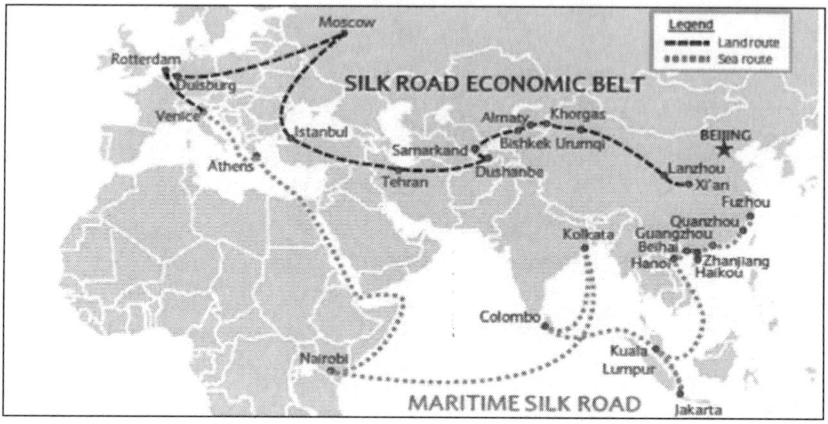

Source: Xinhuanet.com and Barclays Research

To balance the growing influence of China in Central Asia, Russia has long been supportive of India's permanent membership in the SCO and is interested in India playing a more visible geo-political role in the organisation.

Moreover, one has to bear in mind the fact that in order for China to emerge as a global player, it is also in need of stronger partnerships with countries like Russia, as Beijing is concerned about the US' 're-balancing strategy' Strengthening of the US' bilateral ties with India and its 're-balancing' in the Asia-Pacific region are seen as a counter-strategy against China establishing its monopoly over the maritime sphere, as the South China Sea, which contains an enormous amount of natural reserves, will not only determine China's economic and political future but also affect its territorial claims in the region.

The strengthening of relations with Russia only means access to dominate the Eurasian landmass, along with naval bases from the Baltic. Moreover, with the amalgamation of Russia's cutting-edge weaponry and huge energy markets and China's vast population and industrial base,the alliance between the two countries will threaten the preeminence of the US.[37]

Hence, although the bond is multifaceted, Russia's relationship will China is defined by numerous ambiguities and contradictions. Notwithstanding that, China's peaceful rise is only a veiled strategy to create a 'comfort zone' in and around China and to avoid any sort of military adventurism with countries like India and Russia or even the US for that matter, as China's national priorities are to expand its influence globally without any hindrance from major international players.

As for India, while it continues to work towards developing stronger ties with the US, it should also be aware that China is closely watching these developments. Given the long-standing divide between India and China and the territorial dispute, any untoward situation created by either India or China will have a major impact on the wider engagement between the two countries which are showing signs of a positive direction in their relations at various levels.[38] China is indeed way ahead of both Russia and India but the prospects of all three countries developing a stronger partnership will fetch positive outcomes in their global engagements. Both India and Russia should adopt a pragmatic approach in their relationship by way of 'balancing' or 'accommodating' China's status quo in international affairs.

However, the upward trend in Sino-Russia relations is largely aimed at containing the hegemonic position of the US and not to destabilise the alliance between India and Russia. Therefore, Russia and China need to gain India's confidence by forming a partnership that accommodates India as an equal partner in exploring the potential for cooperation in the energy sector, high-tech and common security concerns like Islamist terrorism.

Russia's Relations with Pakistan

Pakistan's evolving relationship with Russia in recent times is, however, undeniable. Moscow concluded a defence agreement on weapons sale to Pakistan in June 2014. This raised the eyebrows of several political analysts and is being interpreted as a setback for India as the decision comes in the wake of India having strong defence ties with Russia and its virtual support to Moscow over the Crimean referendum.

There have been high-level visits between the leaders of both Pakistan and Russia, resulting in Russia's increasing involvement in the country, particularly in investment in heavy industry and energy. Under the project CASA-1000, Russia is also interested to link energy supply in Kyrgyzstan and Tajikistan to Afghanistan and Pakistan, to minimise the effects of an acute energy crisis. The prospective building of the railway and motor roads from Tajikistan to Pakistan under Russian auspices will increase trade and connectivity in the region and help the prospects of Eurasian integration.[39] Trade between the two countries is showing signs of expansion. For Russia, closeness to Pakistan might promote Russian aims of becoming further involved in the management of Asian security along with its strong relations with India and China.

Russia is expected to continue in its attempt to develop a cooperative relationship with Islamabad as the region is too important to ignore—Russia considers Central Asia its strategic backyard, The CAR region faces a combination of challenges, especially radicalisation of Islam from Afghanistan.

The region is also home to Russian ethnic groups. Hence, Afghanistan's security situation is of immense significance to Russia. Russia's foreign policy priorities towards the region are aimed to protect its ethnic groups, prevent drug trafficking, and combat Islamist extremism emanating from the Afghan region. Newly emerging ties with Pakistan are principally driven by these strategic imperatives to manage Afghanistan after the US withdrawal in 2014. From the Russian perspective, the two most important avenues for this cooperation are counter-terrorism and combatting drug trafficking.

Additionally, with the diversification of its defence markets by India and indigenisation of its defence industry by China, Russia is also compelled to diversify its defence export destinations to include countries such as Pakistan.While Moscow's move to sell weapons to Pakistan is perceived by India as an act of betrayal, the move should not actually have come as a surprise since Russia has the prerogative to diversify its defence markets. In 2013, Russia finalised a deal with China for the sale of 48 Sukhoi Su-35 aircraft. India must, of course, persist in communicating its security concerns to Russia and invoke the special relationship the two have historically enjoyed. It is also unlikely that Moscow would shift its perspective of seeing India as its key partner in the South Asian region and also at the global level.

The bilateral relationship is still far more stable and less volatile despite the hiccups in defence cooperation. The decision of Russia to provide India access to signals from the Global Navigation Satellite System (GLONASS) is proof that Russia is the most dependable partner as it is far more willing to share military technology than the Western suppliers. It is also relevant here to understand that India was given the licence to indigenously manufacture defence equipment with Russian assistance. Therefore, India has greater leverage in terms of its relations with Russia rather than Pakistan, as it shares better camaraderie and mutual trust than the latter. However, both sides will have to work at sustaining the specialness of the relationship.

India's Growing Proximity to the US

Since the past decade or so, there has been an upward trend in the relations between the two most successful democratic countries. Of late, India's growing proximity to Washington and diversification of its foreign policy has impacted the traditional partnership between Moscow and New Delhi which has viewed India as a strategic asset in the South Asian region and also as a strong ally in global affairs. The Indian policy makers are aware that to achieve the aspirations of attaining an influential role in the international system for itself, India needs to diversify its foreign policy priorities and establish alliances with countries like the US which is the leading global player.

In the context of the Indo-US strategic partnership, it can be stated that the inking of the Indo-US Defence Framework of 2005, followed by the 123 Agreement of 2007,[40] has resulted in an upward trend in the Indo-US foreign policy approach. According to some political observers, the centrepiece of the Indo-US relationship was the agreement announced in 2005 and formally framed in 2007, for American assistance to India's nuclear programme in exchange for limited inspections of India's civilian nuclear facilities by the International Atomic Energy Agency. As India is a non-signatory to the nuclear Non-Proliferation Treaty (NPT), this development was lauded as a non-proliferation success.

During the talks between former Prime Minister Manmohan Singh and US President Barack Obama in October 2013, both India and the US agreed to a full-fledged defence partnership.[41] The same year, both countries struck the first commercial agreement on civilian nuclear power cooperation that was stalled due to India's nuclear liability law.[42]More recently, President Obama was the guest of honour at the Republic Day parade in New Delhi. During his visit, an agreement was reached on cooperation in the sphere of civil nuclear energy cooperation. The parties succeeded in overcoming disagreements over India's nuclear liability law.

India's growing proximity to the US has to some extent led to a dissonance between Moscow and New Delhi—the Russian policy-makers have been observing the growing partnership between India and the US with concern as this may affect the dominance of the Russian defence market. The two sides also renewed their framework agreement signed in 2005 on military-technical cooperation for an additional 10 years. The US has offered India a range of almost 17 high-end military technologies through the Defence Trade and Technology Initiative (DTTI). This will deepen defence ties between the two countries. This includes joint development and production in India of the Unmanned Combat Aerial Vehicles (UCAVs), Hawk XXI medium range anti-missile system, and other defence equipment.[43] Over the past three years, the US has supplied India with weapons worth $5.4 billion, for the first time surpassing Russia, which supplied $4.2 billion in military equipment.[44] But many political analysts have viewed Obama's visit as being more of political symbolism as the US is yet to tap India's potential as an important entity in global geo-politics.

While there is growing proximity in the relations between the two countries, there is, however, a contrast between America's and Russia's approach towards India, especially in the nuclear status of India which has remained a decisive factor in defining India's relations with the US, and Russia's posture towards India. India realises that Russia had assisted in its civil nuclear and civilian space programmes, especially when the US and other countries had shunned nuclear commerce with India.

Although defence cooperation between the US and India is strong, in total, the volume of military-technical cooperation, through joint projects, is heavily Russia-centric. This includes licensed production in India of Russian military equipment, as well as service contracts for weapons supplied to India. As Bharat Karnad, professor of national security studies at the Centre for Policy Research has rightly said,"Russia has partnered, and continues to partner India in strategically sensitive technology projects ranging from ballistic missiles, ship submersibles, and nuclear submarines to the Fifth Generation Fighter Aircraft". As of today, India and the US have no joint projects in the defence sector.[45] In addition, with rapid economic growth and energy demands, the appetite for hydrocarbons and nuclear energy will be crucial in determining India's potential growth in the international system.[46]

Despite the hiccups in the partnership, the relations between the two countries are far more stable than those between India and the other big powers. India is aware that Russia is its most dependable partner and the Russians are far more willing to share technology than the other big powers. The growth of China in terms of both economic development and its military might,is a potential threat to India. Defence cooperation between Russia and India remains strong because of shared security concerns, geo-political imperatives, and economic benefits. Both countries fear radical Islamic terrorism, share concerns about regional instability and the repercussions post US withdrawal from Afghanistan. Unlike Russia, the US is yet to exploit India's capabilities and relevance as an important entity in international relations.

Diversification of Defence Markets

Though the defence cooperation in what has traditionally been the most successful area in the bilateral relations between the two countries may seem very promising, it is, however, not without its challenges. India's move to diversify its supply of arms and replenishment of its arsenal by a shift in its geo-political orientation towards Western defence markets like those of the US, Israel, France, UK, etc, is not viewed well by the Kremlin. As for India, decline in the quality of Russian military equipment and delay in its delivery comprises a major cause of concern.[47] For instance,the induction of the INS *Vikramaditya* in 2013 brought the curtains down on a 13-year saga of carrier reconstruction which was marred by recurrent time slippages, cost overruns and edgy political negotiations.[48].

With increasing globalisation, transnational disputes and conventional and non-conventional security threats, India is building up its stocks of arms and weapons to protect its boundaries and its national interests from potential threats. And it is evident that as one of the largest suppliers of arms, Russia is in need of a revival of its defence industrial complex as there is growing competition from Western-made weapons, especially by client nations which could soon make the Russian arms market non-competitive and obsolete, even in its traditional markets like India.[49]

The United States and Israel have become major markets for India's defence supplies.[50] Defence cooperation with the two countries has increased exponentially in the last few years and is testimony to the common interests and growing trust between them which is now fast emerging as a strategic partnership.[51]

Assessment of Future Prospects in India-Russia Relations

While pursuing their respective national goals, convergence of security interests has played a pivotal role in strengthening the India-Russia partnership. Despite striking distinctions, India and Russia pursue foreign policies that are largely convergent. Both countries seek to reform the world order with both calling for the establishment of a polycentric world. In this context, the two countries have also expressed their readiness to continue consultations and coordination in multilateral global fora such as the G-20, East Asia Summit (EAS) and Brazil, Russia, India, China, South Africa (BRICS).

It is important to note that the role of BRICS, though a relatively new forum, would be impactful,with its assertion on dialogue and reconciliation. An emphasis on the role of the United Nations, and opposition to sanctions, has not only increased its visibility and role in the international arena but has also elevated it to the status of a global player. In fact, BRICS can play the role of a bridge-builder between Russia and the West: it can be an enforcer of dialogue and deliberation, while, at the same time, playing a role to offset policies that aim to destabilise the global order.[52] The economic and global engagements of the member states have been much evident with the establishment of the New Development Bank by BRICS.

Therefore, both India and Russia have rediscovered the prowess of their partnership in the changing geo-political context and continue to nurture it on the basis of mutual benefits and sustained growth on a long-term basis through political, strategic and economic commitment from both sides.

As for India and Russia relations and converging interests, both countries still back the primacy of the United Nations in solving crises and support the principle of non-intervention in the internal affairs of sovereign states. In the long run, it is mutual confidence,which will help these two powers to play a larger role in global politics.[53] Russia enthusiastically supports India's permanent membership in the UN Security Council and also in the Shangai Cooperation Organisation (SCO).

Russia and India face some of the same security challenges too.

Firstly, the withdrawal of the US led international coalition combat forces from Afghanistan now demands that countries like India and Russia cooperate more closely to help Afghanistan achieve political and regional stability, and combat terrorism in the region.

Secondly, with the growth of the Islamic State in Syria (ISIS) and other terrorist organisations, both India and Russia need to have broader cooperation to meet the challenges of Islamist extremism. Both countries have been soft targets of terrorist attacks. Russia has been the victim of unconscionable terrorist attacks in the Moscow Theatre in 2002, the Beslan school massacre in 2004, the suicide bombing at Moscow's Domodedovo Airport in 2011 and the 2014 December bombings in Volgograd. India too has been struggling with the radical Islamist movement and has also been a soft target of terrorist attacks such as the December 13 Parliament attack, the 26/11 Mumbai attack, and others.

In addition, as India is a fast growing economy but an energy-deficit nation, it is high time that India and Russia take their bilateral relations to the next level by finalising the construction of what is called the daddy of all pipelines that will transport gas from Russia across the Himalayas via China to India. At a projected cost of $30 billion, the pipeline will, when constructed, enable Russia to sell its energy to Asia by lessening its dependence on the Western markets. Both China and India, which are among the world's largest energy consumers, will be pleased to have the Russian energy, thereby reducing their dependence on the highly volatile Middle East.[54]

Moreover, the sanction politics, hostility and tensions between the Western alliance and Russia are seen by many strategic thinkers as the right set of circumstances for India and Russia to enhance their trade and economic relations. But the window of opportunity is transitory, especially because the sanctions have also given way to import substitution from domestic producers and state-led reindustrialisation. The ban on food products, for instance, is only for one year and Russia's search for viable import markets may not be confined to India alone as there is competition from other countries too, to gain access to the Russian market. Under such circumstances, India should focus more on achieving the long-term goal of establishing a strong foothold in the Russian market. Nevertheless, bilateral engagements between India and Russia have stood the test of time, therefore, in order to strengthen the economic ties, the focus should be on exploiting the long-term prospects and tapping into resources that will benefit the two countries.

Hence, for continuity of strong bilateral relations between India and Russia, it is important for both the countries to outline guidelines for the expansion of economic activities. There are several bottlenecks that need to be identified in the economic transactions between the two countries.

India should take the opportunity of the 'de-dollarisation' initiative by Russia. There are suggestions to replace the dollar with the rupee and ruble for trade between the two countries in line with the recently implemented Russia and China mutual trading method of transaction.

The $100 billion BRICS New Development Bank should not only aim to counter the influence of Western lending institutions like the International Monetary Fund (IMF) and World Bank but should introduce measures of economic transaction through national currencies between each other and create a currency reserve pool ensuring the economic security of all BRICS member states.

The contemporary international milieu has strengthened the belief that despite increasing pressure on Russia through international sanctions by the West, India and Russia continue to have a close relationship with each other.

As far as India is concerned, while it continues to work towards developing stronger ties with the US, it should also be aware that China is closely watching these developments. The Chinese are apprehensive of the US strategy of drawing closer to New Delhi as it sees this as a check on its growing influence in international geo-politics, and an attempt to pit the two Asian superpowers against each other.[55]

To conclude, one can state that Moscow and New Delhi should work on areas that have hindered the very nature of this special relationship in order to enhance the future prospects of a strong bilateral relationship, with the defence partnership playing a vital role in calibrating the friendship between India and the Russian Federation.The Indo-Russian relationship has come of age, but in order for India to cement its influential role in the international system, it should attain its goals through cooperation with all the major international powers. New Delhi should expand its global engagements and avoid becoming too closely tied to either Moscow or Washington.

One has to also bear in mind that despite a new government being in power in India,and increasing pressure on Russia through international sanctions, the unprecedented success of the relations between the two countries is evidence that India will not give in to international pressures and will pursue an autonomous foreign policy that benefits its core national interest.

Notes

1. The first part, "Euro,"refers to Europe. "Maidan" is a word of Persian origin, which likely entered Ukraine via the Ottomans, meaning "square" or "open place", however, translating it as "Europesquare". The square was the focal point of the Orange Revolution, the 2004 mass daily protests that forced the annulment of a fraudulent presidential election. In that role, Maidan became a two-syllable encapsulation of peaceful resistance and determined action. The symbolism is powerful enough for the Ukrainian media to have taken to referring to all the current demonstrations as Euromaidan, even if they take place on a "ploshcha," another word for square. Source: Jim Henitz, "Ukraine's Euromaidan: What's in a Name?", December 2, 2013, http://news.yahoo.com/ukraines-euromaidan-whats-name-090717845.html
2. Jim Nichol, "Russian Military Reform and Defense Policy", Congressional Research Service, August 24 2011. www.crs.gov. Accessed on August 8, 2014.
3. Hall Gardner, "NATO, the EU, Ukraine, Russia and Crimea: The 'Reset' that was Never 'Reset', April 3, 2014, p. 6.
4. Arun Mohanty, "Russia at Crossroads", *Mainstream* Weekly, vol. liii, no. 1, December 27 2014, p. 1.
5. Ibid.
6. Oliver Darcy, "Oil Prices Rise After Death of Saudi King", *The Blaze*, January 22, 2015.
7. Phunchuk Stobdan, ed., *India-Russia Strategic Partnership: Common Perspectives*(New Delhi: Institute for Defence Studies and Analyses, 2010), p.3.
8. William Watts, "Oil Above $100? Never Again, Says Saudi Prince Alwaleed",http://www.marketwatch.com/story/oil-above-100-never-again-says-saudi-prince-alwaleed-2015-01-12?mod=MW_story_recommended_default January 12, 2015. Accessed on January 15, 2015.
9. Ibid.
10. David Trilling and Timur Toktonaliev, "Central Asia Hurting as Russia's Ruble Sinks", Eurasianet.org, October 21, 2014, http://www.eurasianet.org/node/70546. Accessed on November 28, 2014.
11. Peter Rutland, "The Impact of Sanctions on Russia", *Russian Analytical Digest*, no.157, December 17, 2014. p.3, www.css.ethz.ch/rad. Accessed on January 12, 2015.
12. Interview—Marin Katusa: Startling Rise of 'The Colder War' "With Anthony Wile," *The Daily Bell,* November 2, 2014, http://www.thedailybell.com/exclusive-interviews/35783/Anthony-Wile-Marin-Katusa-Startling-Rise-of-The-Colder-War/. Accessed on January 16, 2015.
13. "What Western Countries are Most Vulnerable to Russia?", Market Watch, March 5, 2014,http://blogs.marketwatch.com/thetell/2014/03/05/what-western-industries-are-most-vulnerable-to-russia/. Accessed on February 22, 2015.
14. Sergey Denisentsev and Konstantin Makienko, "The Arms Trade Treaty and Russian Arms Exports: Expectations and Possible Consequences", Centre for Analysis of Strategies and Technologies, p.8,www.unidir.org.Accessed on October 3, 2014.
15. Rutland, n.11, p.5.
16. Alex Jones, "Putin Strikes Back: Russia Cuts Off European Gas Supplies, Starts Selling Dollars: The Decision Has Been Made", *InfoWars.com*, January 15, 2015. http://www.infowars.com/putin-strikes-back-russia-cuts-off-european-gas-supplies-starts-selling-dollars-the-decision-has-been-made/. Accessed on January 17, 2015.
17. Arvind Gupta, "Crimean Crisis: A New Phase of Cold War?", Institute of Defence and Strategic Analysis, March 21, 2014, p.3 http://idsa.in/idsacomments/CrimeancrisisANewPhaseofColdWar_agupta_210314. Accessed on May 10, 2014.
18. François Heisbourg, "France Needs Support to Cancel the Misbegotten Mistral Sale", *Financial Times,* July 23, 2014. http://www.ft.com/intl/cms/s/0/f5156478-125c-11e4-93a5-00144feabdc0.html#axzz3PWYTba00. Accessed on January 20, 2015.

19. "Russia Increasingly Worried about US 'Shale Revolution'", *Russian Times*, October 24, 2012. **http://rt.com/business/russia-shale-gas-usa-110/**. Accessed on December 28, 2014.
20. Reaction to Putin's Armaments Conferences, *Russian Defence Policy,* Posted on December 5, 2013, https://russiandefpolicy.wordpress.com/tag/opk /
21. Shortly after Russia's invasion of Georgia and President Barack Obama's election in 2008, the US proposed a reset of relations with Moscow. Few Western leaders took up this suggestion with as much gusto as Nicolas Sarkozy, then French president, with the sale of two naval assault ships of the new Mistral class for €1.2 billion. The Mistral, although barely armed, has great military value as a highly versatile expeditionary command post, helicopter carrier and landing craft platform. It proved its worth when the French used it in the Libyan campaign of 2011, and as the pivot of the maritime component of NATO's rapid response force. Heisbourg, n.18.
22. Charu Sudan Kasturi and JP Yadav, "India Maintains Silence Over Ukraine as Old Friend Russia Gets Cast in Invaders Role", www.abplive.com
23. "Russia Vetoes UN Resolution on Ukraine's Crimea", March 15, 2014 http://www.infowars.com/russia-vetoes-un-resolution-on-ukraines-crimea/
24. Rajeev Sharma, "India's Abstention on Ukraine Resolution Does Not Mean Neutrality", *Business Central Asia,* April 2014,p.32.
25. Ibid.
26. "Druzhba-Dosti: A Vision for Strengthening the Indian-Russian Partnership over the Next Decade" - Joint Statement during the visit of President of the Russian Federation to India",December 11, 2014, http://mea.gov.in/bilateraldocuments.htm?dtl/24486/DruzhbaDosti_A_Vision_for_strengthening_the_IndianRussian_Partnership_over_the_next_decade__Joint_Statement_during_the_visit_of_President_of_the_Russi
27. "Time not Right for Business as Usual with Russia: US to India", *The Economic Times*, December 12, 2014, http://articles.economictimes.indiatimes.com/2014-12-12/news/56990047_1_india-and-russia-russia-yesterday-us-and-eu
28. Rajeev Sharma, "$100 Bn in Just 24 Hours: Putin's India Visit Exerts Immense Pressure on Obama", December 12, 2014, http://www.firstpost.com/world/100-bn-in-just-24-hours-putins-india-visit-exerts-immense-pressure-on-obama-1845487.html
29 R.G. Gidadhubli, "Fifteenth India-Russia Economic Summit: Advantage Russia", *Mainstream Weekly*, vol. 53, no 1, December 27, 2014, http://www.mainstreamweekly.net/article5411.html
30. Arun Kumar Mohanty, "Putin's Visit and India- Russia Summit", *Mainstream Weekly*, vol. 52, no.1, December 13, 2014, http://www.mainstreamweekly.net/article5397.html
31. Ibid.
32. Gulshan Sachdeva, "India's Relation with Russia", in David Scott, ed., *Handbook of India's International Relations*(Routledge, 2011), p.217.
33. Alexi Lossan, "Russia-China Talks Yield 30-year Gazprom Contract Worth $400 Billion", Russia Beyond the Headlines", May 21, 2014, **http://rbth.com/business/2014/05/21/russia-**china_talks_yield_30 year_gazprom_contract_worth_400_billion_36823.html. Accessed on February 2, 2015.
34. Mark N. Katz, "Russia's Security Challenges", *The International Relations and Security Networks*, Acta Slavica Iaponica No 16. 2007,p.135.
35. Tatiana Zakaurtseva, "The Current Foreign Policy of Russia", Social Research Centre, 2007, pp. 88-90.
36. Nyshka Chandran, "'New Silk Road' Highlights China's Two-speed Reform", CNBC, November 17, 2014, http://www.cnbc.com/id/102190017
37. Fred Wier, "Russia, China Plan War Games, Arms Sales. Could Alliance be in the Cards?", *The Christian Science Monitor*, November 21, 2014, http://www.csmonitor.com/World/

Europe/2014/1121/Russia-China-plan-war-games-arms-sales.-Could-alliance-be-in-the-cards

38. Saptashri Dutta, "How Pakistan and China are Covering Obama's India Visit", *Quartz India*, January 25, 2015. http://qz.com/332911/how-pakistan-and-china-are-covering-obamas-india-visit/. Accessed on January 28, 2015.
39. Debidatta Aurobinda Mahapatra, "Reduction of Arms in South Asia: A Role for Russia? *Russia and India Report*, August 7, 2014, http://indrus.in/world/2013/08/07/reduction_of_arms_in_south_asia_a_role_for_russia_28119.html
40. Anuradha M. Chenoy, "India and Russia: Allies in the International Political System", in P. Stobdan, ed., *India-Russia Strategic Partnership: Common Perspectives* (New Delhi: Institute for Defence Studies and Analyses, 2010), p.133.
41. Ksenia Kondratieva, A Project Report on "India and Russia Military and Defense Cooperation", submitted to University of Mumbai Academic Year 2013-2014. Accessed on February 26, 2014.
42. Saurav Jha, "Nuclear Liability Act: Will it Scare Away the Suppliers?", *Deccan Herald*, September 1, 2014, http://www.deccanherald.com/content/91976/nuclear-liability-act-scare-away.html. Accessed on September 1, 2014.
43. Vishal Thapar, "US Offers India High-end Military Technology", *The Sunday Guardian*, January 24, 2015, http://www.sunday-guardian.com/news/us-offers-india-high-end-military-technology. Accessed on February 12, 2015.
44. "Obama's Visit to India No Threat to Russia-India Ties: Volkhonsky", *Russia and India Report*, January 27, 2015. http://in.rbth.com/world/2015/01/27/obamas_visit_to_india_no_threat_to_russia-india_ties_volkhonsky_41029.html. Accessed on February 13, 2015.
45. Vivek Raghuvanshi, "India, US Advance Strategic Relations", *The Defence News*, January 28, 2015, http://www.defensenews.com/story/defense/policy-budget/industry/2015/01/28/india-obama-modi-dtti-us-agreement-weapons-coproduce-bilateral-russia/22457599/. Accessed on February 26, 2015.
46. Stobdan, n.23, p.4.
47. S Anandan, "13-year Saga Comes to an End", November 16, 2013, http://www.thehindu.com/news/national/ins-vikramaditya-inducted-into-indian-navy/article5358030.ece
48. Ibid.
49. Tor Bukkvoll, "Iron Can't Fight: The Role of Technology in Current Russian Military Theory," *Journal of Strategic Studies,* vol. 34, no. 5, October 2011, p.681.
50. Ibid.
51. Deba R. Mohanty and Uma Purushothaman, "India-US Defence Relations: In Search of a Direction", Observer Research Foundation, New Delhi, August 2011, pp.8-9.
52. Debidatta Aurobinda Mahapatra, "BRICS Play Role as Global Balancer", *Russia and India Report*, March 26, 2014, p.29.
53. Niveditha Das Kundu, "Russia-India-China: Prospects for Trilateral Cooperation", http://www.helsinki.fi/aleksanteri/english/publications/contents/ap_3-2004.pdf. Accessed on February 24, 2015.
54. Prakash Nanda, "Why Russia still Matters", *Indian Defence Review*, Net Edition, December 11, 2014, http://www.indiandefencereview.com/news/why-russia-still-matters/. Accessed on January 14, 2015.
55. Dutta, n. 38.

5

India-China Relations: A Defining Partnership for the Asian Century

Sana Hashmi

The current discourse on macro trends of the 21st century seems to be settled in favour of Asia, with the evolution of a broad consensus that the 21st century is the Asian century. This is in contrast with the 19th century, which has been referred to as that of Europe; and the 20th century as the era of the US, the sole superpower of the world. As the European region is still grappling with the Euro Zone Crisis and the US' economic growth is declining, several Asian economies are turning into the economic powerhouses of the world. In fact, China is already regarded as the "manufacturing hub of the world". Gross Domestic Product (GDP), the broadest measure of goods and services produced across the US, notched an annual growth rate of 2.4 percent for 2014, just a touch better than the sluggish average of the nearly six-year-old recovery and far from the 4 percent growth of the late 1990s.[1] While the US growth rate has been declining in the recent past, India and China have grown at an average rate of 5.8 percent and 7.3 percent respectively. According to the International Monetary Fund (IMF), India is projected to grow at 6.3 percent in 2015 and 6.5 percent in 2016, and it is likely to cross China's projected growth rate of 6.3 per cent.[2] India and China are not only the largest economies, but also have the biggest militaries in Asia, with the largest nuclear arsenal stockpiles in Asia. In fact, the 21st century is largely shaped by the rise of India and China that accounts for approximately 38 percent of the global population and 15 percent of the world's GDP. They have also maintained a very complex relationship that is overshadowed by history but also offers promising opportunities in an era of globalisation.[3] However, the stories of the rise of India and China are not rooted in history. In fact, this is a relatively new phenomenon. The initiation of remarkable economic reforms during China's paramount leader Deng

Xiaoping's era in China and India's acclaimed Look East Policy (rechristened as the Act East Policy under Narendra Modi's government) have been the major events which led to the integration of these two countries in the East Asian economy. Internationally, the Chinese leadership has pursued a policy of "peaceful rise" "peaceful development" that has always relied more on reassurance (a good-neighbour policy) and incentives (lucrative trade or investment deals) than on coercion or power politics; therefore, China's expanding economy is now regarded more as an opportunity than a threat, and its polished foreign policy exudes confidence and poise.[4] India, which has traditionally been aloof from the East Asian security dynamics, is engaging with countries and institutions of the region in more ways than one. Thus, adding new dimensions to the regional dynamics. Together, the two Asian giants have injected new energy into the political and economic equilibrium of the region, unseen during the Cold War years. This paper aims to highlight the salient features of this unique development.

Background

Relations between India and China, the two ancient civilisations, are millennia old and both countries are bound through historical, cultural and social linkages. Resistance against their respective colonialists and their common objective of achieving Asian-African solidarity were two of the major reasons which helped these countries to inch closer to each other in the pre and post-independence eras. Since independence, India's ties with China have been of critical importance. In fact, on April 1, 1950, India, after Myanmar, became the second non-socialist country and the 16th state to recognise the People's Republic of China (PRC). Likewise, India has always been of utmost priority in China's strategic calculations, which is, by and large, attributed to India's strategic location and strengthening stature in the international fora.[5]

Though both countries opted for different political structures and social and economic systems after independence, India and China found several reasons to walk together on the international stage. Promoting Asian-African solidarity was one of the major areas of interest for India and China. Their relations, like China's foreign relations with any other country, were laid down on the *Panchsheel Principles/Five Principles of Peaceful Coexistence*. The visit by the first Chinese Premier, Zhou Enlai, to India and the reciprocatory visit by the Indian Prime Minister, Jawaharlal Nehru, to China in 1954, gave a new meaning to India-China relations. With the signing of the "Agreement on Trade and Intercourse between Tibet Region of China and India" on April 24, 1954, India, mainly to prove the depth of its friendship with China, had given up all its extra-territorial rights on Tibet. As per clauses of the agreement, the Government of India agreed to withdraw its armed forces from Tibet and to hand over all the post, telegraph and telephone offices, together with all the equipment to the Chinese government.[6]This friendly approach was not only attributed to their long historical and civilisational linkages but their geographical contiguity also played a great role in shaping their policy towards each other.

Prior to the 1950s, India did not have a border with China; it was only with the Chinese invasion of Tibet that China came closer to India and the strategic buffer between India and China was removed. In fact, the differences over the common border forced India and China into a war in 1962. However, that was the first and the only military conflict between these two Asian countries, and the relationship began to get back on track with both countries trying to shed the historical baggage in the 1970s. The first step in this direction was the restoration of ambassadorial relations in 1976 when K. R. Narayanan was appointed as India's first ambassador to China since 1962 and then the 1988 visit by the then Indian Prime Minister, Rajiv Gandhi, was a watershed event in India-China relations. Later, in 1993, as a part of their Confidence Building Measures (CBMs), the signing of an Agreement on the Maintenance of Peace and Tranquillity along the Line of Actual Control (LAC) on the India-China Border Areas during former Prime Minister Narasimha Rao's visit reflected the growing stability and substance in the bilateral ties.[7] Since then, there has been no looking back for both countries. In the contemporary times, while there are issues which have the potential to derail the relationship, pragmatic cooperation weighs more than competition or rivalry for India and China.

Opportunities in India-China Relations

Economic Relations and Trade Relations

Economic ties between two countries are a driving force in the relationship. In fact, they comprise an indicator of the depth and level of the relationship between the two countries. To some extent, it may be said that economic interconnections act as the enabling environment for generation of greater mutual trust between two countries. Though India-China relations are still marred by mutual trust deficit, their economic relations have not been affected much by any of the irritants. Economic ties between India and China form the basis of their relationship. The signing of the Most-Favoured Nation (MFN) Agreement in 1984 elevated their economic relations to a higher level. In March 2014, China surpassed the United Arab Emirates (UAE) to become India's largest trading partner. In fact, China's share in India's total trade is almost 9 percent and India-China trade is larger than the combined bilateral trade of Germany, the UK and Japan with India.[8] As regards India's share in China's total trade, it is just 2 percent. India's trade with China has increased manifold since 2004. From a meagre figure of just US$ 7 billion in 2004, bilateral trade reached a whopping figure of US$ 65.86 billion in 2013.

Table 1: India-China Trade, 2009-2013

(Figures are in US$ billion)

Year	Exports from India to China	Imports from China to India	Total Trade	Trade Imbalance
2009-2010	11.61	30.82	42.43	-19.21
2010-2011	15.48	43.47	58.95	-27.99
2011-2012	18.07	55.31	73.38	-37.24
2012-2013	13.53	52.24	65.77	-38.71
2013-2014	14.82	51.04	65.86	-36.22

Source: China-India Trade Investment Centre, at http://www.citic.in/. Accessed on February 9, 2015.

Table 2: India's Bilateral Exports to China, 2004-2012*

(Figures are in US$ million)

Description of Products**	2005	2007	2008	2010	2012
Live Animals and Animal Products	139	157	96	274	240
Fruit and Vegetable Products	51	115	87	161	429
Animal or Vegetable Fats and Oil	43	65	70	223	380
Prepared Foodstuff, Beverages, etc.	74	162	241	200	27
Mineral Products	4,130	5,248	6,277	7,032	3,531
Products of Chemicals	857	973	872	1,210	1,517
Plastic and Articles thereof	382	292	229	392	637
Textile and Textile Articles	286	988	836	2,307	3,834
Base Metals and Articles of Base Metals	873	851	423	4,523	2,698

Source: S. K. Mohanty, *India-China Bilateral Trade Relationship: A Study Prepared for the Reserve Bank of India*, (New Delhi: Reserve Bank of India, July 2014), p. 53.

Note: * This table does not include data from all the years since 2004.

** This table does not include all the items which are exported to China.

India's exports to China mainly include animal products, textiles and mineral products. For the last several years, the mineral sector dominated India's bilateral export basket with China, but its prominence declined significantly in recent years and the share of the mining sector declined from 55.4 percent in 2007 to 24.0 percent in 2012; however, both mineral and base metal sectors have complemented each other in focussing exports to the Chinese market.[9] Chemical products, including pharmaceuticals, form a large part of India's exports to China, a trend which has started showing up for the past few years. Chemical products, plastic and articles thereof have also found a place in the list. The nature of India's bilateral export basket indicates that these sectors fall mostly in the categories of resource-based and labour-intensive products and India's attempts to export technology-intensive products have been much below its potential, as seen from its current economic engagement with China.[10]

Table 3: India's Imports from China, 2004-2012*

(Figures are in US$ billion)

Description of Products**	2005	2007	2008	2010	2012
Products of Animals	1.657	3.787	5.135	6.618	9.357
Mineral Products	970	1.376	1.711	758	990
Machinery and Mechanical Appliances	4,313	11,149	12,241	18,488	23,340
Textile and Textile Articles	1,065	1,306	1,398	1,725	2,165
Articles of Stone, Plaster, Cement	220	419	575	685	947
Vehicles, Aircraft and Vessels	217	624	785	1,854	1,861
Natural or Cultured Pearls, Jewellery	181	303	383	524	1,263

Source: S. K. Mohanty, *India-China Bilateral Trade Relationship: A Study Prepared for the Reserve Bank of India* (New Delhi: Reserve Bank of India, July 2014), p. 53.
Note: * This table does not include data from all the years since 2004.
** This table does not include all the items which are imported from China.

India's imports from China are diversified in nature and the dominating sector is machinery imports. In terms of composition of India's bilateral imports from China, sectoral shares are declining for minerals, pulp products, textiles and clothing, and base metals, and India's bilateral pattern of imports clearly indicates that demand for technology-intensive products is becoming strong in the domestic market whereas demand for labour-intensive and resource-based products has been gradually weakening in recent years.[11]

The trajectory of India-China trade relations suggests that these are much below their potential, especially when compared with the hefty US-China trade figure of US$ 562 billion. Both countries aim to reach the US$ 100 billion mark by the end of 2015; however, there was a 7 percent decline in their bilateral trade in the beginning of 2015. It seems unlikely that the two countries will achieve their stipulated target of US$ 100 billion. Despite this, there is still a ray of hope and that is, the trade figure till the end of 2014 stood at US$ 70 billion, ending a two-year decline.

Investments

Of late, India is turning into a favourable investment destination for many foreign countries. That is the reason why Japan, in September 2014, announced investment of US$ 34 billion in India and China plans to spend US$ 20 billion in the next five years. India's attractiveness as an investment destination is visible from the average net inflow that more than trebled from an average net inflow of US$ 3.8 billion to US$ 13.6 million during 2006-11.[12] With the rise in trade volume, both countries are exploring avenues to increase their bilateral investment. In fact, during Chinese President Xi Jinping's maiden visit to India in September 2014, it was agreed that in the next five years, China would invest in:[13]

- Helping bring India's ageing railway system up-to-date with high-speed links and upgraded railway stations.
- Setting up industrial parks in Gujarat and Maharashtra.
- Giving more market access to Indian products, including pharmaceuticals and farm products, mainly to bridge the ever-increasing trade deficit

However, like trade relations, Chinese investments in India are much below its potential. China's economic relations, mainly investments relations, are not untouched by deepening suspicions regarding its intentions. India has blocked Chinese investments in sectors such as telecom, ports, and shipping due to security concerns, and made it difficult for Chinese employees to obtain visas to work in India[14] and for Chinese companies to initiate their ventures independently in India. The same is the case with Indian companies in China. Since a majority of companies in China are state-owned, Indian companies do not get preferable conditions when investing in China. In such a situation, the possibility of an increase in the investment opportunities needs to be explored thoroughly.

Cooperation at Multilateral, Regional and Sub-Regional Fora

The 21st century has also come to be referred to as an era of multilateralism and regionalism. Nowadays, countries are cooperating with each other through multilateral mechanisms which give them opportunities to interact. China and India are also a part of several multilateral and regional institutions that have further helped them in realising their ambitions while projecting a benign image. A few examples of their burgeoning cooperation are BCIM-EC (Bangladesh, China, India, Myanmar-Economic Corridor) and BRICS (Brazil, Russia, India, China and South Africa).

BCIM-EC

BCIM is a sub-regional grouping, set up to improve regional economic integration among Bangladesh, China, India and Myanmar by linking South Asia to Southeast and East Asia. The first and foremost purpose of this grouping is to enhance the connectivity among these four countries and connect India's northeast with China's Kunming through Bangladesh and Myanmar. It was first started on August 17, 1999, as a Track-II dialogue which came to be known as the "Kunming Initiative". The main thrust of the exercise was to exhort the governments concerned to improve communication between the southwestern region of China and the northeastern region of India by developing appropriate road, rail, waterway and air links; more specifically, a call was made to revive the ancient Southern Silk Route between Assam and Yunnan.[15] The idea was to expand bilateral trade among these four countries by establishing an economic corridor.

So far as the sub-regional dynamics are concerned, both India and China are mindful of the fact that their landlocked areas—the seven northeastern states of India and the Chinese province of Yunnan—are underdeveloped in terms of connectivity, infrastructure, and easy access to resources; therefore, sub-regional cooperation through BCIM-EC is perhaps the most suitable way to deal with the issue of lack of connectivity and infrastructure as well as the problems posed by underdevelopment.[16] Once the BCIM-EC is fully established, it will combine India, China and the Association of Southeast East Asian Nations (ASEAN) Free Trade Area (FTA), comprising 7.3 per cent of the global GDP, thus, granting India significant economic outreach to China through easy market access along its northeastern borders.[17] Additionally, for India, it will eventually allow the northeast to open up which will lead to the subsequent and much-awaited development of the region. However, due to uncertainty, in the form of mutual trust depreciation in India-China relations, the project is currently at a halt. In recent years, the developments on the BCIM front include the formation of the Joint Study Group by India and China, the BCIM Car Rally in 2013 and the deliberations on the finalisation of the economic corridor on the K2K (Kunming-Ruili-Bhamo-Lashio-Mandalay-Tamu-Imphal-Sylhet-Dhaka-Kolkata) route which is 2,800 km long. Essentially, once operationalised, BCIM-EC has the potential to give a new meaning to India's Act East Policy, develop its northeastern region and revamp its relations with China.

BRICS[18]

BRICS is an acronym for Brazil, Russia, India, China and South Africa. Of late, BRICS as a grouping has been gaining prominence. It has clearly emerged as one of the most promising groups, considering that it not only involves India and China, the two Asian giants, but also Brazil, South Africa and Russia, the major economies of Latin America, Africa, and the Eurasian regions respectively. BRICS has fast emerged as a key grouping in the world with economic issues as one of the top agenda points. It may be noted that though BRICS is just five years old, it has still managed to cover a wide array of issues. In such a short span of time, many mechanisms have been established. On the financial front, in 2014, BRICS's New Development Bank (NDB) and Contingent Reserve Agency (CRA) were concluded. These mechanisms have made it easier for BRICS member states to exchange ideas so as to promote trade and investment and also to strengthen intellectual and financial support for pragmatic cooperation. Second, there is a sense of equality amongst the BRICS members. For instance, it was agreed that these countries will contribute an equal amount of US$ 10 billion for the BRICS NDB.

The trend shows optimistic results about India-China cooperation in BRICS. It is evident that both sides want to expand their cooperation through multilateral exchanges as such cooperation serves mutual benefits and promotes economic growth and regional integration. There are several indicators to measure the level of cooperation between two countries. One such indicator is economic cooperation, which has already been discussed. Regional, multilateral and institutional cooperation is a natural outcome of strengthened India- China ties, and in that context, BRICS becomes a key grouping. Closer India-China relations would not only make the other members more comfortable in dealing with the two Asian giants, but the BRICS countries would also be able to take a more comprehensive stand on issues that face the World Trade Organisation (WTO). In addition, the BRICS countries can greatly benefit in the climate change negotiations, South- South Cooperation, United Nations Security Council (UNSC) reforms and fighting terrorism, amongst other issues, if India and China are able to achieve a qualitative change in their relationship.

The Seventh BRICS Summit, held at Ufa, Bashkortostan, Russia, on July 8-9, 2015. BRICS enthusiasts are looking at the year with a lot of hope. The year 2015 can indeed be a major milestone for BRICS provided the challenges pertaining to cohesion, sustaining low demands for oil and rapid downfall of oil (especially for Russia) and a mutually agreeable common agenda are pushed with determination. A lot depends on how India and China work with each other and what turn their relationship takes in 2015.

A closer look at India-China relations reveals that there exists pragmatic cooperation between these two countries, which is further pushed by the regional dynamics. It has been seen on various occasions that India and China have a similar perspective on issues such as Russia's Ukraine problem and the Syrian issue which are of international importance. China is cooperating with India at various levels which makes it evident that India holds value in China's multilateral equations.

Bottlenecks in India-China Relations

India-China Boundary Dispute: Genesis of the Dispute

The India-China boundary dispute began when India gained independence on August 15, 1947, and the PRC was established on October 1, 1949. The Chinese Communist Party (CCP) was determined to undo the treaties and agreements imposed on it by the colonial powers, and regain China's so-called 'lost territories'. The CCP leaders wanted to 'correct' the boundaries with neighbours, including India. India accepted and inherited whatever the British left for it after the partition of the country. With regard to the boundary issue with China, the McMahon Line, and a western and more complex dimension was added on the accession of the state of Jammu and Kashmir (J&K) to India on October 26, 1947.[19] After independence, the Chinese leaders became more assertive, and refused to accept the legality of the McMahon Line, an issue on which India had its hands tied. Naturally, therefore, the India-China border disagreement turned into a dispute causing anxieties in the Indian policy-making circles. In 1951, when Jawaharlal Nehru brought to the notice of the Chinese government some Chinese maps which showed traditional Indian territory as part of China, Chinese Premier Zhou Enlai, at first, assured Nehru that these were old maps produced by the "pre-liberation regime" and that China had not had the time to revise them.[20] Sensing that China might flare up the issue and actually go in for the rewriting of history, Nehru clarified that "India's boundaries with China were clear and not a matter of further argument".[21] Later, on August 28, 1959, the boundary dispute came to the public attention with Nehru stating in Parliament that three days earlier, a strong Chinese detachment had crossed into the Indian territory of Longju in the Subansiri Frontier Division at a place south of Migyitun, and opened fire.[22] Keeping in view these developments, Prime Ministers Nehru and Zhou Enlai agreed to hold regular meetings in New Delhi from April 19-25, 1960. Consequently, a Joint Working Group was established to examine the factual data provided by both sides, which would later be produced as a report. Nevertheless, the issue remained unsettled and the relations began to deteriorate.

It was claimed by the Indian government that the arguments extended by it in the discussions leading to the 1961 boundary report were strong, valid and supported by legal documents, whereas the Chinese territorial claims were unconvincing. Unable to succeed in its aim to acquire a large chunk of Indian territory by peaceful means, China, therefore, attacked the northern border of India.[23] Consequently, the 1962 War heavily damaged China's 'good neighbourliness policy' as also its relations with its erstwhile friendly neighbour, India.[24] In addition to this, the popular slogan *Hindi-Chini Bhai Bhai,* announced by Nehru to celebrate India-China bonhomie, lost its sheen, which was never to be regained. The major defeat for India was the loss of Aksai Chin to China. Aksai Chin lies in the western sector, which also has a border with Pakistan. What bothered India more was that after occupying a large tract (approximately 38,000 sq km) of Aksai Chin, which is considered by India as illegal occupation, China built a highway (National Highway 219) through it to connect it with its eastern province of Xinjiang, one of the restive regions in China.[25]

Claims and Counter-Claims

There are no two views about the fact that India-China relations are, by and large, governed by their half-a-century-old border dispute. While China has resolved its land border disputes with 12 out of its 14 neighbouring countries by giving them heavy concessions, it is yet to make advancements in its border disputes with India and Bhutan. As regards their border dispute, India and China each has its own story to narrate. While China's official position has been that the common boundary between India and China had not been formally delimited and, therefore, required to be negotiated between the two governments, and if necessary, settled through joint surveys, the Indian government claims that the McMahon Line is the only valid boundary between India and China.[26] Explaining the reasons behind the long-drawn-out conflict, the Chinese government has been claiming that the temporary alignment of the boundary was the result of British imperialist aggression against China and especially the Tibetan regime of China, and further arguing that the India-China frontier had never been formally delimited.[27] On the other hand, the Indian official position has been that the entire length of the boundary had been defined, either by treaty or by custom, or both.[28]

The India-China border problem is two-faceted as there is a conflict in two of the three sectors, i.e., the eastern and western sectors. As of now, the middle sector remains undisputed since, in 2005, China had accepted India's sovereignty over Sikkim. Therefore, the India-China border dispute appears to include two issues now. The first issue stems from the differing perceptions of India and China about the legality of the McMahon Line in the eastern sector. The second is that China and India are at loggerheads on the ownership of Aksai Chin which is situated in the western sector. Both countries share a long border of 4,000 km out of which 2,000 km is in the western sector. This sector lies between the Indian side of Kashmir and one of China's most restive regions, Xinjiang Uighur Autonomous Region (XUAR). In the western sector, India claims that Aksai Chin, which is currently under China's control, has been India's territory since time immemorial. Additionally, it claims that Pakistan had handed over Indian territory, including Shaksgam Valley, to China in 1963. This territory was compromised during the finalisation of the China-Pakistan boundary treaty in 1963. Coming to the Chinese side of the story, the Chinese government claims that although India occupied more than 90,000 sq km of 'Chinese territory' in the eastern sector, provoked two border clashes in 1959 and laid claim to large tracts of Chinese territory, the Chinese government has always stood for a peaceful settlement of the India-China boundary question through negotiation.[29]

The relations between the two countries began to improve in the years that followed the 1962 War. However, the borders felt the heat again in 1986, when Chinese and Indian patrols began confronting each other in the Sumdorong Chu Valley in Tawang. This area which is situated east of Bhutan, sparked off a border crisis that continued for a few months, with both sides refusing to back down, stepping up their patrols in the disputed area and moving substantial military forces into the region.[30]

The Reasons for the 1962 War

The 1962 War stunned the believers of the '*Hindi-Chini Bhai Bhai*' slogan, shattering the hopes for a peaceful Asia. Nehru, who sacrificed Tibet by recognising it as part of China, was cited as saying that he was "stabbed in the back" by the Chinese in 1962.[31] The unfortunate event of history derailed the India-China relationship, pushing them to such an extent that they had no diplomatic relations with each other for almost 14 years. In this context, it is imperative to explore the reasons for the war.

- While several possible reasons and explanations have been provided for the 1962 War, China's primary explanation has been that it resorted to war in response to India's *Forward Policy*. In early 1960, the Indian armed forces reported several possible incursion attempts by China's People's Liberation Army (PLA). It was claimed that Chinese platoons were trying to occupy the vacant and uninhibited areas along the India-China border. Additionally, what worried the Indian leadership was the construction by the Chinese of seven roads alongside Ladakh, several roads along the middle sector of the India-China border, six to the Sikkim and Bhutan borders, and eight to the North-East Frontier Agency (NEFA) border. Reports also confirmed that seven new posts in Ladakh, 14 in Punjab, Himachal Pradesh and Uttar Pradesh, 12 across Sikkim and the Chumbi Valley, and three across NEFA were established by the Chinese.[32] Seizing more Indian territory wherever possible and to create evidence in support of their 1960 claim by pushing forward the Line of Actual Control was clearly the Chinese objective that they very carefully pursued.[33]Puzzled by the Chinese aggressive postures, India realised the futility of being a 'peacenik', and adopted what has been termed as the *'Forward Policy'*, the brainchild of Gen B. M. Kaul. Deploying the *Forward Defence Policy,* the Indian side stationed troops and established border outposts in large numbers along the border to control and ultimately stop the Chinese incursions into Indian territory. In the opinion of Gen. Kaul, the so-called policy would act as a deterrent and, in turn, rule out the possibility of an India-China War. He stated, "The Chinese would not react to our establishing new posts and they were not likely to use force against any of our posts".[34] However, the policy only added 'fuel to the fire', providing China with another reason to invade Indian territory.

- It is often argued that the Tibet issue was the source of the dispute between India and China, leading them eventually to war. The Dalai Lama and the Tibetans-in-exile are often cited as the reasons for the flaring up of the Tibet issue.[35] That the India-China boundary issue was just a symptom and a result of the deterioration in the relations between the two countries; and that the deterioration had set in because of the official and unofficial Indian support to, and sympathy for, the Tibetan revolt of 1959, is another argument made by several Sinologists—a point that has been accepted to a certain extent.[36]
- Thirdly, it was in the 1950s that the Chinese leadership began to get wary of Nehru's attitude and assessed that Nehru was, on the one hand, a leading member of the "Indian bourgeoisie" that had led the fight for independence and, on the other, could not let go of his "lust for expansion".[37] It is an established fact that the Nehru-Mao ideological rivalry played a major role in the deterioration of India-China relations. When Mao Zedong decided to launch his war against India, he had categorically asserted that he would crush Nehru who he was envious of due to various reasons; one reason, according to him, was that he felt that India was getting undue attention from the international community, attention that he, along with the PRC, deserved for their revolutionary war.[38] Apart from the ideological rivalry between Mao and Nehru, a very important cause for the Chinese invasion of India was the ideological difference between the two countries, one swearing by sectarian Communism and the other by democratic socialism, one by alignment and the other by non-alignment, one by dictatorship and the other by democracy.[39] It was felt that China had a grand design for the Afro-Asian world and for the elimination of India as a serious obstacle to Chinese ascendancy.[40]

China's Claim on Arunachal Pradesh[41]

The reasons for the 1962 War and other issues related with it did not end with this war. Since the boundary issue was never resolved between the two sides, it remains a contentious issue. In addition to the territory China had occupied in the western sector, it still questions Arunanchal Pradesh being a part of India. So far, China has not ratified the McMahon Line—a stand which is bound to have wider ramifications in the context of Chinese sovereignty claims over Arunanchal Pradesh. Historically, Arunachal Pradesh was not a state; it was incorporated in India as a territory on January 21, 1972. Earlier, it was known as NEFA which was created in 1955. Historically, the roots of the Simla Accord lie in the McMahon Line. The Simla Accord was signed in 1914, in which the McMahon Line was drawn, involving the plenipotentiaries of British India, China and Tibet. However, in the later stages, China, under the Nationalist forces, withdrew its consent to ratify the agreement, claiming that Tibet was never an independent nation. China has been opposing and challenging the very legitimacy of the Line on the ground that it was signed by erstwhile Tibetan officials who had no authority to do so. Claiming that Tibet is an alienable part of China, the Chinese also claim that it was a British design to weaken and humiliate China, and regard it as a constituent of British imperialism.[42]

Claiming Tawang as a part of China, the Chinese leadership states that the sixth Dalai Lama was born in Tawang in the 17th century. China cites the Tawang Monastery, one of the last vestiges of Mahayana Buddhism, as evidence that the mountainous district of Tawang in Arunachal Pradesh once belonged to Tibet and that India should hand it back to help settle the issue.[43] While China has cited a number of reasons to prove its legitimacy over Arunachal Pradesh, India has always refuted the Chinese claims. However, despite India's consistent refusal to attend to China's claims, China, which used to claim only Tawang previously, has now expanded its claims from Tawang to the entire state of Arunachal Pradesh. In 2006, just a week before the then Chinese President Hu Jintao's maiden state visit to New Delhi, the then Chinese Ambassador to India, Sun Yuxi, stated, "The whole of the state of Arunachal Pradesh is Chinese territory. And Tawang is only one of the places in it. We are claiming all of that. That is our position."[44] This assertion led China to claim over 90,000 sq km of Indian territory on the northeastern front.

Tibet Factor

Tibet has always been a determining factor in India-China relations. With the Chinese invasion of Tibet in 1949-50, China became an immediate neighbour of India. Though China's presence so close to the Indian border was seen with apprehension, Nehru always downplayed this factor. In fact, so as to alleviate irritants, Nehru signed the "1954 Agreement on Trade and Intercourse between Tibet Region of China and India" with China. This move was not positively received in the Indian corridors of power. On May 18, 1954, Nehru stated in the Lok Sabha (House of the People):[45]

> "We recently made an agreement with China. Several members did not like this agreement. They say that we have shown great weakness, that we have committed the mistake of admitting that China has full authority over Tibet... In my opinion, we have done no better thing than this since we became independent. I have no doubt about this."

However, despite, Nehru's assurance, the 1954 agreement and for that matter, India's reiteration of the "One China Policy" were considered major diplomatic blunders on his part.[46] In this regards, Peter Lyon in *The Foreign Policy of India* has stated:[47]

> "In 1954, the India-China Treaty of Trade and Friendship concerning... India, in effect, **abandoned any historic rights in Tibet, receiving in return nothing more substantial than** Chinese promises of eternal friendship... Having conceded that Tibet is a part of China, India subsequently has had to live with the unfavourable military and other aspects of this (eg., the flight of the Dalai Lama, the influx of Tibetan refugees, the loss of trade with Tibet)..... and has come tardily and at the high cost of recognising that the 1954 agreement, far from inaugurating a peaceful settlement in perpetuity, was but an early, yet major, Chinese move in what it looks like a protracted India-China struggle along the Himalayas and elsewhere."

Nevertheless, India was cautious of the possibility of a Chinese invasion of Tibet. In fact, India set for itself three objectives as the PLA moved into Tibet:[48]

- First, keep India's territorial integrity intact, and ensure that the entry of the Chinese forces into Tibet does not cast a shadow on India's security.
- Second, efforts must be made to ensure a sustained India-China friendship.
- Third, Tibet should enjoy real autonomy.

In contrast, China's objectives were simply aimed at establishing and strengthening its authority over Tibet. At the later stage, China decided to 'demographically annex' Tibet by initiating the Han migration which was basically to undermine the Dalai Lama and establish China's effective control over Tibet.[49]

Nehru's engagement with China failed to yield positive results, and invited criticism from the domestic constituency. Other leaders such as Sardar Patel had forewarned Nehru on his Tibet policy. However, it cannot be denied that Nehru was mindful of the limitations of India. It has been argued that for the Indian armed forces, it was not possible to take on both Pakistan and China simultaneously and, therefore, Nehru wanted to avoid a direct confrontation with the Chinese throughout the 1950s.[50] After the 1962

War, India realised that Tibet was no longer a buffer between India and China, a fact which had huge implications for Indian security:

- First, with Tibet under its complete domination, China now finds itself militarily and strategically in a stronger position vis-a-vis India; diplomatically too, it is in a favourable environment, with considerable scope for diplomatic manoeuvring to its advantage.[51] Considering that the infrastructure on the Chinese side is better than that on the Indian side, China is in a better position to negotiate. More importantly, with the extension of the Qinghai-Tibet Railway Line to Shigatse, the travel time between Lhasa and Shigatse has been reduced to just two hours. This railway line extension which was inaugurated on August 15, 2014, would allow China to fulfil its concealed motives. It has become easier for China to rapidly transport troops and weapons to the southern part of Tibet which is very close to Arunachal Pradesh.[52] In the next Five-Year Plan (2016-2020), China intends to extend this railway line to Kyirong in Nepal and Chumbi Valley which is situated between Sikkim and Bhutan. Furthermore, China also plans to construct a railway line between Lhasa and Nyingchi Prefecture.
- Second, Tibet is referred to as a "water reservoir" of many South and Southeast Asian countries as rivers such as the Brahmaputra, Indus, Salween and Mekong, which originate in Tibet, flow to countries like India, Bangladesh and Thailand. At least 65 percent of the population of South and Southeast Asia is dependent on the water of these rivers. It is no secret that many of China's northern and northwestern regions are water-deprived; hence, China, for a long time, has been involved in diverting river water from Tibet to fulfil the water needs of its northern region. For the same purpose, China has embarked on a water diversion project which has come to be known as the South-to-North water diversion project. This project also includes the diversion of water from the Brahmaputra river (known as the Yarlung-Tsangpo in China). In fact, China has been building huge dams on the rivers and since India is a lower riparian country, and there is no water treaty between the two countries, India may face severe water scarcity in the future.

Huge Trade Imbalance

While there has been a consistent rise in the India-China trade figure, the rise in the trade deficit has also been noticed. The trade advantage is tilted in China's favour. It may be noted that the trust deficit was not alarming in the 2000 decade but the volume of the same has been increasing considerably over the years. The trade deficit which was just US$ 19.21 billion in 2009 rose to US$ 36.22 billion in 2012. The ever-growing trade deficit is mainly because India exports raw material to China, whereas finished goods are being imported from China.

The Indian leadership is aware that this problem of trade imbalance needs to be dealt with, with utmost urgency. It is in this context that India has been raising the issue with China for the last few years now. In fact, India has several mechanisms such as the India-China Strategic and Economic Dialogue (SED) and India-China Joint Economic Group to discuss such issues at length. During Xi Jinping's visit to India, the two leaders assigned the SED to explore new areas for economic cooperation in cross-cutting fields, including industrial investment, infrastructure development, energy conservation and environment protection, high-tech industry, clean energy and sustainable urbanisation.[53] As regards the India-China Joint Economic Group, at its 10th session, held in 2014, both sides decided that several measures would be taken for bridging the prevailing trade deficit. Such measures would include cooperation on pharmaceutical supervision, including registration, speedier phytosanitary negotiations on agro-products for two-way trade, stronger links between Indian Information Technology (IT) companies and Chinese enterprises, and increasing services trade in tourism, films, health care, IT and logistics.[54] While there are no two views on the fact that India is striving hard to address this challenge, the problem of trade imbalance is still intact. In fact, one may argue that the day is not far when this issue will become as problematic as the India-China boundary conundrum.

China-Pakistan All-Weather Friendship

Xi Jinping paid a state visit to Pakistan on April 20-21, 2015. Ahead of his first-ever visit to the country, Xi stated, "I feel as if I am going to visit the home of my own brother". During his address to the Pakistan Parliament on the second day of his tour, Xi termed Pakistan as China's "iron brother".[55] That was not the first time that such vows of friendship were reiterated by a Chinese minister and leader. In fact, China-Pakistan bonhomie has been seen on several occasions. Amid US President Barack Obama's visit to India in January 2015, Chinese Foreign Minister, Wang Yi had referred to Pakistan as China's "irreplaceable all-weather" friend. Additionally, in May 2013, Chinese Premier Li Keqiang also stated that Pakistan is China's "iron brother".

Clearly, both countries attach great importance to their bilateral relationship. For instance, during his India visit, Xi had pledged to invest US$ 20 billion in India's infrastructure development. However, China moved one step ahead while announcing its investment in Pakistan. China has, under the framework of its Silk Road project, announced a whopping figure of US$ 46 billion for the construction of the China-Pakistan Economic Corridor. Through the corridor, a network of roads, railway and oil and natural gas pipelines between China and Pakistan are expected to be constructed. The corridor has long-term ramifications for India. This move will not only bolster China's military presence in Pakistan Occupied Kashmir (PoK) which continues to be a disputed area between India and Pakistan, but also, China's continued presence in PoK and attempts to expand its sphere of influence to the Indian Ocean Region (IOR) have the potential to fuel the regional rivalry, considering that India is also endeavouring to give a fillip to its Indian Ocean strategy.[56]

China has been involved in Pakistan's nuclear programme since its inception. In December 2013, the China National Nuclear Corporation (CNNC) pledged to invest US$ 6.5 billion in the construction of Pakistan's nuclear power projects. Moreover, China will be supplying two of its ACP-1000 nuclear reactors to Pakistan for fulfilling its energy needs. As of February 2015, China has been cooperating with Pakistan in as many as six nuclear power projects. China's civil nuclear cooperation with Pakistan has become a cause of concern for countries like India and the US. Apart from the China-Pakistan nuclear cooperation, China's infrastructure development in Pakistan too is a cause of concern for India. Of all the projects, due to security reasons, China's assistance in the construction of Gwadar port has not been received well by the Indian leadership. It has been argued that the motives behind the construction of a strategically important port like Gwadar were not simply economic in nature but have concealed expansionist, political and militaristic implications.[57] Additionally, for a very long time, China has been Pakistan's largest arms importer. This makes it evident that China is becoming Pakistan's natural defence partner and the China-Pakistan joint military exercise held in August 2014 is testimony to that.

Though China and Pakistan claim that their friendship is not aimed at any third country, this all-time alliance is not baseless; it has emerged out of China's and Pakistan's differences with India at the regional level. With China and Pakistan both possessing nuclear weapons and China, time and again, assisting Pakistan to further develop its nuclear capabilities, India, certainly, does not wish to face a two-way threat in the name of China and Pakistan. However, China needs to take into consideration the fact that while China's friendship with Pakistan is helpful for it to put pressure on India, in the long run, it is deemed to have negative impacts on India-China relations. Given that India is much more influential than Pakistan on the international stage, it is in China's interest to not excessively use the Pakistan card against India. In fact, owing to Pakistan's negative image in handling the terrorism issue, China would not want to be seen as giving/showing undue favours to Pakistan.

The Review of the Year Gone by

The year 2014 comprised a mixed bag for India-China relations. Events such as the commemoration of the 60th anniversary of *Panchsheel,* a change in the leadership in India, the visit of Xi Jinping to India and the 17th round of border negotiations were the key highlights of the year 2014 in the context of India-China bilateral relations. With the change of leadership in India and Narendra Modi assuming the prime minister's office, India's China approach has begun to alter. For instance, while Modi visited countries ranging from Bhutan to the US in 2014, he is scheduled to visit China in May 2015. In fact, he chose the two Himalayan states, Bhutan and Nepal, for his maiden foreign visits as Prime Minister. These visits were indicative of the fact that India is keen to reinforce its strong presence in the South Asian region. The move was seen as India's attempt to counter China's increasing influence in India's immediate neighbourhood. While, on the one hand, India became vocal about resolving the border dispute; on the other, positive developments prevailed over the miniscule element of animosity.

Commemorating Six Decades of Panchsheel: 2014, The Year of Friendly Exchanges

One of the major developments in the year 2014 was the commemoration of the 60th anniversary of the signing of the *Panchsheel* Agreement. The year 2014 was officially pronounced as the "Year of Friendly Exchanges between India and China". To celebrate the *Panchsheel* Agreement as also India-China friendship, India's Vice President Hamid Ansari paid a five-day visit to China in June 2014. The visit was important in the sense that this was the first by an Indian leader to China after the Narendra Modi government took charge in May 2014. It may be noted that the last visit paid by an Indian Vice President to China was in 1994, when the then Vice President K. R. Narayanan had visited China.[58] On the whole, the celebration of the 60th anniversary of *Panchsheel* was seen as a move towards alleviating differences and reinforcing the importance of mutual interests. However, the irony is that while the year gone by was marked by the celebration of 60 years of *Panchsheel,* India and China have hardly coexisted peacefully. It has been 60 years of mutual distrust and uncompromising stances towards each other.

Border Negotiations

In February 2014, Yang Jiechi, who is also the special representative on border talks from the Chinese side, visited India to launch the 17th round of border negotiations between India and China. As a part of the meeting, the Indian and Chinese sides held the fifth meeting of the Working Mechanism for Consultation and Coordination on India-China Border Affairs. It was accompanied by two-day border talks at the special representatives level in New Delhi on February 10-11, 2014.

The then National Security Adviser Shiv Shankar Menon and Chinese State Councillor Yang Jiechi presided over the talks that "reviewed recent developments in the India-China border areas, especially in the Western Sector. Additionally, implementation of the Border Defence Cooperation Agreement (BDCA), additional CBMs and further steps for maintaining peace and tranquillity were also discussed".[59] Clearly, the talks were aimed at checking the military stand-offs along the Line of Actual Control (LAC) as also the BDCA which was signed during former Indian Prime Minister Manmohan Singh's visit to Beijing in October 2013. Additionally, during Xi's India visit, the joint statement affirmed:[60]

> "During the visit, the two sides exchanged views on the India-China boundary question and reiterated their commitment to seek a fair, reasonable and mutually acceptable solution, proceeding from the overall interests of bilateral relations. Recalling the Agreement on the Political Parameters and Guiding Principles for the Settlement of the Boundary Question signed in April 2005, both sides reiterated their commitment to an early settlement of the boundary question and expressed their conviction that this will advance the basic interests of the two countries and shall, therefore, be pursued as a strategic objective. They reaffirmed the utility and significance of the mechanism of Special Representatives for seeking a political settlement of the boundary question and of the Working Mechanism for Consultation and Coordination on India-China Border Affairs for handling border related matters. Pending a final resolution of the boundary question, the two sides would continue to make joint efforts to maintain peace and tranquillity in the border areas."

However, the progress on border negotiations has been rather slow and tardy, having failed to make any headway. Nevertheless, considering the developments on border negotiations so far, it is difficult to predict a timeline on the border settlement. In view of the complexity of the situation, it may be said that the best option for India is to adopt a more pragmatic approach towards resolving the long-standing border issue. In a situation wherein the border dispute seems to be intact, the immediate focus should be on enhancing strategic mutual trust by checking the border incursions and fully implementing the CBMs.

Xi Jinping's India Visit v/s Modi's Japan Visit

Xi Jinping paid a state visit to India from September 17-19, 2014, and signed as many as 20 Memorandums of Understanding (MsoU) and agreements in the areas relating to infrastructural development and strengthening cultural linkages between India and China. It was Xi's first visit to India as the President of China. The main purpose of the visit was to establish closer ties with the new leadership in India and also to give a defining shape to the relationship.

According to Professor Srikanth Kondapalli, the visit will be remembered for five major aspects:[61]

- Firstly, there were many unprecedented departures from the past in these interactions. For instance, agreements were signed at the regional (Gujarat state) level on sister cities, sister states and development related issues.
- Secondly, China and India interactions indicated the tough bargaining at Hyderabad House and both Modi and Xi expressed strong opinions on economic and territorial disputes, and other issues.
- Thirdly, China finally opened up its coffers to India, although just a trickle, at US$ 20 billion in investments in the next five years.
- Fourthly, Indian leaders stood their ground on the territorial dispute, visas, river water and the like. In his media interaction on the conditional normalisation of relations with China, Modi stated: "A climate of mutual trust and confidence; respect for each other's sensitivities and concerns; and, peace and stability in our relations and along our borders are essential for us to realise the enormous potential in our relations".
- Finally, the emerging personal chemistry between the two leaders of the two rising Asian countries was notable which will be important for the long-term economic development of both countries.

A careful analysis of Xi's India visit and for that matter, of events in the year gone by, suggests that China has given India one of the first few positions in its priority list. While the investment of US$ 20 billion was given to India, major issues such as border dispute resolution and huge trade imbalance were also discussed at length. The visit was regarded as a huge success by both leaders. However, amid Xi's visit, on September 18, 2014, around 1,000 PLA soldiers entered southern Ladakh. Though this incursion did not overshadow Xi's visit, it made clear that the boundary dispute is likely to linger for a longer period.

Interestingly, Xi's India visit was followed by Modi's maiden five-day state visit to Japan in August-September 2014. China and Japan are at loggerheads with each other because of the ongoing maritime dispute in the East China Sea. Apparently, the Modi-Shinzo Abe bonhomie sent shock waves in China. In fact, in January 2014, when Japanese Prime Minster Shinzo Abe was visiting India, the joint statement stated, "The relations between Japan and India have the greatest potential of any bilateral relationship anywhere in the world". In a similar context, during a business summit in Tokyo, Modi was heard saying that "Japan and India should strengthen strategic cooperation to promote peace and prosperity in Asia and meanwhile counter an expansionist mindset. Everyone around us..... we see an 18th century expansionist mindset: encroaching on another country, intruding in other's waters, invading other countries and capturing territory."[62] Though no country was named in the statement, considering that India and Japan are involved in territorial disputes with China, it seemed to be directed at China. It may be argued that Modi's Japan visit outweighed Xi's India visit in more ways than one. An opinion piece in *the Economic Times* illustrated the major highlights of Modi's visit to Japan:[63]

- Referring to India as a "low cost manufacturing hub", Modi gave an open invitation to Japanese investors to invest in India under "Make in India" and stated that India offers the three essential Ds for businessmen to thrive, namely, Democracy, Demography and Demand.
- It was agreed that the Prime Minister's Office (PMO) would establish a special management team to facilitate investment proposals from Japan.
- With Japan committing to fund bullet trains, the dream of running high-speed trains on Indian tracks is now a step closer to realisation. Such trains are expected to run between Ahmedabad and Mumbai at an estimated cost of around Rs 60,000-70,000 crores.
- Japan announced that it would invest US$ 34 billion in India over the next five years, whereas China had committed to invest US$ 20 billion.
- Indo-Japan defence relations were elevated to the "Special Strategic and Global Partnership".
- Japan lifted the ban on Hindustan Aeronautics Limited (HAL) and five other Indian entities, which had been imposed in the aftermath of the 1998 nuclear tests.

These developments are indicative of the India-Japan burgeoning relations and that Modi's Japan visit was a landmark event in their relationship. Modi recognises that New Delhi must strategically collaborate with Tokyo to prevent the rise of a China-centric Asia, or else India's world-power aspirations will be stymied for good.[64] These two visits have signalled that Modi is cooperating with China where it is needed, while simultaneously reaching out to strategically important partners in Asia and outside. This approach may be categorised as cautious and India's Japan as well as Vietnam policy may be seen as an answer to the China-Pakistan friendship and the frequent border incursions.

India and the Maritime Silk Road

During his India visit, Xi expressed willingness to include India in his pilot project, constructing the Maritime Silk Road. Xi Jinping's desire to rope in India in his pilot project is indicative of China's willingness to work closely with India. In October 2013, Xi Jinping, while addressing the Indonesian Parliament, proposed to build the Maritime Silk Road (MSR) through the disputed South China Sea. At the substantive level, the MSR is conceptualised to serve two purposes: energise relations with neighbours through effective use of naval diplomacy; and respond to the US' rebalancing towards Asia in diplomatic terms by making its maritime presence felt.[65]

On India's participation in the MSR, Dr. Rahul Mishra, Research Fellow, Indian Council of World Affairs (ICWA), explains that as far as India is concerned, the MSR is "an opportunity in overalls":[66]

- While there can be no two views that the MSR would give China unhindered access to the Indian Ocean, if India strengthens its economic prowess and follows up on promises made, the MSR would be of great value to India.
- One of the big promises of the MSR is that greater maritime cooperation covering the areas from the Indian Ocean to the Bay of Bengal, and Malacca and Lombok Straits would help in humanitarian assistance and disaster relief operations; thereby, help in fighting trans-national, non-traditional security challenges such as piracy, gun-running, human trafficking and natural disasters, effectively.

Clearly, India has been hesitant in joining hands with China with respect to the MSR. There are several reasons for India's reluctance to facilitate China in constructing the MSR. First, the lack of trust between India and China is holding India back. Second, in June 2014, the Secretary of the Ministry of Culture, Shri Ravindra Singh, under the Modi government, initiated "Project Mausam" which has been seen as a counter to China's "String of Pearls" strategy or its efforts to reach the Indian Ocean Region (IOR). The endeavour of "Project Mausam" is to position itself at two levels: at the macro level, it aims to reconnect and reestablish communications between countries of the Indian Ocean, which would lead to an enhanced understanding of each other's cultural values and concerns; while at the micro level, the focus is on understanding national cultures in their regional maritime milieu.[67] The central themes that hold Project Mausam together are those of cultural routes and maritime landscapes that not only link different parts of the Indian Ocean littoral, but also connect the coastal centres to their hinterlands.[68] With this project, India wishes to expand its influence in the maritime domain as well.

As far as China's maritime ambitions are concerned, it is aware that it has to reach out to India if it wants to have access to the IOR. That was why, in February 2015, China called on India to shed its ambivalence about Beijing's ambitious Maritime Silk Road plan, with the Chinese leadership unveiling new details about the more than US$ 100 billion initiative that aims to build a network of ports and maritime infrastructure throughout the Asia-Pacific.[69] However, while the MSR does offer opportunities to countries of the region, including India, it remains to be seen how China manages to realise it while convincing countries to keep their apprehensions at bay.

The Way Forward

While there are several issues of divergence between India and China, issues of convergence are forcing them to take an unconventional path. The forces of globalisation and the surge of regionalism, particularly in the Asian context, have motivated the countries to shed their historical baggage to reap the maximum economic benefits from other countries. This is true in the case of India-China relations also. However, the differences between them cannot be downplayed. Despite cooperation at such a high level, pessimism looms large over India-China relations and the mutual trust deficit continues. This may be attributed to their ongoing boundary dispute, the huge imbalance in bilateral trade, the China-Pakistan nuclear nexus and India's growing bonhomie with Japan and Vietnam.

For decades, China has tried to sideline the issue of the boundary dispute while cooperating with India on several other issues. China's approach towards its territorial disputes suggests that it will only resolve the boundary dispute with India when either China's own internal or peripheral stability is at stake or it is reaping diplomatic gains out of the border deal. As of now, China has nothing to lose if it does not resolve the boundary dispute. In fact, the ongoing dispute is seen as a pressure tactic by the Chinese. Nevertheless, in the long run, this dispute needs to be addressed. Now, when India has abandoned the appeasement policy and is exploring new opportunities to cooperate with several Asian countries and also with the US which is still regarded as the non-resident power in the Asia-Pacific region, CBMs are doing no good to India-China relations. This approach is certainly not going to help China. In fact, it will contribute to the escalation of the mutual trust deficit.

Xi Jinping, during his special address at the Taj Palace Hotel, New Delhi, on September 19, 2014, had stated: "China and India should view the border issue as well as other issues left over from history in a positive light". The time has come to transform talk into action. Concrete steps need to be taken for building mutual trust by resolving the long-standing issues. However, this goal appears unattainable in the near future. In such a scenario, the conventional approach needs to be reviewed and altered. One may argue that resolving the boundary dispute is no longer a prerequisite for the development of other aspects of bilateral relations. Hence, India and China should realise that even if the boundary dispute does not get resolved in the short run, they should keep working towards respecting each other's concerns and injecting a new life in their relationship while they keep looking for solutions to the boundary conundrum in the long run.

India-China relations comprise one of the most complicated relationships of contemporary times. While there are differences between them, cooperation still weighs more than conflict. Therefore, the border dispute should not derail the relationship. For that to happen, India has to deal with China from a position of strength which will be possible only with a calibrated approach comprising a fine balance of strengthened military capabilities and infrastructure along the border and diplomatic finesse.

Notes

1. Josh Mitchell, "US Economy Hits Speed Bumps", *The Wall Street Journal,* January 30, 2015, at http://www.wsj.com/articles/u-s-gdp-growth-slows-to-2-6-in-fourth-quarter-1422624685. Accessed on January 31, 2015.
2. "India's Growth Rate to Surpass China's in 2016: IMF", *Economic Times,* January 20, 2015, at http://articles.economictimes.indiatimes.com/2015-01-20/news/58267866_1_world-economic-outlook-growth-forecast-growth-rate. Accessed on January 26, 2015.
3. Vincent Wei-cheng Wang, "Chindia or Rivalry? Rising China, Rising India and Contending Perspectives on India-China Relations", *Asian Perspective,* vol. 35, no. 3, July-September 2011, pp. 437-469.
4. Ibid.
5. Sana Hashmi, "Can India and China Make a Clean Break with the Past", *Rediff,* September 15, 2014, at http://www.rediff.com/news/column/can-india-and-china-make-a-clean-break-with-the-past/20140915.htm. Accessed on September 15, 2014.
6. "Agreement Between the Republic of India and the People's Republic of China on Trade and intercourse between Tibet Region of China and India" (Beijing: Ministry of External Affairs of India, April 29, 1954).
7. "India-China Relations", January 2014, at http://www.mea.gov.in/Portal/ForeignRelation/China_January_2014.pdf. Accessed on January 16, 2015.
8. S. K. Mohanty, *India-China Bilateral Trade Relationship: A Study Prepared for the Reserve Bank of India* (New Delhi: Reserve Bank of India, July 2014), p. 49
9. Ibid.
10. Ibid.
11. Ibid.
12. KPMG, "India-China Business Investment Opportunities", 2013, p. 20, at http:/en.ccei.org.in/files/India-China-Business-Investment-Opportunities-2013.pdf. Accessed on February 20, 2014.
13. "China's Xi Jinping Signs Landmark Deals on India Visit", *BBC News,* September 18, 2014, at http://www.bbc.com/news/world-asia-india-29249268. Accessed on September 19, 2014.

14. "Five Reasons India Should Not Worry About its Trade Deficit with China", *Forbes,* September 28, 2014, at http://www.forbes.com/sites/anaswanson/2014/09/28/five-reasons-india-shouldnt-worry-about-its-trade-deficit-with-china/. Accessed on February 20, 2015.
15. P. V. Inderisan, "The Kunming Initiative", *Frontline,* vol. 17, no. 7, April 1-14, 2000.
16. Sana Hashmi, "India-China Relations in 2013: An Assessment", in Air Marshal Vinod Patney ed., *Asian Defence Review 2013* (New Delhi: Knowledge World, 2014).
17. Leonora Juergens, "BCIM and BIMSTEC: Two Competing Initiatives for Northeast India?", *IPCS Commentary,* May 20, 2014, at http://www.ipcs.org/article/india/bcim-and-bimstec-two-competing-initiatives-for-northeast-india-4454.html. Accessed on March 2, 2015.
18. This section on BRICS draws heavily from material from the author's previous work published in *India-China Chronicle Magazine*. For details, see Sana Hashmi, "India-China Cooperation in BRICS", *India-China Chronicle,* March-April 2015.
19. A. G. Noorani, *India-China Boundary Problem 1846-1947: History and Diplomacy* (New Delhi: Oxford University Press, 2011), p. 1.
20. B. L. Sukhwal, *India: A Political Geography* (New Delhi: Allied Publishers, 1971), pp. 197-198.
21. *Notes, Memoranda and Letters Exchanged and Agreement Signed between the Government of India and China, White Paper II,* 1959 (New Delhi: Ministry of External Affairs, Government of India, 1959), p. 49.
22. Noorani, n. 19, p. 1.
23. Sukhwal, n. 20, p. 202.
24. The good neighbourly policy was first initiated in 1954 with a clandestine aim of parting ways with China's once prominent foreign policy principle of *Leaning to One Side* towards the Soviet Union.
25. Ramananda Sengupta, "Why China Claims Arunachal Pradesh", *Rediff,* November 16, 2006, at http://www.rediff.com/news/2006/nov/16sld1.htm. Accessed on September 26, 2014.
26. Ministry of External Affairs, Government of India, *Report of the Officials of the Governments of India and the People's Republic of China on the Boundary Question* (New Delhi: Ministry of External Affairs, 1961), pp. 233, 110-115.
27. n. 21, p. 52-57.
28. Ibid., p. 85.
29. *Sino-Indian Boundary Question* (Beijing: Foreign Language Press, 1962), p. 2.
30. V. G. Kulkarni, "Eyeball to Eyeball on the Himalayan Border", *Far Eastern Economic Review*, April 9, 1987, pp. 38-40.
31. A. Appadorai and M. S. Rajan, *India's Foreign Policy and Relations* (New Delhi: South Asian Publishers, 1985), p. 143.
32. B. N. Mullik, *My Years with Nehru: The Chinese Betrayal* (New Delhi: Allied Publishers, 1971), p. 313.
33. Ibid.
34. Quoted in Neville Maxwell and A. G. Noorani, "India's Forward Policy", *The China Quarterly*, vol. 45, 1971, pp. 157-163.
35. T. S. Murty, *India-China Boundary: India's Options* (New Delhi: ABC Publishing House, 1987), p. 66.
36. Ibid.
37. Ranjit Singh Kalha, *India-China Boundary Issues: Quest for Settlement* (New Delhi: Pentagon Press, 2014), p. 100.
38. Ibid.
39. Sukhwal, n. 20, p. 196.

40. Ibid., p. 197.
41. This section on *China's Claim on Arunachal Pradesh* draws heavily on material from the author's previous work on *China's Tawang Temptation* published in October 2012 in *Defence and Diplomacy* Journal of the Centre for Air Power Studies. For details, see Sana Hashmi, "China's Tawang Temptation", *Defence and Diplomacy,* vol. 2, no. 1, October-December 2012, pp. 115-124.
42. Surya P. Sharma, "The India-China Border Dispute: An Indian Perspective", *The American Journal of International Law,* vol. 59, no. 1, January 1965, pp. 16-47.
43. Surya Gangadharan, "Arunachal is Chinese Land: Envoy", *Rediff,* November 20, 2006, at http://ibnlive.in.com/news/arunachal-is-chinese-land-envoy/26108-3.html. Accessed on January 26, 2014.
44. "Arunachal Pradesh is our Territory: Chinese Envoy", *Rediff,* November 14, 2006 at http://www.rediff.com/news/report/china/20061114.htm. Accessed on October 23, 2013.
45. Quoted in K. Gupta, "Sino-Indian Agreement on Tibetan Trade and Intercourse: Its Origin and Significance", *Economic and Political Weekly,* vol. 13, no. 16, April 22, 1978, p. 696.
46. Ibid., p. 696.
47. Peter Lyon, "The Foreign Policy of India", in F. S. Northedge, ed., *The Foreign Policies of the Power* (New York: Praeger, 1969), p. 265.
48. L. L. Mehrotra, *India's Tibet Connection* (Shimla: Indian Institute of Advanced Studies, 2001), p. 18.
49. Ibid.
50. Ibid., p. 27.
51. Dawa Norbu, "Strategic Development in Tibet: Implications for its Neighbours", *Asian Survey,* vol. 19, no. 3, March 1979, p. 245-259.
52. Sana Hashmi, "Tibet Railway Signals Border Imbalance", *Asia Times Online,* September 17, 2014, at http://www.atimes.com/atimes/South_Asia/SOU-01-170914.html. Accessed on September 17, 2014.
53. "Joint Statement between Republic of India and the People's Republic of China on building Closer Developmental Partnership", Ministry of External Affairs, Government of India, September 19, 2014, at http://www.mea.gov.in/bilateral-documents.htm?dtl/24022/joint+Statement+between+the+Republic+of+India+and+the+Peoples+Republic+of+China+on+Building+a+Closer+Developmental+Partnership. Accessed on September 19, 2014.
54. Ibid.
55. Sana Hashmi, "Xi's Pakistan Visit: High on Substance, Low on Values", *Rediff,* April 22, 2015, at http://www.rediff.com/news/column/xis-pakistan-visit-high-on-substance-low-on-values/20150422.htm. Accessed on April 22, 2015.
56. Ibid.
57. For details on Gwadar port, see Rahul Mishra and Sana Hashmi, "Gwadar Port: India's Achilles Heel", *Defence and Security Alert,* vol 3, issue 10, July 2012.
58. "Hamid Ansari Embarks on China Visit", *The Hindu,* June 26, 2014, at http://www.thehindu.com/news/international/world/hamid-ansari-embarks-on-china-visit/article6150938.ece. Accessed on June 26, 2014.
59. For details, see "5th Meeting of the Working Mechanism for Consultation and Coordination on India-China Border Affairs," February 10, 2014, at http://mea.gov.in/press-releases.htm?dtl/22852. Accessed on February 10, 2014.
60. Hashmi, n. 52.
61. Srikanth Kondapalli, "Five Major Takeaways From Xi Jinping's India Visit", *Economic Times,* September 19, 2014, at http://articles.economictimes.indiatimes.com/2014-09-19/news/54109239_1_prime-minister-narendra-modi-president-xi-jinping-maritime-silk-road.

Accessed on September 20, 2014.

62. "Modi-Abe Intimacy Brings Scant Comfort", *Global Times,* September 2, 2014, at http://www.globaltimes.cn/content/879478.shtml. Accessed on March 2. 2015.
63. "PM Narendra Modi's Visit to Japan: 10 Key Takeaways", *Economic Times,* September 2, 2014, at http://articles.economictimes.indiatimes.com/2014-09-02/news/53479892_1_india-and-japan-bullet-trains-pm-narendra-modi. Accessed on September 5, 2014.
64. Brahma Chellaney, "Why Modi's Japan Visit was a Watershed", *Rediff,* September 5, 2014, at http://www.rediff.com/news/column/brahma-chellaney-why-modis-japan-visit-was-a-watershed/20140903.htm. Accessed on March 3, 2015.
65. Rahul Mishra, "What China Must Do to Get India on Silk Route", *Rediff,* September 17, 2014, at http://www.rediff.com/news/column/what-china-must-do-to-get-india-on-silk-route/20140917.htm. Accessed on September 19, 2014.
66. Ibid.
67. "Project 'Mausam' Launched by Secretary, Ministry of Culture", June 21, 2014, at ignca.nic.in/mausam.htm. Accessed on June 25, 2014.
68. Ibid.
69. Ananth Krishnan, "China Asks India to Put Aside 'Maritime Silk Road' Concerns", *India Today,* February 12, 2015, at http://indiatoday.intoday.in/story/china-india-asean-sushma-swaraj-maritime-silk-road-concerns/1/418576.html. Accessed on March 8, 2015.

6

Existential Complexities in Iran's Nuclear Deal

Debalina Ghoshal

The seeds of the Iranian nuclear programme were sown way back in the 1950s. Since then, with regime changes, there has been tumultuous progress in the programme. Until the Iranian Revolution, the US had provided assistance in the country's nuclear programme, but post Iranian Revolution, the US and its European allies **viewed the programme with suspicion**. The nuclear programme further evoked criticism when in 2002, reports revealed that Iran was using it to develop nuclear weapons. Since then, the Iranian nuclear programme has been mired in controversy. In addition, Tehran's progress on its ballistic missile programme has exacerbated the growing mistrust between Iran, on one side, and the US, the E3 (Britain, Germany and France), Israel and the Arabian allies of the US, on the other. Critics of Iran's nuclear programme tried a myriad means to prevent Iran from progressing with **the nuclear programme** but were unable to restrain Tehran. In 2013, a historic deal was signed between Iran and the P5+1 (Britain, China, France, Russia, US and Germany) in which Iran agreed to limit its nuclear programme to ensure that it was meant only for peaceful purpose.

This paper briefly discusses the Iranian nuclear deal which was struck in November 2013 and also the recent Joint Comprehensive Plan of Action (JCPOA). In order to comprehend the nuclear ambitions of Iran, the paper briefly sketches the historical background of the nuclear programme to fathom the complexities that evolved in it and studies Iran's tryst with the nuclear Non-Proliferation Treaty (NPT) and Additional Protocol (AP) and how Tehran has consistently maintained its stance that its nuclear programme is meant for peaceful purposes. The paper studies Iran's threat perceptions from its adversaries. It delves briefly into Iran's nuclear delivery systems and the international responses to these developments in order to comprehend the concerns of the US and E3 countries and Iran's adversaries in West Asia better. The paper also strives to study the great power geo-political game in the region amid the nuclear deal and the implications of the nuclear deal on India.

Iran's Nuclear Deal

Since the disclosure of the 2002 reports, the P5+1 states pressurised Iran to put a halt on its nuclear programme. After many acrimonious debates and negotiations, a consensually agreed upon solution, acceptable not just to the P5+1 states, but even to Iran, was reached, culminating in the signing of the Joint Plan of Action (JPOA) by Iran and the P5+1 on November 24, 2013. Credit for this could be given to President Hassan Rouhani of Iran, under whom relations between Iran and the US have started to improve. In fact, the nuclear deal negotiation process ended the lengthy estrangement of relations between the US and Iran following the Iranian Revolution. Under this deal, Tehran agreed to accept stringent constraints on its nuclear programme for the first time. In return, the P5+1 countries agreed to lift the sanctions imposed on Iran[1] which provided a big respite for its economy. Prior to this, on November 11, 2013, Tehran had signed the "Framework for Cooperation" with the International Atomic Energy Agency (IAEA). This framework aimed to "strengthen their cooperation and dialogue" while also ensuring the "exclusively peaceful nature" of Tehran's nuclear programme. The framework sought to resolve the outstanding issues which have not yet been resolved by the IAEA.[2]

Though the JPOA was a temporary settlement to the nuclear impasse, it had the long-term objective of reaching a permanent solution. The deal demanded that Tehran would:[3]

- Halt production of near-20 percent enriched uranium and disable the configuration of the centrifuge cascades used to produce it.
- Start to dilute half of the near-20 percent enriched uranium stockpile that is in hexafluoride form, and continue to convert the rest to oxide form, not suitable for further enrichment.
- Not enrich uranium in roughly half of the installed centrifuges at the Natanz facility and three-quarters of the installed centrifuges at Fordow.
- Limit its centrifuge production to those needed to replace damaged machines.
- Not construct additional enrichment facilities.
- Not go beyond its current enrichment research and development practices.
- Not commission or fuel the Arak heavy water reactor.
- Halt the production and additional testing of fuel for the Arak reactor.
- Not install any additional reactor components at Arak.
- Not transfer fuel and heavy water to the Arak reactor site.
- Not construct a facility capable of reprocessing at Arak, preventing the separation of plutonium from spent fuel.
- Agree to a cap up to 5 percent on the permitted size of Iran's stockpile of enriched uranium.

- Allow IAEA inspectors to visit the Natanz and Fordow enrichment sites daily and the Arak reactor at least monthly.

The agreement was expected to "cut off Iran's most likely paths to a bomb" and to create "time and space" to negotiate a comprehensive agreement."[4] This deal was welcomed by Rouhani since it recognised Tehran's "right to enrichment" for peaceful purposes.[5]

The deadline for this temporary deal was July 20, 2014. However, the deal failed to achieve the desired success by July 2014, owing to the fact that Tehran could not accept the proposal to restrict itself to 10,000 centrifuges at a time. Tehran claimed it needed 190,000 Separative Working Units (SWUs)[6] and justified its demand for 190,000 SWUs on the fact that of the 19,000 centrifuges, only 10,000 were then operational.

As of now, Tehran has agreed to freeze its nuclear enrichment programme for some years. However, owing to the agreement on fuel supply with Russia for the Bushehr power plant coming to an end in 2021, Iran claims it would need considerable enrichment capacity for the production of fuel for the same post 2021.[7] The US had initially demanded that Tehran restrict its enrichment activities for twenty years, while Tehran had requested for the restriction to be for a decade.

Iran's immediate neighbours in West Asia are not buying Iran's claim that the nuclear programme is peaceful in nature. They believe that it could have a "Possible Military Dimension" (PMD). Post July, 20, 2014, the talks to curb Iran's nuclear programme continued, and Iran and the P5+1 states had hoped that the deal would end on a positive note for both parties. But, states like Israel and Saudi Arabia feel that Tehran is only buying time to be able to develop nuclear weapons. Israel does not support the US policy of allowing Iran to enrich uranium to an agreed level and demands a complete end to its nuclear programme. Israel believes that this deal would not stop Iran from developing the atom bomb and would only pave the way for it to do so.[8]

Israel has also demanded more stringent economic pressure on Iran since Tel Aviv believes that it was the economic pressure which brought Tehran to the nuclear negotiating table. Post **Lausanne** negotiations, Tel Aviv has demanded that Iran recognise the existence of Israel, which experts feel is a "deal breaker" demand.

The November 2014 talks extended the nuclear negotiations until July 2015 while it was decided that a political agreement would be reached by March 2015. The March 2015 Laussanne negotiations under the Joint Comprehensive Plan of Action (JCPOA) resulted in Iran agreeing to reduce its low enriched uranium stockpiles to 98 percent and also to scale back its installed centrifuges.[9] Just like the JPOA, the JCPOA has earned criticism from Iran's immediate neighbours in the region. Saudi Arabia, Iran's immediate Sunni neighbour in the region and its adversary too, is of the view that lifting of the sanctions would enable Iran to fund its proxy Shia organisations in a better way and, therefore, increase terrorism.[10] Moreover, Saudi Arabia has argued that despite the nuclear deal, Iran's ability to develop nuclear weapons would not be affected since its technical capabilities would remain. The deal is only for 15 years, hence, the Saudis fear that Iran could develop nuclear weapons after that.[11]

US President Obama has viewed the deal as a "good deal" and believes that if Iran cheats, "the world will know." Obama's thinking is probably that a "good" nuclear deal with Iran would mean a better relationship with it and, therefore, could enable the US to promote and strengthen peace and stability in West Asia. The US has confirmed that if a deal is reached with Iran, the sanctions would be removed in phases. However, it has clarified that should Tehran be caught conducting any unscrupulous activities concerning its nuclear programme, the sanctions that are lifted, would be imposed again. While it is evident that Israel and Saudi Arabia are not happy with the nuclear deal, their concerns are less to do with the Iranian nuclear programme and more to do with the improving relations between the US and Iran. For Saudi Arabia, this could mean a lesser ability to influence the US in the Middle East, and, may be, a decline in the US demand for Saudi oil.

Back in Iran, the Iranian hardliners may also not view this deal in a positive light. The Iranian Revolutionary Guards Corps (IRGC) that controls the military sites which the IAEA may wish to inspect also, may not view this deal positively. Lifting of the sanctions would receive a mixed response from the Iranians. Iranian citizens who have suffered the most due to the sanctions would heave a sigh of relief and hope for normalisation of the economy. But the hardliners, who have gained power and wealth **as a result of** sanctions might not feel happy about the progress of the deal.

A Brief History (1950-2010)

The Iranian nuclear impasse cannot be fully understood without a brief background knowledge of the history of the nuclear programme. Iran's nuclear programme took off in the 1950s when Tehran began receiving nuclear assistance from the US under the US' "Atoms for Peace" programme. This was in 1957, four years after the military coup.[12] The "Atoms for Peace" programme was initiated when the US realised that the Iranian regime was stable and deserved to get nuclear technology for peaceful use.[13] Iran under Reza Shah Pahlavi, founder of the Pahlavi dynasty, was more inclined towards the US and the European countries which enabled Tehran to receive nuclear technology assistance from these countries. As the US supported the "sultanistic regime", they provided it considerable economic and military aid. Iran became a member of the Central Treaty Organisation (CENTO) in 1955, further facilitating nuclear cooperation between Tehran and Washington.

In 1960, Iran purchased from the US small nuclear reactors at the Tehran Nuclear Research Centre.[14] Owing to Iran's accession to the NPT in 1968, the US supplied Highly Enriched Uranium (HEU) to Tehran for fuelling the nuclear research reactors.[15] Reports suggest that the US supplied Tehran with 5.545kg of enriched uranium and out of this, 5.165kg contained fissile isotopes. Some 112 kg of plutonium was also supplied by the US for use as "start-up sources for the research reactor", of which 104 kg comprised fissile isotopes.[16] However, Tehran had to give an assurance that it would not use these nuclear materials to develop nuclear weapons.

In the 1970s, Iran's nuclear cooperation extended beyond the US. Soon after setting up the Atomic Energy Organisation of Iran (AEOI), in June 1974, Iran invested $1billion in a French uranium enrichment plant. The French company Framatome signed a letter of intent with the AEOI for the construction of two pressurised water reactors near Ahvaz. Iran invested $ 1 billion in the French uranium enrichment plant.[17] This French nuclear plant was called the Eurodiff uranium enrichment plant in which Iran was to have "full access to enrichment technology developed by Eurodiff."[18] However, since Eurodiff was a completely European enterprise, a non-European partner could not ideally venture into it. Hence, with 60 percent French and 40 percent Iranian partnership, France and Iran formed the Sofidif to represent it in the Eurodiff consortium.

Nevertheless, the agreement with France had three major goals:[19]

- Iran's contribution to the uranium enrichment industry in France.
- The construction of a nuclear research and development centre in Isfahan.
- Generation of 5,000 Megawatt (MW) of nuclear power in Iran. The same year, in November, Tehran struck a deal with Siemens Kraftwerk Union (KWU) of West Germany in order to build two 1,200 MW reactors.[20] But, following the Iranian Revolution which led to the downfall of the pro-Western Pahlavi, the project was cancelled by Germany. The Germans decided that they would also cancel the agreement to construct nuclear power plants at Isfahan and Saveh.[21] Despite the revolution, Tehran managed to complete its Safeguards Agreement with the IAEA in the same year. In 1976, Tehran entered into clandestine negotiations with South Africa to purchase uranium concentrate. Following the Iranian Revolution and then the Iran-Iraq War in the 1980s in which Iraq bombed nuclear plants in Bushehr in Iran, Tehran's nuclear programme slowed down. According to Kerry M Kartchner, "The Iranians suffered horrific losses from Iraqi chemical attacks during the Iran-Iraq War, accompanied by the failure of the international community to effectively act against, or intervene with, Iraq."[22] Further, the hostage crisis negated any possibility

of future nuclear cooperation with the US. Iran was subjected to harsh sanctions from the US which hindered the progress of the nuclear programme.

Another important reason for the slowing down of the Iranian nuclear programme in the 1980s was RuhollaMousavi Khomeini's lack of interest in pursuing it. In fact, in an interview with the *Foreign Policy* journal, Mohsen Rafighdoost, the then minister of the IRGC, claimed that throughout the eight years of war, he had requested Khomeini to develop chemical and nuclear weapons, especially as Iraq had used chemical weapons against Iran. However, Khomeini maintained that Islam banned the development of WMD.[23]

He even referred to these weapons as *haram* (sinful). However, Khomeini was in favour of nuclear energy which is evident from the fact that he ordered the scientists to divert the nuclear programme to a nuclear energy programme. In 1988, Iran collaborated with Argentina's Applied Research Institute to alter the Tehran research reactor so that it could run on uranium enriched to slightly less than 20 percent U-235. Due to the Iran-Iraq War, which drained out Iranian resources, only limited resources could be diverted to the nuclear programme.

The nuclear programme gained momentum when a more pro-nuclear leader, Ali Akbar Hashemi Rafsanjani, took charge of the regime in the 1990s. Iran developed close ties with China and Pakistan then in order to avail of nuclear technology from them. Reportedly, in 1991, China secretly exported "natural uranium"[24] to Iran which was consequently utilised in experiments in the uranium conversion process.[25]

In 1992, Beijing also signed a contract for the sale of a 300 MW Light Water Reactor (LWR) and a large research reactor, capable of producing plutonium. By 1993-95, with assistance from the Pakistanis' A.Q. Khan network, Iran managed to get design drawings of Pakistani centrifuges, even though talks regarding the centrifuges had started way back in 1987. Khan is believed to have sold the surplus P-1 centrifuges to Iran since Pakistan was already replacing them with the more sophisticated P-2 centrifuges. By 1996, Tehran also received the design drawings of the advanced P-2 centrifuges.[26]

In 1999, China agreed to provide the design drawing of the Uranium Conversion Facilities (UCF) at Esfahan to the AEOI under which Iran received documents which mentioned the conversion process and engineering designs.[27] However, owing to diplomatic pressure from the US, Beijing had to stop this cooperation mid-way. Even though Beijing succumbed to US pressures and severed nuclear ties with Iran, the Chinese initiated UCF was sufficient for Iran to carry on with its nuclear programme.[28]

During the 1990s, Iran signed a nuclear cooperation agreement with Russia. Under this agreement, Russia agreed to complete the construction of the Bushehr-1 nuclear power plant and offered secretly to supply a large research reactor, a fuel fabrication facility and gas centrifuge plant.[29] In 2002, using the UF6 which was supplied by China, Tehran, in its secret centrifuge, meant for research and development activities, conducted some tests at the Kalaye Electric Company.[30]

However, in 2002, three European countries, Germany, France and Britain (E3) expressed their concerns over Tehran's nuclear programme. Reports suggested that Iran was developing enriched uranium which was not meant only for peaceful purposes, but could even be diverted to develop nuclear weapons. In 2003, an effort was made by the IAEA to initiate an investigation process of the Iranian nuclear programme. The IAEA discovered that Iran had not declared its past enrichment experiences. Documents dealing with the production of nuclear weapons and HEU were also found.[31]

In September 2003, the IAEA adopted a resolution which demanded that Iran abide by the norms of the Safeguards Agreement and of the Additional Protocol (AP). The resolution further demanded that Tehran should suspend its activities related to uranium enrichment and sign, ratify and fully implement the AP.[32]

In the Paris Agreement of November 2004, Iran "affirmed it would not seek nuclear weapons." Tehran "committed to full cooperation and transparency in its dealings with the IAEA" while agreeing to "prolong its suspension of all enrichment-related and reprocessing activities."[33] In 2005, the E-3 undertook an initiative to prevent Tehran from pursuing its nuclear programme. Iran, however, continued to maintain that the nuclear programme was meant for peaceful purposes and "vowed never to give up the fuel cycle."[34] Further, the E3 also criticised Tehran's nuclear programme when it expressed its desire to develop uranium hexafluoride, a component used for uranium enrichment at its UCF.

On the domestic front, in 2006, for Mahmoud Ahmedinejad, while the centrifuge programme became a platform for winning domestic political support, it became a sticking point in relations with the E3, and fearing that Iran could develop nuclear weapons, the European nations sought to provide an incentive package to the country to halt its nuclear programme. The package included the following components:[35]

- Iran has the undeniable right to utilise nuclear energy for peaceful purposes. Assistance would be provided for the Iranian nuclear programme, including the construction of a Light Water Reactor (LWR).
- Iran will suspend indefinitely its activities relating to uranium enrichment, and this suspension will be supervised by the IAEA. The suspension of uranium enrichment is a precondition to any agreement.
- In future, Iran will be permitted to enrich uranium, but only after the IAEA establishes with absolute certainty that the nuclear programme is meant for peaceful purposes

only; all the reported problematic issues are resolved; and Iran has no undeclared nuclear activity or materials. Permitting Iran to enrich uranium will also require the authorisation of the United Nations Security Council (UNSC), and Iran will need to prove that all its nuclear activities are economically justifiable and related to peaceful purposes.

- The Americans believed that the process of verification would take many years and they would be able to prevent Security Council authorisation for uranium enrichment by exercising their veto power.
- Iran will be supplied with nuclear fuel in one of two ways: either it will help operate the enrichment facility in Russia, which will enrich uranium that had been converted in Iran; or, it will receive nuclear fuel under the supervision of the IAEA.
- Iran will receive economic and technological incentives. For example, it will be accepted into the World Trade Organisation (WTO); the European Union (EU) will assist it in the development of its nuclear energy sector; it will be able to purchase American-made spare parts for civilian aircraft; and restrictions on the Iranian use of American technology in agriculture will be lifted.
- In the event that these proposals are rejected, economic and political sanctions will be imposed on Iran, based on a schedule of sanctions assembled by them for that purpose.
- The threat of sanctions was apparently presented to the Iranians separately. In December 2006, on Iran's refusal to suspend its nuclear programme, the UNSC passed Resolution 1737 which imposed sanctions on it. This resolution was passed with the aim to coerce Iran to return to the nuclear negotiating table. At the same time, the UNSC demanded that Tehran should clarify its nuclear desires.[36] However, dismissing the resolution as illegal, Tehran continued with its uranium enrichment programme. In 2007, further sanctions were imposed by the UNSC on Iran under Resolution 1747 which prohibited Tehran from exporting Iranian weapons and freezing the assets of individuals involved in nuclear activities. Yet, Tehran continued with the enrichment activities and also took great pride in its nuclear programme. Finally, this nuclear affair no longer remained confined to just the E3 countries and Iran but involved the other P5 members, Russia, China and the US. In 2008, the IAEA was not premitted by Iran to verify Tehran's past and present nuclear activities, given that the IAEA visits to the nuclear plant sites were not inspections.[37] In 2010, UNSC Resolution 1929 called for cooperation on Iran's part with the IAEA investigation. The resolution further demanded that Tehran suspend its uranium enrichment activities and even suspend the heavy water reactor project.

Iran's Tryst with the NPT and the Additional Protocol

Iran is a party to the NPT, signed in the year 1968 and ratified in 1970, which prohibited Tehran from developing nuclear weapons. However, Article IV of the NPT "guarantees states-parties access to nuclear technology as long as they adhere to their treaty obligations" and, thus, Iran maintained that it had the right to enrich uranium,[38] as the NPT allows "any nuclear process not directly related to weaponisation."[39] Hence, states can develop "weapon components, fissile material, missiles for delivery," to name a few.[40]

In 2003, Iran signed the Additional Protocol (AP), but only came close to ratifying the same. It held back its decision owing to the interference of the UNSC in its nuclear energy programme and, therefore, was in defiance of UNSC Resolution 1929. Had Iran ratified the AP, the E3 members were expected to recognise Iran's rights to nuclear technology and thereby, find solutions to resolve differences over the nuclear issues.

Nuclear Weapons Ambition of Iran: Weapons or Energy?

Iran's incentives to develop nuclear weapons are many. Firstly, the American threat to Iranian territory has been perceived to increase. Secondly, there exists a threat from Israel's virtual nuclear weapon status. Iran's South Asian neighbour, Pakistan, is a nuclear weapon state and its fissile material stockpile is increasing at a rapid pace. Reports have also suggested that Saudi Arabia is believed to be under the nuclear umbrella of the US. Turkey too is under the extended nuclear deterrence of the US and hosts US tactical nuclear weapons.

According to Ephraim Kam, a security analyst, Iran views WMD, nuclear weapons in particular, "as a suitable response" to address these threats. Furthermore, Iran could view nuclear weapons as a requirement for building its position as a regional power and advancing its hegemony over West Asia. Kam further states that "Iran believes that the acquisition of nuclear weapons will free it of its dependence on others in the realm of security, decrease its vulnerability to threats and pressures, force regional and international actors into taking Iran's interests into greater consideration, and assist Iran in achieving these interests."[41]

Despite the threat perceptions, it feels subjected to from its immediate neighbours, Iran claims that it has no desire to develop nuclear weapons and that the nuclear programme is for peaceful purposes. In 2008, despite UNSC Resolution 1803, Ayatollah Khamenei had declared, "No threat can hinder the Iranian nation from its path. We will forcefully continue on our path and not allow the oppressors to step on our rights."[42] Iran has also been accused of working on a laser enrichment programme to avoid detection, however, the source of the technology and the location where such work is being conducted have not been specified.[43] It is reported that Iran is working on atomic vapour laser isotope separation[44] and in the future, this technology could be used to make nuclear weapons (though the process would be complicated). In 2013, the IAEA reported that Tehran has enough information to design and produce nuclear warheads based on an implosion[45] nuclear device.[46] The same year, Iran also attracted criticism for the development of Exploding Bridge Wire (EBWs) detonators. There were concerns that Tehran could use EBWs detonators to develop nuclear weapons.[47] The IAEA evaluates that high-tension firing systems and multiple EBW detonators fired simultaneously are key components of nuclear weapons. In addition the IAEA stated that the EBWs have limited non-nuclear applications.[48] Tehran, on the other hand, claimed the allegations to be "groundless" and insisted that the EBWs were developed as "safe and reliable alternatives to spark gap detonators" meant for conventional purposes.[49] Iran has even provided access to information regarding its nuclear programme and has also allowed IAEA inspectors to visit the Saghand uranium mine and the yellowcake production plant at Ardakan.[50] In 2013, Iranian President Rouhani had reiterated that Tehran has never been after WMD since it did not view such weapons as "legitimate" and affirmed that the country's nuclear programme was transparent.[51]

But, in 2014, Iran agreed to alter the design of IR-40 Heavy Water Reactor (HWR) near the Iranian city of Arak so that it could "limit Iran's ability to forge a second path to a bomb, using plutonium."[52] Iran has been accused of developing nuclear power plants in Natanz. It is reported that Iran possesses a commercial fuel enrichment plant, which is Iran's "largest gas centrifuge uranium enrichment facility"[53] housing more than 16,000 centrifuge units. Tehran also hosts a pilot fuel enrichment plant housing 692 centrifuge units. However, Iran maintains that the Natanz nuclear plant will accelerate its civil nuclear programme and that the nuclear power plant does not have a "possible military dimension". Iran argues that in order to become self-sufficient in nuclear energy, the nuclear facilities in Natanz are crucial. Becoming self-sufficient in nuclear energy would reduce Tehran's dependency of foreign suppliers, namely Russia. In addition under a multilateral agreement in 2009 between France, the US and Russia, on one side, and Iran on the other, Iran was to export 1,200 kg of its 3.5 percent low enriched uranium to Russia for refinement. In return, Russia would enrich the exported uranium to 20 percent purity while France would convert the enriched uranium into fuel rods, thereby, reducing the chances of the enriched uranium being converted into weapons grade uranium.[54]

At present, the research reactors that Iran possesses are too small to produce considerable quantities of plutonium for nuclear weapons. Though it is believed that the IR-40 HWR could be suited for plutonium production, the completion of the reactor is not scheduled in the foreseeable future. Moreover, Iranian Atomic Chief Ali Akbar Salehi confirms that the plutonium that would be produced from IR-40s would not be suitable for producing bombs. Despite this, the reactor has invited suspicion from the P5+1 countries since there is little justification to develop a reactor which is a "40 MWt natural-uranium fueled, heavy water cooled, and heavy water moderated reactor capable of producing roughly 11 kg weapons grade plutonium, enough for at least one bomb per year"[55] solely for peaceful purposes. Such reactors are capable of producing nuclear weapons at a faster pace. Iran, however, has agreed to redesign the IR-40 reactor in such a manner that only 1kg of plutonium will be produced from the reactor as opposed to 9 kg planned earlier.

In February 2014, Tehran claimed that it had developed centrifuge technology which was fifteen times more powerful than the current centrifuges being used to enrich uranium.[56]

Salehi has confirmed that this development was not a violation of the nuclear deal and that such developments are permitted in the deal. But Iran's critics have justified their concerns that the nuclear deal does not allow Tehran to install new centrifuges, only to replace damaged machines.

Centrifuge technology has earned Iran a lot of criticism and it has also been a "sticking point" in the nuclear deal talks.[57] Tehran claims that its nuclear technology is meant solely for peaceful purposes, most importantly for generating electricity.[58] Compared to nuclear reactors and gaseous diffusion plants, centrifuge plants use less electricity and produce less detectable signals and so "evade safeguards altogether."[59] What is of concern to the IAEA is the fact that centrifuges make easy the rapid conversion of reactor grade fuel to bomb grade. By the time, an IAEA inspector is able to arrive at the location for verification of the fuel, whether it is reactor grade or bomb grade, it may be difficult for him to verify whether the centrifuge has been used to develop a bomb or not.

The P5+1 countries are of the view that Tehran could use the Fordow enrichment plant for developing nuclear weapons, as Iran has failed to disclose the facility.[60] This, along with the IAEA reports in 2013, which mentioned that Tehran has enough information to design and produce nuclear warheads based on an implosion nuclear device,[61] is alarming for the P5+1 countries. Following the JCPOA in 2015, Israeli Prime Minister Benjamin Netanyahu commented that the nuclear deal in a few years "would remove restrictions" on the nuclear programme while "enabling Iran to have a massive enrichment capacity that it could use to produce many nuclear bombs within a matter of months."[62] However, Iran has clarified that it would take at least eighteen months for it to develop nuclear weapons. The timeframe could even be three years if the process of converting the material into uranium metal and moulding to make bombs is included.[63] Iranian Foreign Minister Mohammad Zarif further revealed that the weaponisation process is not simple for Iran due to lack of capabilities and these capabilities, according to Zarif, would need to be developed from scratch.[64]

However, in June 2014, an analysis by the *Wall Street Journal* predicted that in the near future, Tehran could "outsource" the completion of the bombs to North Korea due to their close ties and mutual hatred for the US.[65] This possibility cannot be eschewed completely given that North Korea has its nuclear weapons programme and close military cooperation with Iran—North Korea has assisted in Iran's missile programme.

But the March 2015 negotiations at Lausanne under the JCPOA have had some positive outcomes. Iran has agreed to allow the IAEA inspectors to travel throughout the country for investigating any suspicious sites or in case of any allegations of covert enrichment. The JCPOA also requires Iran to reduce its installed centrifuges, not enrich uranium over 3.67 percent for 15 years and reduce the current stockpile of Low Enriched Uranium (LEU) for 15 years;[66] the advanced and excess centrifuges would be under IAEA monitoring and would be in operation only as a replacement to an existing centrifuge and no centrifuge facilities would be built for 15 years; Iran also agreed not to continue any enrichment activity at the Fordow facility for 15 years and to convert the facility for peaceful purposes only. Iran is also prohibited from maintaining any fissile material at the Fordow facility and two-thirds of the centrifuges would be removed while the remaining centrifuges would not be used for enrichment purposes; and the centrifuges and related infrastructure would be under IAEA safeguards.

Iran's Nuclear Delivery Systems

The Iranian nuclear programme issue got further aggravated as Tehran made an effort to continue developing nuclear capable ballistic missiles, defying all the sanctions. The Iran-Iraq War was one of the important factors behind Tehran concentrating on the development of ballistic missiles. Iran's limitation in air power and the success of the Scud category of missiles as terror weapons during the war, have led to the development of ballistic missiles. The credit for Iran's liquid-fuelled missile systems goes to North Korea, while for its solid-fuelled missile systems, the credit goes to China. Beijing has even provided Tehran with gyroscopes and accelerometers for advanced radar systems, missile guidance systems and computerised tools.[67]

Iran's ballistic missile programme is indeed progressing at an impressive (and alarming) pace. According to the Congressional Research Services (CRS) Reports of December 2012, Iran has the "largest inventory of ballistic missiles in the Middle

East" and that "it is expanding the scale, reach and sophistication of its ballistic missile forces, many of which are inherently capable of carrying a nuclear payload."[68] In less than a generation, Tehran has managed to transform itself from a "non-player" to a "significant missile power."[69] At present, Iran's ballistic missile arsenal includes Short Range Ballistic Missiles (SRBMs) with a range up to 1,000 km, Medium Range Ballistic Missiles (MRBMs) with a range from 1,000-3,000 km, and Intermediate Range Ballistic Missiles (IRBMs) that range from 3,000-5,500 km.

Iran's SRBMs include the liquid-fuel propelled Shahab-1 with a range of 300 km, the solid-fuel propelled Fateh-110 with a range 200 km, and the 750 km range Fajr. Tehran also possesses the Chinese solid fuelled M-11s, called the Tondars. The Nazeat missiles have a range of 100-130 km, and the Zelzalfamily of missile systems include the Zelzal-1 with a range of 150 km, Zelzal-2 with a range of 100-210 km, while the Zelzal-3 has a range of 200 km.[70]

The Zelzal and Nazeat families of missile systems are not as advanced as the Fateh missile system. Iran's Shahab-1 missile is reported to be capable of carrying nuclear warheads similar to the Soviet Scud-B[71] and is carried by a Transporter Erector Launcher (TEL)[72] for road mobility, ensuring the survivability of the missile system. The liquid fuelled Shahab-2 missile, on the other hand, has a greater range (500 km) and probably greater accuracy than the Shahab-1. Tehran's solid-fuelled, road mobile Tondar-68 ballistic missile is the Chinese version of the M-11, with a range of 400 km. Iran has also developed the Ghadr-101 missile, called the Samen, with a range of 750-800 km,[73] derived from the Chinese M-9 missiles.[74]

Among MRBMs, Iran possesses the Ghadr with a range of 1,800-2,000 km, Ashura with a range of 2,000 km, and Shahab-3 with range of 1,200-1,900 km. Iran's Sejjil-1 and Sejjil-2 or Ghadr-110 missiles with "extremely high capabilities,"[75] comprise a solid-fuelled, land mobile missile system.[76] The Shahab-4 has a range of 1,350-1,500 km, and is derived from the North Korean No Dong missile system. Among IRBMs, Iran possesses the 2,500-4,000 km range Musudan ballistic missiles which are reported to be capable of carrying nuclear warheads. The Shahab-5, also called Kosar, ranges from 3,500-3,750 km to 4,000-4,300 km.[77] Reports suggest that Iran is even developing Intercontinental Ballistic Missiles (ICBMs) which include the Shahab-6 missiles with a range of 5,470-5,500 km to 5,632-6,200 km. This increased range would depend on the number of stages used in the launch vehicle and their performance.[78]

Tehran's advancements in ballistic missiles have raised concerns and many analysts feel that the issue of ballistic missiles should be dealt with in the nuclear deal itself. Iran, however, maintains that ballistic missiles are "part of conventional armed forces." Thus, for Iran "to seek Iran specific limits on conventional weapons", which it regards as crucial to its self-defence would jeopardise the key objectives of the negotiations.[79] Ballistic missiles are also an integral component of Iran's deterrent capability and a symbol of its technological prowess. This capability further provides a boost to Iran's military strength and its national pride. The IRGC has an unprecedented influence and control over Iran's strategic forces. Thus, it would never be acceptable to the IRGC to give up these strategic weapon systems which give it a sense of pride and prowess.

Moreover, Tehran is also developing long range cruise missiles. In March 2015, reports confirmed that Iran had developed the long range Soumar cruise missiles with a range 2,500 km which could be capable of carrying nuclear warheads and can target the Middle Eastern as well as southern European countries. It is unclear if the missiles belong to the Meshkat family or whether Iran has a separate Meshkat family of cruise missiles.

Iran's threat perceptions would prevent Tehran from including the issue of ballistic missiles in the nuclear deal. Israel, its staunch adversary, is not a party to the NPT and is said to be developing ballistic missiles capable of delivering nuclear warheads. Saudi Arabia, another adversary of Iran, has acquired long range ballistic missiles from China, while Turkey too has been reported to be developing MRBMs and IRBMs.

Tehran is subjected to missile threats also from its South Asian Sunni neighbour, Pakistan. The European countries like Britain and France possess submarine launched ballistic missiles which can reach Tehran. Tehran also faces missile threats from the US. Britain, which has fought its Falkland War against Argentina, would watch the Iranian military cooperation with the South American countries carefully. Any Iranian military cooperation with the South American countries could tilt the balance of power in the South Atlantic region which may not be acceptable to Britain. In 2011, reports had come in that Tehran was developing missile bases for its Shahab missiles in Venezuela. Though, the reports were denied later by both the US and Iran, Iran's growing relations with the South American countries could make these missile bases a reality in South America, a move unacceptable to both Britain and the US.

The UN sanctions impose a prohibition on the development of ballistic missiles, including on launchers using ballistic missile technology. The JPOA, however, imposes no such prohibition. There is no legal international treaty yet, which binds Iran to limit its ballistic missile capabilities, unlike the NPT which binds Iran to confine its nuclear programme to civil use only.

The Great Power Game

Geo-political issues always have spiralling effects and one issue could give rise to another. The Iranian nuclear deal will have cascading effects in not just the Middle East but also in Europe. The US' softening of its stance on Iran's nuclear programme has not been accepted in good spirit by Israel which wanted a complete halt on it.

There has been an appeal to include Iran's ballistic missile programme in the nuclear deal. Claude Chafin, the communications director at the House Armed Services Committee of the US had stated in 2014 that unless there was a comprehensive deal to "limit" the Iranian ballistic missile programme, and "eliminate" its ability to enrich uranium, Tehran could be a threat to the US.[80] Netanyahu has not viewed Iran's ballistic missiles in a positive light, and feels that such a development highlights Tehran's "insincerity" regarding the nuclear negotiations. In the meanwhile, the UN panel of experts has expressed concerns over Iran showing no signs of halting its missile development programme. However, Wendy Sherman, the undersecretary of state of the US Senate Foreign Relations Committee, maintaining a different stand, has said that if the nuclear deal is struck with Iran, then the ballistic missiles would become "almost", though "not entirely", "irrelevant."[81]

In addition, Moscow also has raised concerns over the European Phased Adaptive Approach (EPAA). The EPAA is an effort by the US to field its missile defence systems in the European countries as a counter against Iran's nuclear capable missile threats. By March 2014, the US had decided that the Missile Defence Agency (MDA) would invest $ 100 million to "initiate the redesign" of the ground-based interceptor kill vehicle.[82] US Secretary of Defence Chuck Hagel had stated that the Iranian nuclear deal "does not eliminate the need for US and European allies to continue implementing missile defence plans in Europe." However, he affirmed that the missile defence would "pose no threat to Russia."[83]

However, Russian Foreign Minister Sergey Lavrov feels that the missile defence in Europe is not required if the nuclear deal is "put into practice".[84] President Vladimir Putin has also been critical of the US missile defence system in Europe, calling it "defensive in name" while in actuality, it is an "essential element of a strategic offensive potential." He has further raised concerns over the system being a trigger for the US to initiate a "disarming nuclear strike" and, therefore, it could upset "the strategic balance of power."[85]

The US' shipboard SM-3 missile interceptors in the eastern Mediterranean Sea under Phase 1 of the EPAA presently provide the North Atlantic Treaty Organisation (NATO) and the US the capability to defend against the present Iranian missile threats. By 2015, it is expected that the US will field the SM-3 interceptors in Poland and by 2018, in Romania that could intercept longer range ballistic missiles. In response, Russia has threatened to deploy its ballistic missiles capable of delivering nuclear weapons **in the**

Kalingrad region, pointing towards Central Europe. Moscow has also warned that the US missile defence in Poland is within the reach of these missiles.[86]

In West Asia, there has been some alteration in equations between certain states following the nuclear deal. The power houses of West Asia, namely Israel and Saudi Arabia, **which** have been at loggerheads with each other since the inception of Israel as a state, are now strengthening their ties with each other. For long, Israel has viewed its Arabian counterpart in West Asia with suspicion owing to the Zionist-Arabian ideological differences. In fact, it is interesting to note that until the Iranian Revolution in the 1970s, Israel shared good relations with Iran as a step to counter the Arabian influence in West Asia. In the present context, the Iranian nuclear impasse has increased the amiability towards each other of long standing rivals, Israel and Saudi Arabia, to lessen any scope of a Shia dominated Iranian influence in the region. However, this is not for the first the time that Israel and Saudi Arabia are putting aside their differences and joining hands. In the 1960s, during the Yemen Civil War, both Riyadh and Tel Aviv organised joint airlifts against the Egyptian forces.[87] Both Saudi Arabia and Israel have not been satisfied with the US policy towards the Iranian nuclear ambitions. The two countries feel that the US needed to be stricter with Iran and stop the nuclear programme completely. This has led them to build closer ties with each other, despite the unresolved Arab-Israeli conflict.

Russia, on the other hand, has been supportive of the nuclear deal, but not supportive of a pro-Western Iran. In order to prevent any such developments, in April 2015, soon after the Lausanne negotiations, Russia decided to send Iran the S-300 air defence systems.[88] This is expected to provide an impetus to Iran's military capability. This deal was signed by Russia in 2007, but was cancelled later in 2010 owing to pressures from the US and Israel. Moreover, the fact that Iran is allowed to carry on with its peaceful nuclear programme would mean opening of doors for Russia's state run Rusatom nuclear company which is already expanding its business in the Middle East. Russia has been enthusiastic about Iran joining the Shanghai Cooperation Organisation (SCO) and according to Lavrov, Iran's accession to the SCO would mean good prospects for the organisation.

For China too, there is scope for nuclear and defence cooperation with Iran. China and Iran have been signing deals on oil projects, and until 2012, Iran was China's third largest exporter of oil. China has made sure that Tehran is officially accepted as a founding member for China's Asian Infrastructure Investment Bank (AIIB) which would enhance Iran's interaction with the international community. Beijing has expressed its keenness to include Iran in the Shanghai Cooperation Organisation (SCO).

Surprisingly, following the Iranian nuclear impasse, even Islamabad has played safe in its diplomatic ties with the powers in the West Asian region. During the 2015 Yemen crisis, when Saudi Arabia expected Islamabad, the Saudis' loyal ally, to support Riyadh with military forces to attack the Shia Houthi rebel forces in Yemen, Pakistan chose to stay neutral and did not provide military forces to Saudi Arabia. This decision was taken by Islamabad soon after Iranian Foreign Minister Mohammad JavadZarif visited Pakistan during the debate in Pakistan on whether to send troops to Yemen. Islamabad's refusal to send troops to Yemen has disappointed Riyadh but, despite that, Pakistan chose to try and be a mediator rather than actively join Saudi Arabia militarily to attack the Shia rebels.

Does the Iranian Nuclear Deal Benefit India?

India has been in support of the Iranian nuclear deal which was evident from the statement of the a Ministry of External Affairs spokesman, Syed Akbaruddin in 2013, wherein he said India hoped that the nuclear issue would be solved through "dialogue and diplomacy."[89] New Delhi is hoping for the nuclear deal to take a positive shape since it would relieve Tehran of the harsh sanctions and thereby, improve trade relations between the two states. New Delhi had already experienced the brunt of Iranian sanctions when, in Financial Year (FY) 2012-13, Iranian supplies comprised 7.2 percent of India's oil imports, which was a reduction from 10.5 percent from 2011-12.[90] Also, the lifting of sanctions would be a great impetus to the Chabahar port in Iran in which India is investing, and which will provide India easy access to Afghanistan. Moreover, New Delhi and Tehran could even cooperate in enhancing stability in Afghanistan,[91] and cooperation with Iran could provide India greater scope for influence in the Central Asian region.

Also, if Tehran developed nuclear weapons, Pakistan would beef up its nuclear arsenal. This is because Islamabad would need to counter two nuclear powers in its neighbourhood, India and Iran. Increase in Pakistan's nuclear arsenal would affect not just stability in South Asia, but also become a global concern. An Iranian nuclear weapons capability could also have a spillover effect in West Asia which could result in Israel accepting its 'Nuclear Weapons State' (NWS) status. Pakistan has always been apprehensive of Israel, especially after the 1980s and 1990s when there were reports that Tel Aviv was planning to bomb Pakistan's nuclear facility at Kahuta. This too could result in an arms race in South Asia, with Islamabad trying to keep pace with not only India, but with Iran and Israel as well. Moreover, Iran's nuclear weapons capability could increase Pakistan's nuclear arsenal since Islamabad may need to cater to Saudi Arabia's nuclear ambitions. This is because Pakistan is reported to have received funding from Saudi Arabia for its nuclear programme, so that in case the need arises in Riyadh for nuclear weapons, it could avail of these from Islamabad.

Conclusion

The nuclear deal is no doubt a face saver for the US, especially as it realises that cracking down on the nuclear programme is next to impossible. Iran too has cooperated in the nuclear deal to the best of its abilities. However, as regards the nitty-gritty of the nuclear deal, it may be expected that Iran would only agree to a deal which caters for its nuclear ambitions for peaceful purposes. As regards the Arak reactor, while efforts could be made in feeding the reactor with LEU instead of natural uranium, Iran is not likely to accept this solution. Tehran would redesign the reactor to suit its own needs and in a way that would be technically feasible for it. Nevertheless, the deal has been a pleasing one to some states like the US, Russia and China while states like Israel, Saudi Arabia have expressed their concerns regarding it.

The JPOA and the JCPOA do not deal with the issue of ballistic missiles and the need to include the issue of missiles in the JPOA and JCPOA is minimal since the UNSC Resolutions already lay down stringent measures on the Iranian missile development programme. Therefore, the nuclear deal should be separate and any effort to include the ballistic missiles development programme in it could jeopardise the progress of the deal and lead Tehran to withdraw from it. Further, as the nuclear deal progresses, Russia's concerns pertaining to the US missile defence system in Europe would need to be addressed by the US.

Also, while states like Israel have continued to oppose any enrichment activity of uranium in Iran, the US has maintained a different stance on the Iranian nuclear programme. Washington is working out the level of enrichment that could continue in Iran and trying to prevent Iran from acquiring nuclear weapons. However, it remains to be seen whether Obama will be able to successfully strike the nuclear deal or not.

"Facts and analysis presented in this article are based on the progress on the deal until April 2015. The nuclear deal that came through in July 2015 will allow Iran to pursue nuclear program for peaceful purposes in return for lifting of sanctions."

Notes

1. Julian Borger and SaeedKamaliDehgan, "Iran Seals Nuclear Deal with West in Return for Sanctions Relief," *The Guardian,* November 24, 2014, <http://www.theguardian.com/world/2013/nov/24/iran-nuclear-deal-west-sanctions-relief>
2. "IAEA, Iran Sign Joint Statement on Framework for Cooperation," *IAEA,* November 11,2013, <https://www.iaea.org/newscenter/pressreleases/iaea-iran-sign-joint-statement-framework- cooperation>
3. Media Note, "Summary of Understandings Related to the Implementation and Extension of the Joint Plan of Action," *U.S. Department of State*, July 22, 2014, <http://www.state.gov/r/pa/prs/ps/2014/07/229658.htm>
4. Kelsey Davenport, "Iran, P5+1 Sign Nuclear Agreement," *Arms Control Association,* December

2013, <https://www.armscontrol.org/act/2013_12/Iran-P5-1-Sign-Nuclear-Agreement>

5. Ibid.
6. An SWU "is a complex unit which is a function of the amount of uranium processed and the degree to which it is enriched, i.e., the extent of increase in the concentration of the U-235 isotope relative to the remainder."
7. "Iran Nuclear Crisis: Can Talk Succeed," *BBC News*, November 25, 2015, <http://www.bbc.com/news/world-middle-east-11709428>
8. Chris Mitchell, "Obama: Military Strike on Iran Won't Stop Nuke Program", *CBN News*, June 2, 2015, <http://www.cbn.com/cbnnews/insideisrael/2015/june/obama-military-strike-on-iran-wont-work/>
9. Elise Labott, Mariano Castillo and Catherine E. Shoichet, "Optimism as Iran nuclear deal framework announced, more work ahead," *CNN*, April 3, 2015, <http://edition.cnn.com/2015/04/02/world/iran-nuclear-talks/>
10. Taylor Luck, "Iran Nuclear Deal: Saudi Arabia Fears Rival's Regional Footprint," *The Christian Science Monitor*, April 6, 2015, at http://www.csmonitor.com/World/Middle-East/2015/0406/ Iran-nuclear-deal-Saudi-Arabia-fears-rival-s-regional-footprint
11. "Why Saudi Arabia and Israel Oppose Iran Nuclear Deal," *Al Jazeera*, April 14, 2015, http://www. aljazeera.com/news/2015/04/saudi-arabia-israel-oppose-iran-nuclear-deal-150401061906177.html
12. Reported to be a CIA-assisted coup.
13. David Patrikarakos, "The Peacock Wants To Strut: Nuclear Power Under The Shah," in *Nuclear Iran: The Birth of An Atomic State* (London: IB Tauris and Co Ltd: 2012).
14. David Albright and Andrea Stricker, "Iran's Nuclear Program," *The Iran Primer,* <http:// iranprimer.usip.org/resource/irans-nuclear-program>
15. "Iran," *NTI,* Updated November 2013, <http://www.nti.org/country-profiles/iran/nuclear/>
16. "Chronology of Iran's Nuclear Program," Oxford Research Group 1957-2007, <http:// www.oxfordresearchgroup.org.uk/oxford_research_group_chronology_irans_nuclear_ programme_1957_2007>
17. Ibid.
18. NamiraNegm, "Case II: Iran," in *Transfer of Nuclear Technology under International Law* (Boston: MartinusNijhoff Publishers, 2009).
19. SeyedHosseinMousavian, "Iran's Nuclear Program," in *The Iranian Nuclear Crisis: A Memoir* (New Delhi: Knowledge World, 2013). p. 46.
20. "A History of Iran's Nuclear Program," *Iran Watch,* March 1, 2012, <http://www.iranwatch.org/our-publications/weapon-program-background-report/history-irans-nuclear-program>
21. Thus, two nuclear power plants were cancelled in Isfahan and two more at Saveh.
22. Kerry M. Kartchner, "Strategic Culture and WMD Decision Making," in *Strategic Culture and Weapons of Mass Destruction: Culturally Based Insights into Comparative National Security Policymaking* (US: Palgrave Macmillan, 2009), p.60.
23. Ibid.
24. The NPT Safeguard Agreements do not cover uranium ore and, hence, neither Iran nor China needed to have informed about the transfer of uranium ore.
25. David Patrikarakos, "Prologue to the Nuclear Clash-1989-97," in Patrikarakos, n.9, p.157.
26. David Albright and Corey Hinderstein, "The A.Q. Khan Illicit Nuclear Trade Network and Implications for Non-Proliferation Efforts," in James A. Russell and James J. Wirtz, eds.,*Globalization and WMD Proliferation: Terrorism, Transnational Network and International Security* (US: Routledge, 2008).
27. Ibid., pp.158.
28. Robert J.Reardon, "Iran's Nuclear Program: Past, Present, and Future," in *Containing*

Iran (Santa Monica: RAND Corporation, 2012).

29. Iran, *NTI,* Updated July 2014, <http://www.nti.org/country-profiles/iran/nuclear/>
30. Ibid.
31. Houston G.Wood, Alexander Glaser and R.Scott Kemp, "The Gas Centrifuge and Nuclear Weapons Proliferation," *Physics Today,* September 2008, <https://www.princeton.edu/~rskemp/ Kemp%20-%20Gas%20Centrifuge%20and%20Nonproliferation%20-%20SPLG.pdf>
32. David Patrikarakos, "From Tehran to Paris and Beyond," in Patrikarakos, n.9, p.209.
33. Reardon, n. 24.
34. Ephraim Kam, "Can Iran Be Stopped?," in *A Nuclear Iran: What Does it Mean, and What Can Be Done* (Israel: Institute for National Security Studies, 2007), p.24.
35. "Chronology of Iran's Nuclear Programme, 1957-2007," Oxford Research Group, <http:// www.oxfordresearchgroup.org.uk/publications>
36. Raja Menon, *Weapons of Mass Destruction: Options for India,* (United Kingdom, Sage Publications, 2004), Pg.169.
37. David Albright and Serena Kelleher-Vergantini, "LashkarAb'ad: Iran's Unexplained Laser Enrichment Capabilities," *Institute for Science and International Security Imagery Brief,* July 29, 2013, <http://isis-online.org/uploads/isis-reports/documents/Lashkar_Abad_29July2013. pdf>
38. Kelsey Davenport, "Iran, P5+1 Sign Nuclear Agreement," *Arms Control Association,* December 2013, <https://www.armscontrol.org/act/2013_12/Iran-P5-1-Sign-Nuclear-Agreement>
39. David Patrikarakos, "Arms and the Shah: Nuclear Weapons Under the Shah," in Patrikarakos, n.9, p.69.
40. n.12.
41. Ibid., p.26
42. Ibid.
43. Ibid.
44. Laser enrichment is of three main types: atomic vapour laser isotope separation, molecular laser isotope separation and separation of isotopes by laser excitation. In laser isotope separation, uranium isotopes are separated more efficiently than in gas centrifuges. Each isotope of an element has unique set of electronic energy state. Electrons of atoms of each isotope absorb light of a specific colour and if illuminated by a laser beam containing light of this precise colour, the electrons of the atoms of the selected isotope will absorb photons and become excited. The atom may give up the excited electrons and become positively charged ions. The atoms of other isotopes would not absorb photons since they do not have the "right" energy and, hence, will not be ionised. The ionised atoms can be separated from the neutral ones by an electromagnetic field. (Source: Frank Barnaby, "Iran's Nuclear Activities," *Oxford Research Group,* March 2006, <http://www.oxfordresearchgroup.org.uk/ sites/default/files/IranNuclearMar06.pdf>)
45. This would include weapons-grade uranium (or plutonium) and a neutron initiator surrounded by conventional high explosives designed to compress the core and set off a self-sustaining nuclear chain reaction.
46. As given by Colin Kahl, "What Would it Take to Build Bomb," in Garrett Nada, ed., *The Iran Primer,* April 5, 2013, <http://iranprimer.usip.org/blog/2013/apr/05/part-ii-what-would-it-take-build-bomb>
47. "Iran Nuclear Negotiators to Start Work on Final Accord," *BBC News,* May 13, 2014, <http://www.bbc.com/news/world-middle-east-27371534>
48. David Albright, "Background Information on the Explosive Bridge Wire Issue: A Crack in the Door," *ISIS*, February 12, 2014, *at* http://isis-online.org/uploads/isis-reports/documents/

EBW_issue_12Feb2014_final_1.pdf

49. Ibid.
50. n.48.
51. **n.42.**
52. David E. Sanger, "Building Nuclear Weapon Would Take Years, Not Months, Iran Says in Report," *The New York*, **June 12, 2014, <http://www.nytimes.com/2014/06/13/world/** middleeast/ iran-building-nuclear-weapon-would-take-years-not-months-us-disputes-estimate. html>
53. Natanz, *IISS*, <http://www.isisnucleariran.org/sites/detail/natanz/>
54. Ariel Farrar-Welleman, "Germany-Iran Foreign Relations," *Iran Tracker*, July 27, 2010, <http:// www.irantracker.org/foreign-relations/germany-iran-foreign-relations>
55. **Reardon, n. 24.**
56. "Iran Says New Centrifuge Developed to Enrich Uranium," *Phys.Org*, February 10, 2014, <http://phys.org/news/2014-02-iran-centrifuge-enrich-uranium.html>
57. Ibid.
58. Fredrik Dahl, "U.S., Iran Experts Dispute Nuclear Bomb 'Breakout' Timeline," *Reuters*, June 18, 2014, <http://www.reuters.com/article/2014/06/18/us-iran-nuclear-breakout-idUSKBN0ET1JV20140618>
59. Houston G. Wood, Alexander Glaser and R.Scott Kemp, "The Gas Centrifuge and Nuclear Weapons Proliferation," *Physics Today*, September 2008, <https://www.princeton.edu/~rskemp/ Kemp%20-%20Gas%20Centrifuge%20and%20Nonproliferation%20-%20SPLG.pdf>
60. **Ibid.**
61. Kahl, n. 41.
62. "Benjamin Netanyahu: Iran Must Recognize Israel," *The Telegraph*, **April 3, 2015,** *at* http:// www.telegraph.co.uk/news/worldnews/middleeast/israel/11514936/Benjamin-**Netanyahu- Iran-must-recognise-Israel.html**
63. Dahl, n.56.
64. **Ibid.**
65. Claudia Rosett, "Iran Could Outsource Its Nuclear-Weapons Program to North Korea," *The Wall Street Journal*, June 20, 2014, <http://online.wsj.com/articles/iran-could-outsource-its- nuclear-weapons-program-to-north-korea-1403303442>
66. Michelle Dover, "Jargon in the Nuclear Deal Discussions," *Iran Fact File*, **April 3, 2015,** <http://www.iranfactfile.org/category/analysis-backgrounds/background/>
67. "Iran Missile Milestones: 1985-2014,"*Iran Watch*, April 17, 2014,< http://www.iranwatch. org/ our-publications/weapon-program-background-report/iran-missile-milestones-1985-2014>
68. Steven A. Hildreth, "Iran's Ballistic Missile and Space Launch Programs," Congressional Research Service, December 6, 2012, <http://fas.org/sgp/crs/nuke/R42849.pdf>
69. Uzi Rubin, "Showcase of Missile Proliferation: Iran's Missile and Space Program," Arms Control Association, January/February, 2012, <https://www.armscontrol.org/act/2012_01-02/ Showcase_of_Missile_Proliferation_Irans_Missile_and_Space_Program>
70. Anthony H. Cordesman, "Iran's Rocket and Missile Forces and Strategic Option," Centre for Strategic and International Studies, October 7, 2014, <http://csis.org/files/ publication/141007_ Iran_Rocket_Missile_forces.pdf>
71. "Iran's Ballistic Missile Programme," Iran's Strategic Weapons Programme, IISS (New York: Routledge, 2005), p.96. However, the North Korean Scud-Bs were capable of delivering high explosive warheads.
72. "Scud B Shahab-1," Federation of American Scientists, <http://fas.org/nuke/guide/ iran/ missile/shahab-1.htm>

73. Charles P Vick, "Sejjil," *Global Security,* <http://www.globalsecurity.org/wmd/world/iran/ sajjil.htm>
74. Charles P Vick, "Samen," *Global Security*, <http://www.globalsecurity.org/wmd/world/iran/ samen.htm>
75. "India and Iran Both Test-Fire Nuclear Missiles," *Mail Online,* November 12, 2008, <http:// www.dailymail.co.uk/news/article-1084999/India-Iran-test-nuclear-missiles.html>
76. "Iran's Arsenal of Missiles," *BBC News,* May 20, 2009, <http://news.bbc.co.uk/2/hi/7499601. stm>
77. "Shahab-5/IRSL-X-3, Kosar/IRIS," Federation of American Scientists, <http://www.fas.org/nuke/guide/iran/missile/shahab-5.htm>
78. Charles P. Vick, "Shahab-6/ Simorgh-5,6?", *Global Security,* May 25, 2010, <http://www.globalsecurity.org/wmd/world/iran/shahab-6.htm>
79. Ibid.
80. Bill Gertz, "Iran-North Korean Missile Cooperation Undermines Recent Geneva Nuclear Deal," *The Washington Free Beacon,* November 27, 2013, <http://freebeacon.com/national- security/iran-north-korea-missile-cooperation-undermines-recent-geneva-nuclear-deal/>
81. Quoted by Patrick Goodenough, "U.S. Nuclear Negotiator: If Iran Can't Get the Bomb, Its Ballistic Missiles Will Be Almost Irrelevant," *CNS News,* February 5, 2014, <http://www.cnsnews.com/news/article/patrick-goodenough/us-nuclear-negotiator-if-iran-can-t-get-bomb- its-ballistic-missiles>
82. Eric Auner, "Missile Defense Budget Holds Steady," *Arms Control Association,* April 2014, <https://www.armscontrol.org/act/2014_04/Missile-Defense-Budget-Holds-Steady%20>
83. "US to Deploy ABM Systems in Europe Despite P5+1 Deal with Iran," *RT.com,* December 17, 2013, <http://rt.com/news/hagel-shoigu-missile-defense-356/>
84. Patrick Goodenough, "Russia Wants to Use Iran Nuclear Deal to Shut Down Missile Defense Shield,"*CNSNews.com*, December 6, 2013, <http://cnsnews.com/news/article/patrick- goodenough/russia-wants-use-iran-nuclear-deal-shut-down-missile-defense-shield
85. Ibid.
86. AsherOrakby,"RivalswithBenefits:IsraelandSaudiArabia'sSecretHistoryofCooperation," *Foreign Affairs*, March 13, 2015, at https://www.foreignaffairs.com/articles/middle- east/2015-03-13/rivals-benefits
87. Debalina Ghoshal, "P5+1 Nuclear Deal: A Concern or Solution for Putin," *Journal of Turkish Weekly*, August 11, 2014, <http://www.turkishweekly.net/2014/08/11/op-ed/p5-1-nuclear-deal-a-concern-or-solution-for-putin/>
88. "Russia-Iran Relations is a Marriage of Opportunity," *Washington Post*, April 8, 2015, at http://www.washingtonpost.com/world/russia-iran-relationship-is-a-marriage-of-opportunity/2015/04/18/5de80852-e390-11e4-ae0f-f8c46aa8c3a4_story.html
89. SandeepDikshit, "Iran Nuclear Deal Consistent with our Stand, says India" ,*The Hindu*, November 25, 2013, <http://www.thehindu.com/news/national/iran-nuclear-deal-consistent-with-our-stand-says-india/article5386560.ece>
90. AnchalVohra, "Iran Nuclear Deal: What it Means for India", *NDTV*, November 25, 2013, <http://www.ndtv.com/india-news/iran-nuclear-deal-what-it-means-for-india-542375>
91. Jayant Prasad, "Iran Deal Spells Good Tidings for India," *The Hindu*, April 10, 2015, at http://www.thehindu.com/opinion/lead/lead-article-iran-deal-spells-good-tidings-for-india/article7085906.ece

7

Internet Governance: Taming the Virtual Juggernaut

M K Sharma

The only sure bulwark of continuing liberty is a government strong enough to protect the interest of the people and a people strong enough and well enough informed to maintain sovereign control over the government.

— Franklin Roosevelt, former president of the US

Introduction

Invariably, cyber space is insecure, loosely governed, and yet critical to the world's economy. It is a battle ground for international strategic competition and potential conflict. One country's development of advanced cyber weapons might mean another country's heightened insecurity, thus, increasing the miscalculation and risk of misunderstanding of cyber espionage for military action, that may escalate an international tension into a conflict. While the international society reaps the benefits of this evolving technology, the danger of cyber misuse for the economies, national critical infrastructures, and national sovereignty raises many questions. What kind of internet governance norms would be acceptable to all nations? What constitutes responsible cyber space behaviour by nations? How does the international law of war apply to cyber space? Internet governance is on the top of the agenda of most bilateral and multilateral talks, resolutions, Memorandums of Understanding (MoUs) involving nations, Non-Governmental Organisations (NGOs), private agencies, the users, technical community, global and regional organisations. The interests of multiple stakeholders have given rise to a multitude of turf wars only to exacerbate the discussion environment.

'Internet governance' is a loosely defined term with no unanimous acceptance. It broadly means technical and political management of the global core resources that make up the internet such as the root server system, Internet Protocols (IP), IP addresses, domain name assignment, software, hardware and media.[1] As of now, there is no Code of Conduct (CoC) or set of rules for internet governance agreed upon by all nations. Various organisations like the International Telecommunications Union (ITU) of the UN, Internet Corporation for Assigned Names and Numbers (ICANN) of the US, Organisation for Economic Cooperation and Development (OECD), European Union (EU), Internet Governance Forum (IGF) and World Summit on the Information Society (WSIS) are engaged as debating platforms for internet governance, reflecting multiple and conflicting shades. However, there seems to be a consensus amongst nations on considering the internet as the only man-made 'global commons' similar to other natural ones such as the atmosphere, outer space or oceans, while approaching cyber governance through multistakeholder, multilateral or bilateral models.[2] Unlike the nuclear domain and, to some extent, outer space, cyber space continues to be shaped more by generally accepted principles rather than driven by specific treaties, agreements, institutions or norms.[3] Would it be prudent, as we move towards signing treaties that we remain inclusive in our approach rather than restricting the process to the privileged few, given the pervasive nature of cyber space? Answers to such questions would probably emerge only with experience and time.

There are nations that are not yet directly involved in cyber governance but in the near future, large sections of whose populations will be connected to the internet, reaping economic advantages of Information and Communication Technologies (ICTs) in a big way, like India, Brazil, South Africa, Turkey, etc. These so-called 'swing states' are investing heavily to have their say in this already complicated debate to secure their national interests. This paper seeks to map the international architecture, organisations and actors involved in the internet governance ecosystem with an aim to understand its implications for India.

Before proceeding to understand internet governance issues, it is only prudent to look into the underlying cyber security scene in our area of interest, including Asia and other relevant nations.

Cyber Security Scan of Asia and Other Relevant Nations

While the global nature of cyber space is irrefutable, it has a distinct regional character both due to the level of technology penetration and the presence of geo-political hotspots. There seems to be evidence of heightened cyber attacks in the locations suffering geo-political turmoil all the world over, suggesting the congruence of cyber space as a tool with the traditional means of perpetrating conflict. Asia, more than any other part of the world, is affected by cyber insecurity because of two main reasons; firstly, in terms of internet governance, organisational frameworks for collaborations and experience (at both domestic and international fronts), Asia is still a greenhorn as compared to the West. Secondly, while the rate of penetration of cyber technology is the highest in Asia, giving rise to unprecedented vulnerabilities with no clear 'rules of the road' to follow, the saturated on-line regions such as the US and Europe are exerting pressure through their off-line influence to steer the international cyber governance discourse, standards formulation, and development of future technologies in their favour. In fact, some[4] would go to the extent of stating that the US and other countries are deliberately pursuing the agenda of continued status quo of fragmented multiple agency-multiple controls for international cyber governance.

Today, with more than 44 percent of internet users residing in Asia, it is for sure a hotspot for cyber activities. There are over a billion internet users, accounting for internet penetration at 26.2 percent against the world average of 32.7 percent.[5] However, within Asia, China is distinctly ahead with 513 million internet users, while India and Japan are trailing with 121 million and 101 million internet users respectively.[6]

A broad scan of Asian cyber space shows quite interesting hues. While China's prowess lies in hardware manufacture, with economy of scales unparalleled in the world, it is marred with the suspicion of factory floor level compromises in networking products, with far-reaching strategic implications. India is an Information Technology (IT) Enabled Services (ITES) and software development leader but has almost no hardware building capacity of its own, jeopardising National Critical Information Infrastructure (NCII) protection. In terms of economy, cyber space accounted for 3.5 percent of the Gross Domestic Product (GDP) of the 13 countries (including India and China) surveyed by McKinsey in the year 2011.[7] It is also characterised by increasing reliance of governance activities on the internet. For instance, India has earmarked an outlay of Rs 3,929.10 crore in the union budget of 2014-15 for the electronics and information technology sector. This is double the money the IT Ministry spent in 2013-14.[8] With regards to peak broadband speeds, Hong Kong leads with 54.1 mbps while South Korea and Japan follow closely with 48.8 mbps and 42 mbps. China and India trail far behind with 7.1 mbps and 2 mbps respectively.[9]

Under such non-linear and disproportionate developments in cyber space, each nation adopts an approach it finds most suitable to guard its sovereignty. On the one hand, we have countries like North Korea, that choose to remain cut off from common cyber space and Iran, that is developing its own intranet, not connected to the internet; and, on the other, hand, China and Saudi Arabia employ various policy filters to create cyber borders and to allow for content filtering/monitoring in the name of national security. Other cases in point are the single gateway policy of Saudi Arabia for internet traffic in and out of the country, and the great Chinese firewall, and the mandatory installation of software such as a 'green dam' on any computer placed in China that allows monitoring by government agencies. India's position is probably marked by the 'search for balance'between its ability to manage ever growing threats in an increasingly vulnerable cyber space through techno-legal, policy and organisational means, and its responsibility towards the global community to keep cyber space 'open, secure and global' through bilateral, multilateral and global efforts.

Online LICO in Asia

Asia could be called a flashpoint for cyber space as its vibrant economies are dependent on cyber space and there is a lack of mature inter-governmental institutions to deal with political stresses, giving rise to a kind of Low Intensity Conflict Operation (LICO) in cyber space. On the one hand, the rise of China and India as cyber powers is being considered a part of the tectonic power shift from Europe to Asia, challenging the role of post World War II global institutions; and, on the other, the US is able to sustain its global reach and influence over Asia through a mix of cooperation and competition, not restricted to the military domain, but over the cyber governance rules-making process, the control structures of cyber governance, industry and finance. It would be worthwhile to take a look the cyber security faultlines within Asia and the US to better understand the internet governance aspects.

West Asia: In West Asia, one may observe that cyber war-making tools have become adjunct to the hostilities offline and cyber space is being used to fuel the ongoing conflict without any regard for geographical boundaries. A case in point is the Stuxnet malware that destroyed the centrifuges of the Iranian nuclear facility based at Natanz. Being touted as the first cyber weapon, when it came to light in the year 2010, Stuxnet targeted the National Critical Infrastructure's (NCI's) Supervisory Control and Data Acquisition (SCADA) systems. Suspicions about of the involvement of the US and Israel grew stronger when some estimates suggested that the development of Stuxnet would have cost around $1.5 million and around six man years of time. It raises two important issues: one, that while supply chain vulnerability could be a most feared thing, the second tier Zero day vulnerabilities (the electrically operating convertors) could be easily targeted to launch a cyber attack. Two, the integrity of, and relationship with, the country that manufactures the equipment being used in NCI assume a renewed importance.

Within a year of the discovery of Stuxnet (i.e. by the year 2011), a range of malicious ware like Duqu, Mahdi, Gauss and Flame surfaced, with DNA similar to Stuxnet's, primarily spreading through the USB drive; however, unlike Stuxnet, that was a sabotage weapon, the purpose of the other malware was limited to espionage into government departments, banking systems and energy networks. Of these, Flame's sophistication with a smart 20 MB size module, is worth mentioning. It could record Skype conversations, take screen shots, exfiltrate data from smart phones, including audio recordings and network traffic recordings. Mahdi followed the route of phishing e-mails and is believed to have infected machines in Saudi Arabia, Syria, Lebanon, Israel, the UAE, Afghanistan and Egypt.[10] By the year 2012, a virus like Shamoon, believed to be an Iranian reverse engineered version of 'wiper', started to launch Distributed Denial of Service (DDoS) attacks on US banking systems, costing them dearly. Whether it is a state sponsored effort by Iran or the group named 'Izz ad-Din al-Qassam Cyber Fighters'[11] is solely responsible, what stands out is that cyber capabilities can be built within a short period of time, given Iran's virtually nil cyber capability pre-2009.

East Asia: East Asia presents a unique mix of a cooperative, competitive and conflicting geo-political environment coexisting concurrently. It is interesting to observe the reflections of the physical domain conflicts in the cyber domain so profoundly. North Korea, as one of the protagonists of East Asia, treats South Korea (being highly networked) as an easy target for cyber attacks and has been using every kind of cyber weapon against it, achieving noteworthy success. In March 2013, a virus with DNA signatures similar to the Shamoon virus that deleted huge data from the systems of Saudi Armaco, was detected in the systems of several banks and media houses of South Korea, deleting data from their systems. While North Korea does not even qualify for a target surface for cyber attacks owing to its poor IT infrastructure, it is supposed to have more than 3,000 cyber warriors to inflict damage on its adversaries.[12] China presents a common source of cyber skirmishes in this region, be it with Japan, Vietnam[13] or the Philippines. In the year 2013 alone, Japan witnessed a record 12.8 billion cyber attacks on government and other organisations as the Diaoyu/Senkaku Islands dispute remains unresolved. The territorial dispute between China and the Philippines over the Scarborough and Spratly Islands saw heightened exchange of cyber attacks immediately after Chinese military vessels transgressed into disputed waters on April 7, 2012.[14] There have been constant attacks on Vietnamese websites, especially government domains, apparently by Chinese hackers, including the famous attack on 220 websites on May 12, 2014.[15]

Almost all the East Asian countries are developing cyber warfare capabilities but in isolation, except for China, that is far ahead in integrating cyber warfare at every level, including its doctrine, policy, strategy, operations and tactics. South Korea has also made some strides through its National Intelligence Centre that focusses on detecting, preventing and responding to cyber attacks in collaboration with the Korea

Communications Commission (KCC).[16] Japan declared "responding to cyber attacks" as one of its key priorities in its 2012 Annual White Paper post incidents of massive exfiltration of industry data from Mitsubhushi Heavy Industry and others in August 2011.[17] Presently, the Self-Defence Forces (SDF) of Japan do not only defend their own networks but are tasked with "accumulating advanced expertise and skills needed to tackle cyber attacks".[18] Japan announced a $270 million budget to raise a 100-strong cyber unit in September 2012, as recommended by a panel, yet more sophisticated cyber attacks like 'Deputy Dog'[19] which targeted Defence Industrial Base (DIB) companies, US government entities, mining companies and Non-Governmental Organisations (NGOs) keep surfacing, as was discovered in 2013. Also interestingly, Japan has entered a cyber defence cooperation programme with Australia, the only one outside of its programme with the North Atlantic Treaty Organisation (NATO).[20]

Pakistan: While understanding the cyber space governance approaches within the South Asian Association for Regional Cooperation (SAARC) countries, two factors stand out in the context of India: one, how China places cyber warfare in the national overall defence strategy; and, two, the status of cyber security regulations in Pakistan. There are some notable initiatives within Pakistan regarding internet security issues with respect to India. The Pakistan Information Security Association (PISA) is of the opinion, "If Pakistan and India can have an agreement not to attack nuclear installations, why not an agreement seeking the prevention of cyber warfare against each other".[21] Baffled by the Snowden revelations that the National Security Agency (NSA) of the US has been spying on Pakistan with 13.5 billion pieces of intercepted e-mail, phones and fax communications, Pakistan has come up with a seven-point agenda to safeguard its national defence, security, intelligence, diplomacy, nuclear and missile programme, economy, energy, education, civil aviation as well as industrial and manufacturing units, in both the private and public sectors.[22] The action plan for the cyber security of Pakistan, as enumerated by Senator Mushahid Hussain is as follows;

- Relevant legislation to preserve, protect and promote Pakistan's cyber security, drafting for which has already begun. Bills are to be presented in Parliament for cyber security.
- Cyber security threat should be accepted and recognised as a new, emerging national security threat by the Government of Pakistan, similar to threats like terrorism and military aggression.
- Establishing a National Computer Emergency Response Team (PKCERT).
- Establishing a Cyber-Security Task Force with affiliation with the Ministry of Defence, Ministry of IT, Ministry of Interior, Ministry of Foreign Affairs, Ministry

of Information and the security organisations plus relevant and leading professionals from the private security so that Pakistan can take steps to combat this new emerging threat and formulate a cyber security strategy for Pakistan.

- Under the office of the chairman, Joint Chiefs of Staff Committee, an Inter-Services Cyber Command should be established to coordinate cyber security and cyber defence for the Pakistan armed forces.
- Within the framework of SAARC, Pakistan should take the initiative to initiate talks among the 8-member states, particularly India, to establish acceptable norms of behaviour in cyber security among the SAARC countries so that these countries do not engage in cyber warfare against each other.[23]
- The Senate Defence Committee, in cooperation with the Pakistan Information Security Association (PISA), will have a special media workshop to promote awareness among the public and educate opinion leaders on the issue of cyber security.[24]

China: While some would assume that the tenets of traditional warfare such as proportionality, territory and distinction are not easily adaptable to the domain of cyber warfare, thus, probably requiring a paradigm shift, as reflected in the Chinese theory of "Unrestricted Warfare" propounded by two colonels of the People's Liberation Army (PLA), Qiao Liang and Wang Xiangsui, the counter view of the liberal school of thought which also deserves merit, states that this concept comprises "lazy intellectual thinking and a sure recipe for global chaos".[25] More importantly, China's view of future wars is marked with three negatives: non-contact, non-linear, non-symmetric.[26] Under the non-contact category are all the cyber warfare efforts of China to "effectively nullify an opponent's forces without having to directly confront or engage them".[27] The non-symmetric war justifies cyber espionage, hacking and exfiltrating Research and Development (R&D) material in violation of Intellectual Property Rights (IPRs) which are only country specific. Cyber exploitation serves at least two purposes: one is that it allows China to leapfrog and come to parity with the advanced technologies of the US without having to spend on actual R&D; and, two, as a tool of psychological war, it creates a kind of cyber instability when other countries see mass penetration of their National Critical Information Infrastructures (NCIIs).

United States

For maintaining hegemony over the cyber domain, the US was the first nation to declare cyber space as a domain of warfare, though a formal cyber warfare doctrine is yet to be released owing to lack of understanding of the tenets of this dynamic technology. The first exposure of the US government's cyber warfare policy was the leak of its Presidential Directive 20 which revealed:

> The US government shall integrate DCEO (Defensive Cyber Effect Operations) and OCEO (Offensive Cyber Effect Operations) as appropriate, with other diplomatic, informational, military, economic, financial, intelligence, counterintelligence, and law enforcement options, taking into account cost, risks, potential consequences, foreign policy and other policy considerations.[28]

While there is no specific mention of cyber weapons in the document, the US possesses the world's best hardware and software for cyber coercion. To mention a few: the infamous PRISM programme for cyber surveillance that obtained information directly from the servers of nine listed partner companies vis-a-vis Microsoft, Yahoo, Google, Facebook, Paltalk, AOL, Skype, You Tube and Apple. X-Keyscore, posed as a lawful foreign signals intelligence collection system of the NSA, is supposed to have information collection partnerships with Australia, Canada, Great Britain and New Zealand, as revealed by Snowden.[29] Tailored Access Operations (TAO), a Texas based special department of the NSA, is active in end-point operations. Housed in a disbanded Sony Chip Company location, TAO employs more than 60 officers, including 30 military officers, for network penetration and installing spyware into the targets' systems. The target countries include Iraq, Cuba, Venezuela, Afghanistan, Mexico, and Columbia. Spyware operations such as Olympus Ticket, Sharpfocus-2, Parchdusk and Foxacid messages are followed by the NSA's QUANTUM method to insert the malware.[30] In many ways, the motto of TAO epitomises the intent and approach of the US to carry out covert and clandestine operations in cyber space: *"Your data is our data, your equipment is our equipment – any time, any place, by any legal means"*.[31] Apparently, the legality of such endeavours is being maintained through the loopholes in the existing law. The powers of the US PATRIOT Act 2001 were used by then President George W Bush to authorise the intelligence agencies to conduct surveillance without warrants in "support" of the Global War on Terror, bypassing the provisions of the Foreign Intelligence Surveillance Act (FISA), 1978 (amended in 2008), which requires approval from a three-judge court for intelligence agencies, if surveillance is needed to be carried out over foreign targets. Also, there have been secret rulings of FISA courts to facilitate the NSA to collect call records and metadata of millions of US citizens through service providers like 'Verizon'.[32]

In its bid to achieve 'global network supremacy,'[33] the US is also investing heavily institutionally, on developing spy hardware and software. NSA's ANT (Access Network Technology) catalogue, a 50-page document listing the digital toolkit available with the ANT division of the TAO special department for use by NSA employees, is one such example. Analogues to digital elite forces, these tools belong to a family of clandestine tools called "Angryneighbour" and may cost up to $250,000.[34]

From the ongoing, what becomes unambiguous is that the cyber domain is becoming a future battleground, and proliferation of covert cyber capabilities is inevitable as this provides nations with the hard intelligence related to national security and economic R&D material. The road to global internet governance is not without upheavals.

Situating the Internet Governance Debate

Arms Control and Internet Governance Analogy

One of the serious concerns for legitimate governments regarding cyber space is that the attribution technology is not matured enough to pin-point the source of attacks, providing for anonymity, besides the trans-border permeating, low cost and distance-less nature of ICT. In order to secure cyber space, one may think of applying time-tested traditional measure such as arms control. Russia, for instance, has suggested "measures limiting the spread of information weapons; regime prohibiting the development, proliferation and use of information weapons", among others.[35] However, approaching the cyber domain in the traditional arms control fashion may not be a good idea, chiefly for two reasons. Firstly, unlike nuclear arms that were in only the hands of the major powers, cyber technology resides with individuals and the base and reach of this power is too strong to get steered by changing the behaviour of nations alone through treaties. And, secondly, though terrorists, anti-social elements and non-state actors wield enough cyber power to effect large scale disruption to a nation's critical infrastructure, they are not likely to get deterred by a replication of traditional arms control measures amongst nations.

Climate Change and Internet Governance Analogy

In some ways, it seems the debate on internet governance is going the way of the climate change debate. Even though it is known quite definitely that by the year 2050, temperatures are going to rise to alarmingly high levels and the consequent rise in sea levels is going to sink a few countries, not much is being done. Nations wish to protect themselves and the interest of their citizens first. Those who have the wherewithal, would seek to empower themselves first and, at times, this may mean disempowering other nations. In the politics of the high table of international cyber policy-making, there is a lack of faith amongst nations, preventing them from arriving at some favourable consensus internationally. Consequently, this lack of faith translates into the necessity for survival and security that drives nations to build cyber power, both offensive and defensive.[36] In cyber space, the frontrunners will create more information and will own the lion's share of information infrastructure and, thus, will want to protect their information as a priority in order to continue to reap the benefits of being 'providers of goods' in this low cost 'free trade zone' created through cyber power. For India, this realist approach doesn't seem to echo in our military cyber warfare strategic discourses as yet, however, it has been reflected in India's grand strategy formulation document, *Nonalignment 2.0: A Foreign and Strategic Policy for India in the Twenty-first Century*.[37]

Rights and Responsibility Approach

On the other end, the liberal perspective believes in open and equitable access for all wherein privacy and freedom of expression and speech are ensured. Cyber space technologies enable large scale surveillance and monitoring of citizens that has brought these human rights issues to the forefront of internet governance while sovereign governments try to hide behind the shield of national security. At this juncture, both the liberal and realist approaches essentially strengthen the position of cyber space as a global commons that needs to be governed, however, both emerge from two opposite poles tending to converge on the golden mean of individual privacy and the national/international security balance. It is opined that whether one views cyber space through the prism of the universal declaration of human rights or that of a collective responsibility of not allowing any individual nation's domination in this man-made 'global commons', it serves well to take both the rights and responsibilities approaches forward towards achieving the stated aim of keeping cyber space 'open, global and secure'.

Privacy and Security Debate

There is yet another debate, perhaps being falsely portrayed as dichotomous, between privacy and freedom of speech, on one side, and cyber space security, on the other. As in the case of any other global commons like air, climate and oceans, in cyber space also there are no absolute rights or absolute obligations. What is expected of the world community is to arrive at an agreeable level of regulations, a set of norms for all stakeholders. Privacy and security are not either/or options but are to coexist, governed by some laws, to be obeyed by all stakeholders. For instance, all the data protection, monitoring or regulating activities that the Indian government takes on are governed by the law of the land (Indian Telegraph Act and IT Act) that does not discriminate between Indian and foreigner.[38]

Internet: A 'Global Commons' or The Domain of 'More Equals'

Is cyber space a true 'global commons'? At least, that's what the general international consensus seems to suggest. For instance, in the context of Indo-US relations, managing the security of the 'global commons' was identified as a main area of cooperation for the two countries in the joint statement issued at the end of Obama's visit.

> In an increasingly inter-dependent world, the stability of, and access to, the air, sea, space and cyber space domains is vital for the security and economic prosperity of the nations. Acknowledging their commitment to openness and responsible international conduct, and on the basis of their shared values, India and United States (will) explore ways to work together, as well as with other countries, to develop a shared vision for this critical domain to promote peace, security and development.[39]

Similar reflections may be observed in Japan's recently published cyber security doctrine.[40] But as C Raja Mohan[41] points out, the US has been tacitly shifting its stance on considering cyber space as a global commons. While the US National Military Strategy of 2004 refers to the global commons of air, seas, space and cyber space, the US National Military Strategy published in 2011, distinguishes between global commons and the "globally connected domains" such as cyber space. In fact, the apprehensions shared by many nations while considering cyber space as a global commons are mainly three-fold: one, cyber space consists of networks of networks connected through various media, including sea lanes of communication, owned by a few nations and/or corporations, including the servers that are owned by a handful major powers. Therefore, how can cyber space be considered a global commons at par with the air, seas and space? Two, there is a growing perception amongst the have-not nations that everyone's responsibility is no one's responsibility when it comes to the security of cyber space. Not many stakeholders are doing enough towards this owing to their own priorities, thereby giving opportunities to cyber miscreants in the bargain.[42] Three, the ground reality is not reflective of the essence and spirit of the global commons. Many nations, including China and Russia, are working towards establishing controls and authority over this domain, at least in their own territories, as opined through various multilateral fora, including the UN Governmental Group of Experts (GGEs).[43]

India thinks, albeit wishfully, that conceptually the internet must become the equinet where there is equitable space for all so as to protect everyone's security, be it an individual, an organisation or a nation. Obviously, this calls for a collaborative and cooperative approach as no nation can guarantee safe cyber space alone. While this would lead to a debate on international cyber treaties or soft law options, many nations are also taking the route of the bilateral mechanism with like-minded partners to approach cyber governance issues. The question at this juncture is: why and how would bilaterally agreed upon norms become acceptable multilaterally? Hypothetically, should we presume that the cyber governance norms agreed upon by the US and Russia would be accepted by all other participating countries? And even if that happens, what about the non-participating countries which might take to proliferation of cyber weapons in the future, not being signatory to such a treaty?

Internet Governance Through Treaties: How Viable?

There are serious concerns on the effectiveness of any international cyber treaty when viewed from a neo-realist perspective. In such a multilateral approach, the actions of the major powers may not always match with the expectations of other member nations. More often than not, the positions of the major powers are more consequential than the actual conclusions/agreements arrived at through multilateral discussions. There are always some individual national objectives that the major powers seek to fulfil through international cyber conventions/norms. Russia and China would want to seek government control over information flow through a multilateral model, whereas the West, led by the US, is looking for protection of information networks through a multi-stakeholder approach. Furthermore, there is no absolute digital equality amongst nations and the outcome of any international cyber convention is bound to have a differential impact on the digitisation process of different countries. This digital asymmetry entails some cyber activity to be taken as 'normal' by one nation while another may perceive it as a 'threat'.

However, international cyber treaties serve the purpose of providing definitional clarity on the common and relevant issues. Treaties also allow for policy space on Confidence-Building Measures (CBMs) between nations, rationalising their cyber behaviour in the international arena. One of the international initiatives towards seeking cooperation in dealing with cyber crimes is the Budapest Convention, with the signatories including the US, Japan, Australia, South Africa, and Canada. It is still open for ratification by all the countries and has witnessed very limited success. Countries have different priorities and expectations from international treaties. For Germany, the privacy of its citizens is paramount, however, Russia's understanding of dealing with cyber crime is influenced more by the apprehension that the public data so shared under the garb of convention could be used as Big Data for analyses by foreign intelligence agencies to destabilise its internal security. As described by Boris Vasiliev, Russia "stands for the development of a convention on crimes in the use of information and communication technologies, which should be universal and take into account specialties of all countries without exception, should be based on the principle of sovereign equality of its participants and non-interference in the internal affairs of the state".[44]

With increasing integration of the real world happenings with cyber world activities, crime in the cyber world can be best handled by a prompt response in real time, specially when tackling transnational crimes. Presently, there are mainly two options to seek international cooperation: Interpol or by the way of Mutual Legal Assistance Treaties (MALTs). The limitation with MALTs is that, on an average, it takes around 10 months to get a response as has been brought out by the Review Group on Intelligence and Communication Technologies set up by US President Obama, post the Snowden revelations. Given the speed, reach and anonymity of cyber crime, MALTs fall well short of the law enforcement requirement. Some of the measures suggested by the review group to speed up the process include streamlining of a number of steps, provision of records to foreign countries, and provision of online submission of MLATs. At this stage, it is important to understand that the top internet service provider companies (Microsoft, Yahoo, Google, Facebook, PalTalk, YouTube, Skype, AOL, Apple, etc.) that are required to share intelligence under MLATs and much of global cyber space infrastructure through which intelligence would be shared, are owned by the US. Therefore, revision of the law enforcement cooperation process in the US would greatly impact the way cyber crimes are combated internationally.

Swing States' Dilemmas: Does India Stand or Swing?

Why are the 'swing states'[45] so important for international cyber governance? While it is true that the inventors of the internet (the US and Western economies) continue to be the 'producers of goods' over the internet , there is a growing belief that cyber power is slowly but surely being transferred to the highly populated swing states like India, Brazil, South Africa, Peru, Turkey, Argentina, Kenya and Malaysia. In essence, international behaviour is governed by national interests; therefore, any global consensus on international cyber governance will depend upon the clarity of the national policy objectives of other nations. For instance, the US, keeping its national interests at the forefront, always advocates keeping the internet 'global, open and secure' through its politicians, bureaucrats, researchers or corporations, as it benefits US corporations in the long run to keep the internet infrastructure (please note, not the content!) decentralised and securitised so as to convert it into a global free trade zone—of which they are the major goods providers. This approach was declared in a report of the Council on Foreign Relations. On the other side of the spectrum, China's national objectives drive it to have an open internet within its borders but put a 'great firewall' to disconnect its people from the global internet and censor its content to suit the regime.[46] Therefore, as cyber power moves to swing states, their national priorities would only become more crucial to the cause of international cyber governance.

While India seems to be favouring the multilateral approach, that chiefly means government to government agreements/treaties to govern the internet, it is also being categorised as a swing state. It is opined that a stable major regional power like India would not like to seen as a swing state. From the beginning, India has been seeking a policy of autonomy in foreign policy, be it the Non-Aligned Movement (NAM) during the bipolar era of the Cold War, or strategic autonomy in today's multipolar world order, as the guiding vector of its foreign policy. India is also not a small or weak state, so dependent that it is compelled to swing. As opined by Dr Latha Reddy (former deputy national security adviser, India) during the India-ASEAN Cyber Security Conference 2014, the debate on whether India favours multilateralism or multi-stakeholderism has ill situated it in the 'either/or' paradigm choice space.

India takes a more pragmatic approach while engaging and working with the rest of the world to contribute towards democratic and representative international cyber governance while preserving the strengths that come from the open nature of the domain, with interference at the minimum, to keep it socially responsible and legal.[47] India also feels that a global commons like the internet should not be regulated as a private entity by corporations like the Internet Corporation of Assigned Names and Numbers (ICANN). The time is propitious to put in place governance and architecture that make the internet unyielding to misuse and manipulation by both state and non-state actors, and is not seen as a US corporation by other nations. A point in case (out of many) is the total disregard for cultural sensitivities while allocating generic Top Level Domains (TLD) like 'dot budha', 'dot ram' or 'dot Indians,' etc.

Internet Governance: The Story So Far

The Early Years

A little bit of the history of internet governance would serve well to understand the evolution of the myriad organisations, structures, actors and stakeholders that we see today in the governance domain. Initially, to manage the internet, the US Department of Defence's (DoD's) ARPANET used to issue a series of memos called Requests for Comments (RFCs) to document technical decisions or work methods.[48] Back in the year 1979, the Defence Advanced Research Projects Agency (DARPA) founded the Internet Configuration Control Board which got renamed as the Internet Advisory Board (IAB) in 1984, and later (by the year 1986), the Internet Activity Board.[49]

During same period 1984-86, the Transmission Control Protocol/Internet Protocol (TCP/IP) came into being as the backbone of the US National Science Foundation Network (NSFNET) that spread the internet to Australia, Germany, Israel, Italy, Japan, Mexico, Netherlands, New Zealand, and the UK by the year 1989. Also to develop and promote internet standards, the Internet Engineering Task Force (IETF) was formed in 1986 by the US. Alongside, the US DoD entered into a contract with the University of South California to oversee address allocation, internet protocol numbering and assignments under the computer network division at the Information Science Institute of the university. As the internet expanded, this function became more and more important and included the management of the global Domain Name System (DNS) root servers and came to be known as the Internet Assigned Number Authority (IANA). In fact, the Division Director, Mr Jon Postle remained in command since the early days till his death in 1998. Till the early 1990s, he almost singly (with just one assistant, from his California office in Marina del Rey) managed the DNS with a simple 'bottom-up' system of TLDs. Perhaps, he was uninterested in getting involved with policy matters as the world at that time was ignorant of the impending .com bubble.

With introduction of the World Wide Web (www) as a commercial platform and the number of domain name holders crossing one million, Postel, in 1995, proposed the merger of IANA with the Internet Society (ISOC) for a more comprehensive and stable DNS management considering the economic and political dimensions of this technical resource called the internet. But the move was vehemently opposed by the US government and the private industry, specially the Network Solutions Inc. (NSI). NSI was in contract with the US Department of Commerce (DoC) to function as the registrar for generic TLDs (eg .com, .org, .net, .edu) that was a multi-million business as DoC has permitted it to charge an annual registration fee of $35 per domain name. Postel's idea of introducing 150 more new generic TLDs under ISOC would have stalled the US business strategy. Just by the year 1996, NSI registered more than 10 million domain names. Meanwhile, Postel's alternate plan of creating an Interim Ad Hoc Committee (IAHC) represented by IANA, ISOC and IAB as technical bodies with ITU and World Intellectual Property Organisation (WIPO) as inter-governmental bodies and International Trade Mark Association (INTA) as a business group, to prevent pure governmental and commercial control over DNS, was turned down under NSI's lobbying of the US Congress. In fact, the US government did not approve of Postel's idea of shifting the A-root servers from Herndon, Virginia, to Geneva, Switzerland, as part of the solution. Later, in September the same year, IANA got merged with ICANN which was established as a no-profit organisation under contract with the US Department of Commerce.

ICANN has been criticised about its functioning and lack of transparency in the decision-making process as a truly neutral governing body. Also, there have been demands for its subordination to a political organisation under the UN.[50] In 1992, a more inclusive organisation called the Internet Society (ISOC) was established, amalgamating the IAB and Internet Engineering Task Force (ITEF) within itself. It has an open membership of corporations, organisations, academia and individuals.

UN Initiatives Towards Internet Governance

In December 2002, it was noted in the United Nations General Assembly (UNGA) debate that the growing dependence on ICTs would necessitate having global cyber security measures in place. Since then, cyber issues have remained central to the constantly evolving international security agenda. Matters concerning cyber space governance are well documented in the UN Security Council's Counter Terrorism Committee.[51] The cyber governance debate flows seamlessly with the traditional security policy debate and, in particular, along with the threat of terrorism within the UN, that gets reflected in the form of UN Security Council Resolutions.[52] Going a step further, the UN Global Counter Terrorism Strategy has an objective of not only "countering terrorism in all its forms and manifestation on the internet" but also to proactively exploit the "use of the internet as a tool for countering the spread of terrorism".[53] Emphasising the inadequacy of the "law enforcement alone approach" the need for a "culture of information security in the application and use of information technologies"[54] was emphasised upon at the December 2002 UNGA debate. During Kofi Annan's tenure as general secretary of the UN, the tone was set for a "global culture of cyber security" when he epitomised this concern at the World Information Society Day in May 2006:

> In an increasingly interconnected and networked world, it has become critically important to safeguard our vital systems and infrastructures against attack by cybercriminals, while instilling confidence in online transactions in order to promote trade, commerce, banking, telemedicine, e-government and a host of other e-applications. As this depends on the security practices of each and every networked country, business and citizen, we need to develop a global culture of cyber security.[55]

Further, at the UN level, in the year 2003, the first World Summit on Information Society (WSIS) was held in Geneva that drew strong criticism, specially from China, Brazil and South Africa on the legitimacy of ICANN's status which led to the constitution of the Working Group on Internet Governance (WGIG) to clarify the issues before the second WSIS was held in 2005 in Tunis. In the second WSIS also, after much debate, the US declined to give away the control on the Root Zone file and the participants agreed to establish an Internet Governance Forum (IGF) which has been taking the debate further through the Multi-stakeholder Advisory Group (MAG) with its latest 9th IGF meeting in Istanbul, Turkey, on September 2-5, 2014. IGF is a multi-stakeholder forum for policy dialogue, which is a regional, national and subject area initiative, and the Commission on Science and Technology for the Development Working Group (CSTDWG) on improvements to IGF was established in the year 2011. Additionally, the International Telecommunications Union (ITU) hosted a treaty level conference titled World Conference on International Telecommunications (WCIT) in December 2012 in Dubai.

This legal-cultural approach echoes well in the work of ITU in a more pragmatic fashion.

ITU Initiatives: Global internet governance has seen many upheavals, with no overarching laws and regulations in place.[56] ITU,[57] with a membership of more than 191 countries and 750 IT companies, is the mother organisation under the UN, responsible for regulating the Information and Communication Technologies (ICTs) for the governments and private sector, and for creating and sustaining security and confidence in this domain by developing appropriate networks and services.[58] And, not surprisingly, ITU has kept for itself ambitiously idealistic objectives, as enshrined in its mission statement:

> ITU's mission is to enable the growth and sustained development of telecommunications and information networks, and to facilitate universal access so that people everywhere can participate in, and benefit from, the emerging information society and global economy. The ability to communicate freely is a pre-requisite for a more equitable, prosperous and peaceful world. And ITU assists in mobilizing the technical, financial and human resources needed to make this vision a reality.[59]

But what it has been able to rather provide are some broad guidelines, besides the Group of Government Experts' (GGEs') reports. Furthermore, these "still evolving" sets of norms remain non-binding, are, thus, left to the decency of a nation for implementation.

According to the ITU secretary general, there are five key principles that should govern cyber space; one, every government should commit to giving its people access to communications; two, every government should commit to protecting its people in cyber space; three, every country should commit to refrain from harbouring terrorists/criminal in its territories; four, every country should commit to not be the first to launch a cyber attack on other countries; and five, every country must commit to collaborating with other countries within an international framework of cooperation to ensure that there is peace in cyber space.[60]

In a bid to develop a framework for international cooperation, in the year 2007, the ITU came up with Global Cybersecurity Agenda (GCA) with five 'strategic pillars' (including legal and technical procedural measures, organisation, capacity building and international cooperation) as well as seven 'main strategic goals' (ranging from cyber crime legislation to software security and international digital identity protocols).[61] However, presently, the GCA has been co-located with the International Multilateral Partnership Against Cyber-Threats (IMPACT) at the latter's headquarters in Cyberjaya, Malaysia, since September 2008.

In December 2012, the ITU hosted the World Conference on the International Telecommunications (WCIT-12) in Dubai that was believed to become the 'Rio Summit for Cyber Space' in order to achieve the overarching cyber governance values such as openness, security, growth, freedom and enforcement of the rule of law.[62] The major emphasis was to review International telecommunication Regulations (ITRs). The ITRs were last negotiated in Melbourne, Australia in 1988, and there is broad consensus that the text now needs to be updated to reflect the dramatically different information and communication technology (ICT) landscape of the 21st century.[63] However, the Westphalian minded ITU has been criticised for its old fashioned thought process, top-down approach, multilateral (government-exclusive) character and non-transparent decision-making process that does not auger well for the governance of an all pervasive cyber space, with stakeholders ranging from the public, private, academia and research and development arenas.[64]

- **Progress Story Through UN GGE Mechanism:** While many nations have attempted to address the cyber governance issues by creating national level mechanisms, the trans-border nature of cyber space has forced the international community to initiate rules and a norms making process. As early as the year 1998, the Russian Federation introduced a draft resolution on "developments in the field of information and telecommunication in the context of international security" in the UN General Assembly, but it did not have many serious takers among the member nations. It was only when the cyber disruption activities started to affect the real world that in the year 2004, the first Group of Governmental Experts (GGE) was constituted to "examine the existing and potential threats from the cyber sphere and possible cooperative measures to address them". [65]

- **Geo-political Dynamics of Cyber Governance:** The discourse on cyber governance had many ups and downs due to different perceptions held by the two major blocs – the West, led by the US, on one side, for multi-stakeholderism, and Russia and China on the other, for multilateralism. While the West stood for freedom in the functioning of the internet, Russia and China held a strong view seeking the controlling role of governments on the flow of information on the internet. Also the differences in perceptions between the two sides came to the fore on the basic premise of challenge identification. The US and the West primarily sought containment of criminal activities and economic espionage in cyber space, whereas Russia and China were aiming for border rules so as to curb the offensive use of cyber space by any nation.[66] Beijing and Moscow unsuccessfully tried to formalise an international treaty to govern cyber space in the face of strong opposition from the US and other Western countries, and the first GGE resulted in lack of consensus amongst the 15-member expert group.
- There were chiefly two issues on which the two blocs had different opinions: firstly, on the question of the impact of developments in ICT on national security and military affairs. Beijing and Moscow wanted to include "new threats posed by state exploitation of ICT for military and national security purposes" that was not acceptable to the US and the West. Secondly, the GGE failed to specify the focus area for further discussions on "information content" or "information infrastructures" and also on the issue of exercising state control over trans-border information content as a matter of national security. However, Russia continued to pursue the member nations for international cooperation through the GGE apparatus and met with grand success when the second draft resolution was adopted by a vote of 163 to 1 (the only opposition being from the US) in the year 2005. Russia was able to garner co-sponsorship for the resolution by countries like China, Belarus, Kazakhstan, Kyrgyzstan, Armenia, Myanmar, Tajikistan, and Uzbekistan by the year 2006, paving the way for establishing the second GGE in the year 2009.[67]
- **Altered Cyber Threat and Shift in US Cyber Policy post 2009:** Barack Obama's arrival at the White House saw a contrast in how the US viewed cyber governance. A draft resolution was adopted at the 65th UN General Assembly (GA) session (2010) as proposed by the second GGE and this time without a vote and without any opposition from the US. This change in the cyber policy stance could be seen in the background of some significant developments in the cyber domain in the intervening period. Firstly, the Distributed Denial of Service (DDoS) attack on the Government

of Estonia in April-May of the year 2007 that crippled the government websites for weeks, and was believed to have been carried out by Russia over the removal of the Bronze Soldier from the Soviet war memorial in central Tallinn. The incident prompted the North Atlantic Treaty Organisation (NATO) to come to the rescue of Estonia for cyber defence. Secondly, and very soon after, the preemptivecyber attacks on Georgia that coincided with the Russian military's advance in the country almost established a more prominent role of the state in utilising cyber space in the military conflict. These events left the US and the West, and many other states, including India, in an "international cooperation-national security" dilemma as to what sort of response a state could choose to take in such circumstances.

- **Evolving International Code of Conduct for Information Security:** In order to take the process forward, despite many views in sharp contrast to each other, the UN adopted another resolution in 2011 to constitute the third GGE that submitted its report in June 2013. For the first time, the experts agreed on the applicability of international law to cyber space, the issue which had been a bone of contention for long as Russia wanted separate laws for governing cyber space that would provide states exclusive control over this ubiquitous medium. The report stated that "state sovereignty and international norms and principles that flow from sovereignty apply to state control of ICT related activities, and to their jurisdiction over ICT infrastructure within their territory".
- **The Issues of Concern:** The report cautions the states to maintain respect for human rights and fundamental freedoms as stated in the Universal Declaration of Human Rights and other international instruments while addressing national security concerns in cyber space. Furthermore, the report seeks harmonisation of legal approaches adopted by states by strengthening "practical collaboration between respective law enforcement and prosecutorial agencies". The other suggestions include: enhanced sharing of information on cyber security incidents between "national CERTs bilaterally, with CERT communities, and in other forums" and states should restrict themselves from using "proxies to commit internationally wrongful acts". UN Secretary General Ban Ki-moon's statement that "the UN plays an important role in promoting dialogue among member states on the issue of security in the use of ICTs and in further developing international cooperation in this field... (and the third GGE report provides) a sound basis for future efforts to enhance security and stability on the issue of ICTs," only highlights the importance of the UN.[68]

In a nutshell, while, on the one hand, the UN deals with the cyber security issues at par and along with the challenges of global terrorism at the highest echelons, on the other, it talks of some non-binding 'soft' efforts on the part of world society at large, more as an issue of cultural adoption. Whereas, the ITU, in particular, has demonstrated many pragmatic efforts to cohesively integrate the otherwise fragmented domains of policy, technology and industry to empower nations for building secure cyber capability.

Making Sense BeyondITU, ICANN, and WSIS

The internet governance debate is broadly divided into the positions taken by the two major blocs. The US and the West desire that ICANN, as a private US corporation, with a narrow technical mandate, should continue as the mother body to govern the internet in its present form. On the other hand, China and Russia along with other G-20 nations such as India, Brazil, South Africa want acceptance of a far broader definition of "internet governance" to include cyber malware, spam and illegal/objectionable content flow, apart from the root servers, protocols and domain names. And, more importantly, the governing body should work as an independent global organisation under the ITU of the UN. While the controversy between the ITU and ICANN factions continues to brew, India's stand, along with the civil societies of many G-20 nations has been beyond the "either/or" paradigm. ICANN as a multi-stakeholder platform is criticised because it is a private body in contract with the US Department of Commerce (DoC) and functions under US law. However, a governance solution purely inter-governmental (read multilateral) is also undesirable and counter-productive, given the dependence of the economy, business and day-to-day functioning of civil society on the internet. India stands for a revamped organisation with a "decentralised mechanism" to carry out a new set of responsibilities.

Meanwhile, what transpired in the WSIS process in Geneva was interesting. While no compromise could be reached on the governance model other than "agree to disagree and postpone the discussion till WSIS phase II", the conceptual framework enumerated in Articles 48, 49 and 50 of the WSIS Declaration was quite promising and futuristic which could be summarised as:

- Policy authority for internet-related public policy issues is the sovereign right of states. They have rights and responsibilities for international internet-related public policy issues.
- The private sector has had, and should continue to have, an important role in the development of the internet, in both the technical and economic fields.
- Civil society has also played an important role on internet matters, especially at the community level, and should continue to play such a role.
- Inter-governmental organisations have, had, and should continue to have, a facilitating role in the coordination of internet-related public policy issues.

- International organisations have also had, and should continue to have, an important role in the development of internet-related technical standards and relevant policies.[69, 70]

But, the essence got lost in the competition for "important role" and "facilitator's role" between the ITU and ICANN. On one hand, the ICANN lobby believes that internet governance is a technical matter and is best left to the private corporation that has been handling it since the beginning. On the other hand are the supporters of the ITU, who proclaim internet governance to be a political issue concerning the sovereignty of the member nations of the UN, thus, feel that internet governance should be handed over to the ITU. A solution could have been reached by giving the technical responsibilities to ICANN and the political responsibilities to the ITU, but that did not happen because of the inseparability of technical decisions and their economic and political fallouts. For example, control of the root server system is essentially a technical function but as this ensures the stable and secure working of the internet, a prerequisite for the global economy today, it becomes a political issue. For that matter, introduction of Top Level Domains (TLDs) such as generic TLDs (.com, .org, .mil, .edu, etc.) or country name TLDs, would inevitably attract economic and political attention.

Power is shifting from the industry rich to the information rich, and the power shift is not expected to happen without a power struggle. The issue of internet governance is essentially one of creating an inclusive mechanism which would have the speed and flexibility of private organisations, the stability features of governmental set-ups, and the transparency expected of civil society organisations. It demands innovation, as the internet can be governed neither by a private corporation nor purely through inter-governmental bilateral or multilateral treaties. The challenges of diplomacy for the information society are more complex than the simpler 'give and take' balance between governments in the industrial age. The stakeholders are not only the governments, private sector and civil society, but also different interest groups within those stakeholders. The changed economic environment brought in by the globalisation process requires a flexible approach to governance that would accommodate the rights, freedom and legitimate interests, on the one hand, and the duties and responsibilities, on the other, of the global civil society as well as all of the involved affected actors.

Internet governance requires us to go beyond the paradigm of real space and how the systems are regulated and governed in the physical space. It demands insights into what cyber space is made up of and how a code/policy software or hardware regulates this. This may mean at times that the 'law maker' in cyber space is a technician/programmer rather than a politician, hence, its governance requires a different approach. The conflict is not merely of how to manage various stakeholders or governments but is more conceptual at its root. It is about the collective understanding (or individual differences of opinion) of information society, of how it would want to organise cyber space and how it would want to govern it.

Notes

1. Wolfgang Kleinwachter, "Beyond ICANN and ITU", *InternationalJournalfor Communication Studies*, vol. 66. (3-4), pp. 233-251, http://www.sagepublications.com. Accessed on March 4, 2015.
2. MAhima Kaul, 'Global Internet Governance: India's Search for A New Paradigm', *ORF Issue brief # 74, August, 2014,* http://www.orfonline.org/cms/export/orfonline/modules/issuebrief/attachments/issue-brief_74_1409826216579.pdf
3. Dr. Rajeshwari Pillai Rajagopalan, 'Global and National Security Imperatives', http://cyfy.org/global-and-national-security-imperatives/
4. MahimaKaul, "Global Internet Governance: India's Search for a New Paradigm," *ORF Issue Brief*, August 2014, p. 2. www.orfonline.org. Accessed on February 21, 2015.
5. Internet world stats at http://www.internetworldstats.com/stats3htm. Accessed on February 24, 2015.
6. Ibid.
7. James Manyika et al., eds., *Internet Matters: The Net's Sweeping Impact on Growth, Jobs, and Prosperity, Rep.*, McKinsey Global Institute, May, 2011, http://www.mckinsey.com/Insights/MGI/Research/TEchnology_and_innovation/Internet_matters.
8. S Ronendra Singh, "Cyber Security, E-Governance Projects get Major Allocation in Budget', http://www.thehindubusinessline.com/features/smartbuy/cyber-security-egovernance-projects-get-major-allocation-in-budget/article6210201.ece. Accessed on March 4, 2015.
9. Christy Choi, "Hong Kong has Fastest Peak Internet Speed in World", *South China Morning Post,* January 25, 2013. http://www.scmp.com/news/hong-kong/article/1135480/hong-kong-has-fastest-peak-internet-speed-world?page=all. Accessed on March 4, 2015. And Akamai State of Internet Report, Akamai, August 1, 2012. http://www.akmai.com/stateoftheinternet. Accessed on September 21, 2014.
10. "Cyber War on Iran More Widespread than First Thought, say Researchers", *Guardian*, September 21, 2012, http://www.guardian.co.uk/technology/2012/sep/21/cyberwar_iran_more_sophisticated. Accessed on February 12, 2015.
11. "Bank Hacking was the Work of Iranians, Officials say", *New York Times*, January 8, 2013, http://www.nytimes.com/2013/01/09/technology/online-banking-attack-were-work=of-iran-us-officials-say.html. Accessed on December 15, 2013.
12. "N.Korea Commands 3000-strong Cyber Warfare Unit:Defector", *Yonhap*, June 1, 2011, http://english.yonhapnews.co.kr/northkorea/2011/06/01/46/040/1000000AEN20110601004200315EHTML.
13. Vietnam: officially part of Southeast Asia geographically, although culturally it is a part of the East Asian cultural sphere. Politically, it is related to both Southeast Asia and East Asia.
14. Pierluigi Paganini, "China vs Philippines, Cyber War or Activism?" May 3, 2012, http://securityaffairs.co/wordpress/4899/intelligence/china-vs-philippines-cyber-war-or-hacktivism.html. Accessed on February 15, 2015.
15. "China Increases Cyber Attacks on Vietnam During South China Sea Dispute — Vietnam Fears

All-Out Cyber War," *Peace and Freedom Policy and World Ideas*, https://johnib.wordpress.com/2014/05/14/china-increases-cyber-attacks-on-vietnam-during-south-china-sea-dispute-vietnam-fears-all-out-cyber-war/. Accessed on February 15, 2015.

16. "Korea Charts Out National Cyber Security Strategy", *Yonhap*, August 8, 2011, http://www.engilsh.yonhapnews.co.kr/techscience/2011/08/08/45/0601000000AEN20110808006500320f.html. Accessed on February 12, 2015.
17. "Japan Defence Firm Mitsubhushi Heavy in Cyber Attack", *BBC*, September 20, 2011, http://www.bbc.co.uk/news/world-asia-pacific-14982906. Accessed on September 24, 2013.
18. *Annual White Paper 2012*, Ministry of Defence, Tokyo, Japan, http://www.mod.go.jp/e/publ/w_paper/2012.html. Accessed on February 15, 2014.
19. "Operation Snow Man: Deputy Dog Actor Compromises US Veterans of Foreign Wars Website", *FireEye Blog*, February 13, 2014, http://www.fireeye.com/blog/technical/cyber-exploits/2014/02/opearation-snowman-deputydog-actor-compromises-us-veterans-of=foriegn-wars-website.html#more-4514. Accessed on March 30, 2014.
20. Lolita Baldor, "Cyber Cooperation Added to US-Australia Treaty", *Businessweek*, September 15, 2012, http://www.businessweek.com/ap/finacialnews/D9POVN5G0.htm. Accessed on October 25, 2014.
21. Senator Mushahid Hussain, chairman of the Senate Committee on Defence and Defence Production, stated in a seminar on "Defending Pakistan Through Cyber Security Strategy" on July 12, 2013, http://www.dawn.com/news/1023706
22. Ibid.
23. Ibid.
24. http://propakistani.pk/2013/07/09/7-point-action-plan-proposed-for-cyber-secure-pakistan/ as accessed on May 12,2015
25. Samuel Cherian, "Cyber Security: Global, Regional and Domestic Dynamics", *IDSA Monograph Series No. 42,* December 2014, p. 60.
26. Dean Cheng, "The Chinese People's Liberation Army and Special Operations", *Special Warfare*, 25 (3).
27. Ibid.
28. "Obama Tells Intelligence Chiefs to Draw up Cyber Target List – Full Document Text", *The Guardian*, June 7, 2013, http://www.guardian.co.uk/world/interactive/2013/jun/07/obama-cyber-directive-full-text. Accessed on February 12, 2015.
29. "NSA X-Keyscore", Exposed document in http://www.documentcloud.org/documents/743244-Xkeyscore-slidedeck.html. Accessed on August 6, 2013.
30. "Secret Documents: The Special Department TAO NSA Introduces Itself", *Der Spiegel*, December 30, 2013, http://www.spiegel.de/fotostrecke/nsa-documente-die-abteilung-tao-der-nsa-fotstrecke-105355-3.html. Accessed on April 09, 2014.
31. "The ROC: NSA's Epicentre for Computer Network Operations", *SIDtoday*, NSANet, September 6, 2006.
32. "Verizone Forced to Hand Over Telephone Data – Full Court Ruling", *The Guardian*, June 6, 2013, http://www.theguardian.com/world/interactive/2013.jun/06/verizone-telephone-data-court-order. Accessed on March 3, 2014.
33. n. 28.
34. "Inside TAO: Documents Reveal Top NSA Hacking Unit", *Spiegel Online International*, December 29, 2013, http://www.spiegel.de/international/world/the-nsa-uses-powerful-toolbox-in-effort-to-spy-on-global-networks-a-940969.html. Accessed on April 12, 2014.
35. Statement by the Russian participant at the UNIDID Cyber Security Conference, "What does a Stable Cyber Environment Look Like?", Geneva, November 8-9, 2012, http://www.unidir.ch/files/coneference/pdfs/looking-towards-the-future-of-cyber-security-what-does-a-stable-

cyber-invironment-look-like-russian-federation-en-1-794.pdf
36. Cherian Samuel, 'Cybersecurity and cyberwarfare', http://www.india-seminar.com/2013/650/650_cherian_samuel.htm
37. Cherian, n. 22, p. 41.
38. Ibid.
39. https://www.whitehouse.gov/the-press-office/2010/11/08/joint-statement-president-obama-and-prime-minister-singh-india
40. "Towards Stable and Effective Use of Cybespace", Ministry of Defence, Japan, September 2012, p. 2, http://www.mod.go.jp/e/d_act/others/pdf/stable_and_effective_use_of_cyberspace.pdf
41. C Raja Mohan, "Rising India: Partner in Shaping the Global Commons", *TheWashington Quarterly*, 33 (3), pp. 133-148.
42. "NATO in the Cyber Commons", NATO Allied Command Transformation Workshop, Tallinn, Estonia, October 19, 2010.
43. Rahul Prakash and Darshana M. Baruah, "The UN and Cyberspace Governance," *ORF Issue Brief,* No 68, February 2014, http://www.orfonline.org. Accessed on November 20, 2014.
44. http://www.bic-trust.eu/files/2014/04/CYFY-2013-Report-WEB-version-15Apr14.pdf
45. Swing States: As identified by the Centre for International Governance Innovation (CIGI) taking into consideration various factors, including, their voting pattern at the World Conference on International Telecommunication (WCIT) hosted by ITU, memberships to relevant organisations, etc. Tim Maurer, Robert Morgus, "Tipping Scale: An Analysis of Global Swing States in the Internet Governance Debates", Centre for Internet Governance, Canada, Internet Governance Papers, Paper No. 7, 2014.
46. Kaul, n. 2, p. 3.
47. Shivshankar Menon, former national security advisor, GOI, while delivering keynote address at CyFy2013, New Delhi, October 14, 2013.
48. PaulBaran, On Distributed Communications, "RFC's, Internet Request for Comments," http://www.livinginternet.com/i/ia_rfc.htm. Accessed on April 3, 2012.
49. "Recommendations From the IBSA (India-Brazil-South Africa) Multistakeholder Meeting on Global Internet Governance", September 1-2, 2011, Rio de Janeiro, Brazil, http://www.culturalivre.org.br/artigos/IBSA_recommendations_Internet_Governance.pdf. Accessed on February 3, 2015.
50. History page from IAB website, http://www.iab.org/about/history/. Accessed on November 11, 2014.
51. UN Security Council Counter-Terrorism Committee, http://www.un.org/sc/ctc/index.html. See also UN Security Council, "Report of the Counter-Terrorism Committee to the Security Council on the Implementation of Resolution 1624 (2005)' (S/2006/737, September 15, 2006), paras 6, 16, 43, http://daccessdds.un.org/doc/UNDOC/GEN/N06/520/37/PDF/N0652037.pdf?OpenElement.
52. UN Security Council Resolution 1373; reference to "use of communications technologies by terrorists groups", September 28, 2001, para 3 (a), http://www.un.org/News/Press/docs/2001/sc7158.doc.htm.

    UN Security Council Resolution 1624 refers to the need to "prevent terrorists from exploiting sophisticated technology, communications and resources", September 14, 2005, p. 2, http://daccessdds.un.org/doc/UNDOC/GEN/N05/510/52/PDF/N0551052.pdf?OpenElement
53. UN General Assembly, "The United Nations Global Counter-Terrorism Strategy" (A/Res/60/288, September 20, 2006), paras 12(a), 12(b), http://daccessdds.un.org/doc/UNDOC/GEN/N05/504/88/PDF/N0550488.pdf?OpenElement.
54. UN General Assembly, "Creation of a Global Culture of Cyber Security", A/RES/57/239,

December 20, 2002

55. "Message for World Information Society Day: Secretary-General Calls for International Countermeasures to Enhance Cybersecurity", May 17, 2006, http://www.un.org/News/Press/docs/2006/sgsm10433.doc.htm.
56. Rajeswari Pillai Rajgopalan, "Global and National Security Imperatives", *Digital Debates, CYFY Journal*, vol.1, 2013, October 2014, p. 38.
57. ITU was established in Paris in the year 1865 as the International Telegraph Union. It took its present name in the year 1934 and became a specialised agency of the UN. Dr Paul Cornish, *CyberSecurity and Politically, Socially and Religiously Motivated Cyber Attacks* (London: Chathan House, February 2009), p. 18.
58. Hamadoun I. Toure, secretary-general of the International Telecommunication Union and the Permanent Monitoring Panel on Information Security, World Federation of Scientists, "The Quest for Cyber Peace," January 2011, http://www.itu.int/dms_pub/itu-s/opb/gen/S-GEN-WSF.01-1-2011-PDF-E.pdf
59. "ITU Mission", http://www.itu.int/net/about/mission.aspx
60. Ibid.
61. "Global Cybersecurity Agenda Strategic Pillars and Goals", http://www.itu.int/osg/csd/cybersecurity/gca/pillars-goals/index.html. A full account of the aims and activities of the GCA is available in the form of the GCA Global Strategic Report (Geneva: ITU, 2008), http://www.itu.int/osg/csd/cybersecurity/gca/global_strategic_report/global_strategic_report.pdf
62. JoachiKnodt, "Global Cyber (Security) Governance – Facing a Decisive Decade", *Global Policy*, November 5, 2012, http://www.globalpolicyjournal.com/blog/05/11/2012/gg2022-global-cyber-security-governance-%E2%80%93-facing-decisive-decade. Accessed on February 24, 2015.
63. WCIT-12: Conference Overview, http://www.itu.int/en/wcit-12/Pages/overview.aspx
64. Joachi Knodt, "Global Cyber (Security) Governance – Facing a Decisive Decade", *Global Policy*, November 05, 2012, http://www.globalpolicyjournal.com/blog/05/11/2012/gg2022-global-cyber-security-governance-%E2%80%93-facing-decisive-decade. Accessed on February 24, 2015.
65. http://www.un.org/disarmament/HomePage/factsheet/iob/Information_Security_Fact_Sheet.pdf
66. Rahul Prakash and Darshana M. Baruah 'The UN and Cyberspace Governance', *ORF Issue Brief No. 68*, February, 2014. http://cyfy.org/the-un-and-cyberspace-governance/ and http://orfonline.org/cms/export/orfonline/modules/issuebrief/attachments/issuebrief68_1394871027354.pdf
67. Ibid.
68. http://orfonline.org/cms/export/orfonline/modules/issuebrief/attachments/issuebrief68_1394871027354.pdf
69. WSIS Declaration of Principles, December 12, 2003, www.itu.int/dms_pub/itus/md/03/wsis/doc/S03-WSIS-DOC-0004!!PDF-E.pdf. The declaration is also reproduced in this issue of the *Gazette* in the Documentation Section.
70. Kleinwachter, n. 1.

8

South Asian Cyber Security Environment: An Analytical Perspective

E Dilipraj

Prelude

Cyber space, the virtual world of computers and its related technologies, is the new domain of conflicts in the 21st century. With rapidly growing technology and a steadily increasing user base from all walks of life, cyber space is expanding at a fast pace in terms of sheer size as well as vulnerabilities. As the cyber domain was not built with the concept of ensuring security during its genesis, it becomes difficult for the security agencies of the world to induce unsusceptible security mechanisms into such an intense and vibrant realm. As a result of which, it is vulnerable to numerous security threats pertinent to this domain. By the same token, the fact that cyber space operates without boundaries, challenges the very nature of the operating procedures of the real world in terms of governance, maintenance, ownership and legal jurisdictions. Additionally, in recent years, cyber space has been marred by various espionage and surveillance scams by various countries of the world, as revealed by Edward Snowden about the US. Disclosure of facts related to various covert cyber operations by various players has created a tectonic shift in the cyber governance policy of the world which might result in a sea-change in the future of cyber space.

In this scenario, as one of the most vibrant regions of the world, South Asia, actively participates in the world's cyber politics, as both perpetrator and victim of cyber security challenges. However, the South Asian cyber security scenario is dominated not only by the activities of both India and Pakistan but also by the rest of the South Asian countries: Afghanistan, Nepal, Bhutan, Bangladesh, Sri Lanka and Maldives, although these countries remain dormant in this realm. Nevertheless, the sheer size of the user base, the amount of digital information usage and the relevance of this region in the geo-political calculations make it an important case for studying the region's overall cyber security environment. Therefore, this paper aims to study the general cyber environment of the region along with its various cyber security threats, and analyse the existing security initiatives undertaken by the countries of South Asia.

Cyber Landscape of South Asia

The reputation of the South Asian region, especially in the field of security and threats in the physical world is a well established fact. This volatile region is subject to almost all kinds of threats ranging from inter-state wars, terrorism, civil war, insurgency, illicit trafficking of arms, drugs and humans, and water conflicts to environmental degradation, etc. Moreover, in recent years, due to the rapid expansion of cyber space around the world, the threats prevailing in this domain have also started affecting the South Asian region's virtual space, thereby allowing access to a new battlefront for the region's states to defend.

The cyber security threat landscape of South Asia is dominated by threats like data breaches and hacktivism. With the recent revelations of cyber espionage by various countries, this has augmented concerns for the region's cyber security as most of these countries are predominantly identified as 'sitting targets' of such espionage operations. Though South Asia is one of the most populous regions of the world, cyber technology penetration rate is minimal and there is very limited awareness about cyber security. However, the recent developments in mobile technology with internet enabled services have increased the access rate of internet services to more people in this region. Table 1 below shows the statistics of internet and mobile phone subscriptions in each country of South Asia.

Table 1: Internet and Mobile Phone Subscriptions in South Asia

	Fixed (Wired) Broadband		Mobile Phone		
Country	Total Subscriptions (2013)[2]	Subscriptions per 100 inhabitants (2013)[3]	Total Subscriptions (2013)[4]	Subscriptions per 100 inhabitants (2013)[5]	Percentage of Individuals using Internet (2013)[1]
Afghanistan	**1500**	**0.00**	21,588,228	70.00	5.90%
Bangladesh	989,521	**0.63**	**105,051,000**	67.08	6.50%
Bhutan	20,481	2.72	560,890	77.80	29.90%
India	**14,540,000**	**1.16**	886,304,245	70.78	**15.10**
Maldives	**20,140**	5.84	**625161**	181.19	44.10%
Nepal	208,773	0.75	19,864,855	71.46	13.30%
Pakistan	1,077,970	0.59	127,737,286	70.13	10.90%
Sri Lanka	423,522	1.99	**20,315,150**	95.50	21.90%

According to the data given in Table 1, Maldives seems to lead in the percentage of individuals using the internet in their country with 44.10 percent, but the actual number of users, which is approximately 152,155, is much less than the number of users in Afghanistan that has the lowest percentage of individuals using the internet in their country—5.90 percent—which is approximately 1,892,549 users.[6] India has a moderate percentage of 15.10 percent, but the highest number of internet users among the South Asian countries with, approximately 189,073,079 users.[7] This dichotomy between percentage and actual numbers occurs due to the huge difference in the total population of these countries.

However, the number of internet subscribers of a country does not indicate the level of cyber awareness of the population of any country as the latter is analysed based on factors like cyber policies, level of security provided to the cyber infrastructures, and knowledge of cyber security by the users. For instance, India, which has the largest number of internet subscribers in the South Asian region, has faced 15,330 website defacements in 2014 alone.[8] Apart from this, there are other forms of cyber threats faced by the country like cyber frauds, cyber vandalism, cyber bullying, cyber terrorism, etc which all amount to thousands of more incidents.

In fact, the region's Information and Communication Technology (ICT) infrastructures are at a nascent stage and the governments are struggling to provide basic cyber security protection to their national critical information infrastructures which are under persistent cyber threats. Among the eight countries in the region, three countries namely, India, Pakistan and Sri Lanka have an established Computer Emergency Response Team (CERT), which is considered to be the nodal agency for active monitoring and defensive actions to oversee network and system security, ensuring perimeter protection and assuming system/network analysis capabilities. The other five countries have recently initiated setting up of a Computer Incidence Response Team (CIRT) which is a service organisation responsible for receiving, reviewing, and responding to reports of computer security incidents and activity.[9] Due to the existing void in creating a secured environment in the cyber realm, there is a growing trend in the threat landscape to the cyber security of the region. Let us study each country in order to understand in depth the various aspects of cyber security, including cyber threats and government initiatives in their respective cyber domain.

Afghanistan

Afghanistan, which has a fragile political history, continues to struggle in its journey of nation building, especially after the prolonged war since 2001 against the then Taliban regime by the US led allied forces. While the US troops are yet to completely withdraw from the country, the fate of the country is highly debated by the academic community and government officials alike. In this volatile situation, the country has to make inroads into securing the cyber world with utmost caution as this domain would only increase the already existing risks and threats in the country.

However, since 2003, under the transitional administration, followed by a democratically elected government, Afghanistan has made moderate attempts to modernise its ICT domain and has achieved success to some extent. The government has spent approximately US $2,398,763,897 on its telecommunication sector since 2003 and is receiving annual revenue of $200 million from it.[10] The country is also in the process of connecting with the Optical Fibre Cable (OFC): according to government sources, 12 provinces have already been connected with fibre optics network and expansion of this network is underway to connect 20 more provinces. It is expected that, once all the regions of the country are connected to the fibre optics network, the number of internet subscribers would dramatically increase from the current approximate strength of 1,500. Apart from providing intra-state connectivity, the fibre optics network has also connected Afghanistan to its neighbouring countries like Pakistan, Iran, Uzbekistan and Tajikistan. The Afghan government has made an overall investment of $104 million in fibre optics and is reaping annual revenue of $60 million from it.[11] Nevertheless, the internet service is expensive in Afghanistan as the current price of 1 MB internet service costs $35 for the Global System Mobile Communications (GSM) and Internet Service Providers (ISPs) operators.

While the OFC laying process is still underway, the population is highly dependent on mobile phones for internet connectivity. Although it is progress worth welcoming, the fact that mobile based money transfer services like m-paisa, which are slowly creeping into the market, can be used for online trafficking/ cyber trafficking of illicit funds by terrorists, should not be neglected. Moreover, due to lack of stable internet connectivity and also lack of awareness among the public, the Afghan government is unable to provide e-government services. However, the Ministry of Communication and Information Technology (MCIT) has identified a few e-government programmes which would provide value added service and also increase efficiency, effectiveness and transparency in the functioning of the government. The various components of this programme are as follows:

- National ID cards.
- E-governance resource centre.
- Websites for service delivery or interoperability.

- Automated National Registries, including for land ownership, ID cards, passports and other licences.
- Establishing an ICT village.
- Developing electronic government applications.
- Improving ICT training and digital literacy.

Realising the need to secure data location for achieving the above mentioned ambitious e-government programmes, the ministry has set-up state-of-the art infrastructure called the Afghanistan National Data Centre (ANDC), with an investment of $4.7 million, to provide data centre services to the Afghan government for its various ICT applications and systems under the e-government and m-government programmes of the ministry. This facility became operational on October 14, 2009, and offers services like web and e-mail hosting, co-location – providing space for installing customer servers/ racks, dedicated servers for hosting and data back-up services.[12]

The Afghan government has also set up an agency called the "Afghanistan Network Information Centre" under the ICT Directorate, MCIT, which oversees the administration of IP address assignment in association with another agency called the "National Internet Registry of Afghanistan" which is a non-profit government organisation responsible for providing the service of allocating and registering internet resources in the country.[13] The government is also in the process of setting up an AFCERT [Afghanistan Computer Emergency Response Team (CERT)] for detecting, protecting and responding to cyber security threats to the country.

On the policy front, the country has a "Telecom and ICT Policy," framed in 2003 and an "Information and Communication Policy" also framed in the same year. The drafts of the ICT law and "National Cyber Security Strategy" were submitted to the Parliament for its approval by 2014.[14]

Apart from government led initiatives, a few banks in Afghanistan are providing online banking services, but the customers are restricted only to viewing their account details, and are not allowed to do online transactions. Some universities have also introduced courses in computer science and related subjects. Despite various initiatives by the Government of Afghanistan to modernise its ICT infrastructures, the general public is unable to reap much benefit because the initiatives undertaken by the government are mere fundamental steps which do not have much effect on the public. Also, all the government initiatives are focussed on establishing nationwide ICT infrastructures—not on securing the existing networks of communication which has increased the vulnerability of these networks.

In addition to the various initiatives by the government to enhance the cyber security of Afghanistan, the North Atlantic Treaty Organisation's (NATO's) contribution in this process also plays a crucial role. Realising the existing vacuum in cyber expertise in the country, the contribution of NATO focusses on filling up the knowledge gap by organising various seminars, conferences, workshops and training programmes for Afghan officials in order to enhance their knowledge and skills in this highly technical domain. For instance, in 2012, NATO organised a Cyber Defence Training Programme for the Afghan network and system administrators for 10 days. The participants were lectured on topics like security awareness, best practices, and threat identification and response in the cyber realm.[15] In addition to lectures, laboratory sessions were also conducted in which the participants were asked to experiment with responding to attacks and employing defensive measures studied during the course.

Although Afghanistan has not faced any large scale cyber attack so far or at least none has been reported so far, there has been some common misuse of cyber technology. For instance,

- The Afghan Police have received many complaints regarding misuse of SIM cards for making long distance calls without having to pay for them.
- Owing to the recent popularity of credit cards, there have been many instances of credit card frauds.
- In 2008, the Government of Afghanistan banned a web-based pyramid scheme, Quest Net, in which 28,000 Afghans had already become members and had bought a gold coin for five times its price from the organisation's website. It was unveiled to the public that this scheme was a scam masterminded by a Hong Kong based organisation and everyone who had invested in it had lost money.[16]
- There are also various other instances of Denial of Service (DoS) and Distributed Denial of Service (DDoS) attacks, phishing attacks, insider threats and other miniscule hacking incidences in various networks in Afghanistan.

Besides the existing risks and threats to cyber networks and infrastructures of Afghanistan, there are also risks and threats in the cyber domain emanating from the country and threatening targets beyond its borders. Hacker groups like the "Afghan Cyber Army (ACA)", which claims to be the defender of Afghanistan's cyber space in its official Facebook page,[17] have made numerous hacking attacks on various targets which include both government and private websites and networks in Pakistan, the US and China. They have listed their successful hacking attacks in the form of a video in their official YouTube channel.[18] Threats from such hacking groups are irritants to the cyber security of the world as their attacks on any target cannot be predicted or easily detected.

Although the threat landscape of Afghanistan's cyber space seems to be so dire, the prevailing atmosphere is even without the lack of widespread use of cyber resources by the general public for their day to day activities. Once this ratio increases in numbers, the associated risks and threats will also increase proportionately. But, if Afghanistan's officials and policy makers act in the right direction at this present juncture, when the usage is minimal, the country would be able to contain cyber security issues in the future even if the entire population becomes cyber-centric.

Bangladesh

As the most recently emerged sovereign state in the South Asian region, Bangladesh has a very short history of just four decades dominated by political instability and economic recession at many intervals. But in the recent years, under the democratic government, Bangladesh has been able to stabilise its political environment and has taken several steps to boost its economy. For its economic progress, the country has initiated many modernisation processes in which ICT plays an important role. In fact, the policy document named "Perspective Plan of Bangladesh 2010-2021" or in short "VISION 2021", details the policy initiatives to be followed to make Bangladesh a middle income economy. In this document, a chapter called "Digital Bangladesh" is dedicated to ICT initiatives. This idea of Digital Bangladesh was driven by an older ICT policy of the government, called the "National ICT Policy – 2009", prepared by the Ministry of Science and Information and Communication Technology to identify methods to maximise the use of ICT facilities for the growth of the country. In this policy document, it was identified that ICT facilities can be harnessed for achieving the following: social equity, productivity, integrity, education and research employment, strengthening exports, health care, universal access, environment, climate and disaster management and support to ICTs. Although, the policies seem appealing, with an internet penetration rate of merely 6.50 percent, it is not clear as to how the government's ICT initiatives would reach the population.

IT activities began way back in 1993 with the introduction of e-mail services using dial-up connections; Bangladesh tested its internet only in 1996.[19] Owing to the high cost, the usage was initially limited to business users but later it slowly spread to other users too. After the expansion of the optical fibre cable network across the country and the connectivity with submarine optical cable, the country's connectivity, both internationally and internally, increased considerably.

Fig 1: BTCL Optical Fibre Link of Bangladesh

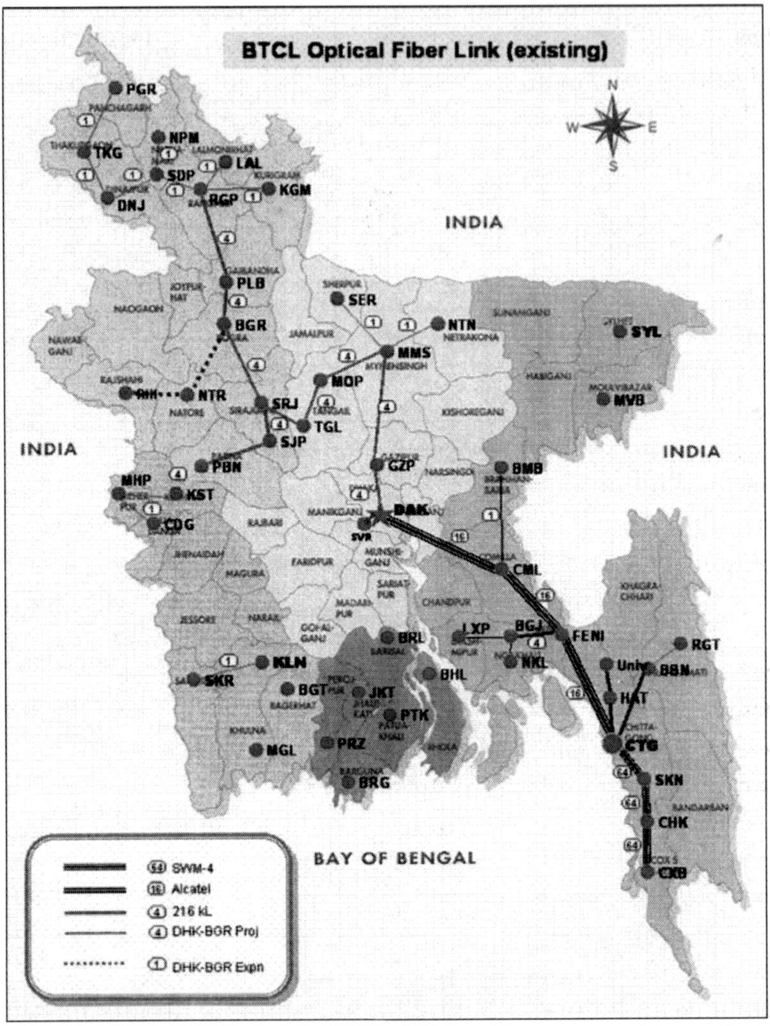

Source: http://www.btcl.gov.bd/home/main/statistics/Optical_Fiber_Network-2009.gif. Accessed on January 24, 2015.

With approximately 989,521 broadband subscribers and approximately 105,051,000 mobile subscribers, the country is currently seen as a possible place for growth of internet usage. The country's government is encouraging cyber activity and has also introduced the e-government framework at the ministerial level. All ministries, divisions, directorates, departments and autonomous organisations have a web presence in the form of websites where all policy documents, forms, circular, orders, notifications and information relevant to the public, etc are posted and regularly updated. Banks in Bangladesh are also providing various e-services like e-banking, e-commerce, e-recruitment, e-tendering, mobile banking, and automated clearing house services.[20]

On the policy front, the country has an Information and Telecommunication Act since 2001 which guides the Bangladesh Telecommunication Regulatory Commission (BTRC) which is the nodal agency for regulating the establishment, operation and maintenance of telecommunication services in the country. In 2009, the Bangladesh government came up with a National Information and Communication Technology Policy for fulfilling the country's "Vision 2021".

Recently, in 2014, the "National Cyber Security Strategy" was released to guide the country's efforts in the cyber world and also to secure its cyber infrastructures. This document is a long-term measure for protecting the country's cyber space against security threats, risks and challenges to national security. The document also outlines a framework for organising and prioritising efforts to manage risks to its cyber space or critical information infrastructure. The document identifies three ways for achieving robust national cyber security: legal measures; technical and procedural measures; and organisational measures.[21]

In spite of various threats to Bangladesh's cyber security, an incident which became an eye opener for the government was the attack on Bangladesh government websites, operating from the Prime Minister's Office (PMO) which was hacked on March 20, 2010. Nineteen out of 64 district portals were hacked allegedly by a hacker pseudo named "*MIL INDIAN HACKER*" who held out the threat of a possible cyber war.[22] Although the websites were retrieved after 16 hours, the widespread hacking of government websites alerted policy makers, and, as a result, two committees were formed after a high level meeting was held at the PMO on March 29, 2010. The committees which were formed were: one for formulating a policy regarding cyber security and the second for taking the necessary steps, if a cyber attack takes place.

Other cyber security threats that affect Bangladesh include threats from malicious software, electronic fraud, web defacement, e-mail account hacking, identity thefts, cyber espionage, phishing, credit card frauds, DoS and DDoS attacks, etc.[23]

With the growing trend in internet connectivity and also with the increase in nomadic connectivity through mobile technology, the country will become more vulnerable to various risks and threats in the cyber realm in the future. With the government's goal for digitalising the nation, it should also be ready to face the challenges emanating from the domain. Though the country is producing policies related to ICT, successful execution of these would actually create a safer situation. Also, the country should focus on improving and increasing the number of its technical experts and in enhancing the capabilities of its CERT organisation. Moreover, there is an immediate need for robust cyber security legal frameworks in the form of concrete laws which will not only act as deterrents but also provide legal solutions to the government on the cyber front.

Bhutan

Bhutan, a landlocked country sandwiched between two giants, China and India, is one of the most isolated countries of the world but which has close relations with India. This country is, in fact, majorly dependent on India for a large part of its economy and national defence. With a constitutional monarchy form of government, Bhutan is the only country in the world that calculates its growth in terms of Gross National Happiness Index. Being a self-isolated country, due to the traditional inward looking and conservative approach, Bhutan had remained a nation untouched by the dramatic modernisation process till the end of the 20th century. Bhutan was, in fact, one of the last countries in the world to get television, which was permitted by the government only in 1999. It was in the same year that the government allowed internet technology to venture into Bhutan which enabled a proper digital link between this mountainous state and the rest of the world.

Realising the need for modernising the country, the Government of Bhutan made serious efforts and invested substantially in the telecommunication sector from 1996 to 2001. Since 2001, Bhutan Telecom, the government telecom operator company, has made efforts to initiate the country's mobile phone technology and achieved a breakthrough in 2003, when it was able to provide coverage to five towns, including the capital, Thimphu. This limited coverage slowly started spreading to other towns too and with the advent of private telecom service provider 'Tashi Group' starting their service in 2008, the mobile network expanded rapidly.[24]

According to the "Bhutan e-Government Master Plan", a policy document from the Government of Bhutan released in January 2014, the country is in the process of implementing its National Broadband Masterplan connecting all 20 Dzongkhags (administrative districts) and 205 Gewogs (groups of villages under districts) of Bhutan. It is also stated that more than 90 government organisations are connected through the Thimpu Wide Area Network (WAN) for secure, efficient and reliable communication across all public agencies in the capital. This WAN is accessible only in the capital but the government is considering expanding this network to all 20 Dzongkhangs of the country. Also, all the 10 ministries of the Bhutan central government and the local governments of 20 Dzongkhags are equipped with video conferencing facilities for easy communication and with the aim of contributing towards realising the role of ICT in enhancing good governance. In addition, on March 26, 2012, Bhutan gained a second International Gateway at Gelephu, which paved the way for increased internet speed for the country. Bhutan was earlier connected to the internet through its only international gateway at Phuentsholing.[25]

Moreover, for realising the country's dream of achieving greater capabilities in ICT and to create more opportunities for the country's future generations, the Royal Government of Bhutan opened the country's first IT Park at Babesa on November 1, 2011. This IT Park, also known as Thimpu Tech Park, operates with the mission to attract respected IT/ITES companies from both within Bhutan and around the world to work in a stimulating environment which provides opportunities for technology based collaboration, learning and innovation. This Tech Park also houses the Bhutan Innovation and Technology Centre (BITC), aimed to function as a business incubator for new start-ups and a shared technology centre – as a one-stop shop for business ventures in Bhutan for their technical needs and as a data centre for data storage and management for the government and the private sectors.[26] However, it is widely opined that it will take a few more years for this Tech Park to become fully operational and it is highly unlikely that foreign companies will venture into the ICT sector of Bhutan due to the lack of market attraction and lack of expertise in the ICT sector among the local population.

The country does not have any agency that can detect, track and mitigate any possible cyber attack on its cyber infrastructures. As mentioned earlier, the country also has an insufficient number of experts in the ICT sector. However, according to the policy document "Bhutan e-Government Master Plan", it is identified that there are 350 highly professional ICT experts in the Government of Bhutan under the Department of Information Technology and Telecom.[27] Apart from these claimed experts, there is no other agency which can secure the country's cyber space. This void in security has opened the gates for all sorts of cyber threats and intrusions into the country without being detected. Bhutan's government sites are prone to hacking from time to time and other sites of the country are not safe either. In fact, while researching for this paper, it was found that the official blog of the Thimpu Tech Park was allegedly hacked by a hacker who goes by the pseudo name '*Latino Saber*'.

Fig 2: Screenshot of the Hacked Site.

Source: http://www.thimphutechpark.com/blog/. Accessed March 1, 2015.

Moreover, Bhutan's cyber space is infested with all sorts of malware and spyware like GhostNet which creates an insecure cyber environment for the country. Individual users of the internet are prone to online scams and other social engineering methods of cyber thefts and cyber crimes like the Nigerian 419 scams and phishing due to lack of proper cyber awareness among the general public.

On the legal front, there is no comprehensive cyber law yet and ICT related crimes are tried under the existing penal code of Bhutan. All provisions related to cyber security are generally referred to the Bhutan Information Communication and Media Act 2006 (BICMA) under Chapter 7 – Provisions Relating to Cyber Issues. The BICMA is expected to be amended after being submitted to the Parliament and the amended Act would make way for a cyber security agency tentatively named the Bhutan Computer Incidence Response Team (BCIRT), which might become the nodal agency for addressing all cyber related issues in Bhutan, if established.[28]

However, the Royal Bhutan Police has taken the initiative to temporarily fill the existing gap in cyber security. It has set up a sub-division to deal with cyber security and the police officers are trained to deal with various forms of cyber crimes. Moreover, under the aegis of Prime Minister Tshering Tobgay, a separate cyber unit monitored by the attorney general was planned to be set up on August 31, 2014 after a high-level meeting in the PMO.[29]

Despite these initiatives, cyber security will remain an unachieved capability in Bhutan until at least the next decade due to lack of proper awareness, resources and expertise, and also because of the fast changing nature of cyber space which would be difficult for Bhutan to catch up with. Also, Bhutan's overreliance on India for everything makes the case worse as India itself is struggling to keep its cyber space secure from various high level threats. However, due to the landlocked nature of its location, and geo-demographic constraints, including harsh terrain and small scattered population, Bhutan is forced to rely on its traditional partner, India, for any sort of assistance in the cyber domain and also in other fields. Therefore, Bhutan's development in the ICT sector is highly dependent on Indian support and strategy for this 'happy' country.

India

India, the second most populous country and one of the leading developing nations of the world is clearly much advanced in terms of technology, policy and legal measures, and by virtue of institutional / organisational frameworks in the cyber space, compared to its South Asian counterparts. It has, in fact, the largest number of internet subscribers and mobile phone users in the South Asian region owing to its massive population. Moreover, according to the website 'Internet World Stats,' India has the third largest number of internet users in the world after China and the United States of America.[30] India is one of the leading exporters of IT products and has a large IT industry, worth billions of dollars in the country.

The ICT sector in India is considered as one of the crown jewels of the country as it contributes a huge share for the economy, creates a lot of employment, generates huge profits for the companies and enables easy communication for the people. Internet was introduced to India on August 15, 1995, in Delhi. Since then, the user base has grown rapidly and reached a total of 85.74 million subscribers in December 31, 2014.[31] Similar is the case of the number of mobile phone subscriptions which has increased tremendously and comprised more than 943.97 million subscribers on December 31, 2014.[32] Both government and private service providers have large numbers of customers. 'Bharti', in association with Airtel, is the leading mobile network service provider and BSNL, the state owned company, is the largest service provider of wired telephone service in the country.

Fig 3: Market Share of Mobile Phone Network Service Providers

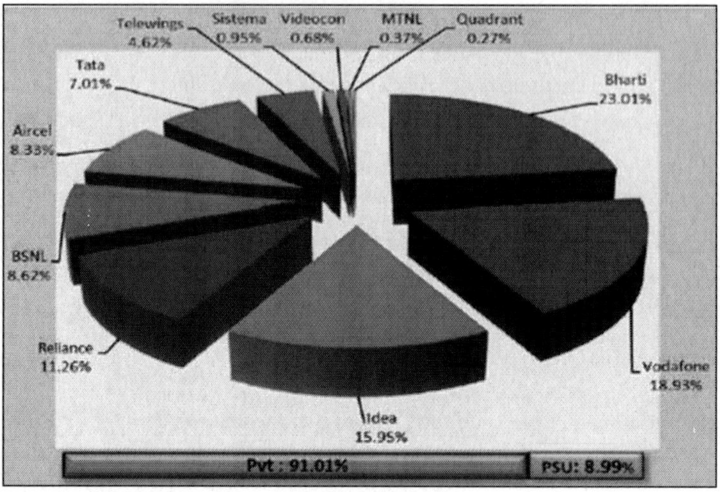

Source: Press release on "Highlights on Telecom Subscription Data as on December 31, 2014", Telecom Regulatory Authority of India, Press Release No 11/2015, February 6, 2015.

Fig 4: Market Share of Wire Line Telephone Service Providers

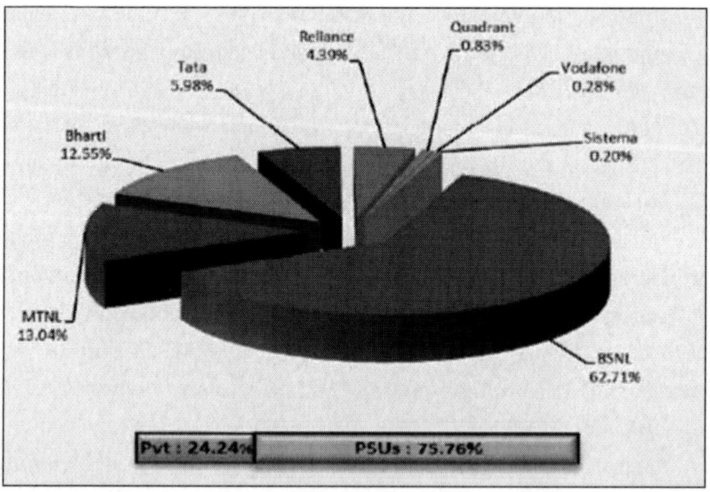

Source: Press release on "Highlights on Telecom subscription Data as on December 31, 2014", Telecom Regulatory Authority of India, Press Release No 11/2015, February 6, 2015.

The widespread use of smart mobile phones has increased the number of internet users of the country in recent years. As a result, the internet market has expanded rapidly, in which both public and private companies are reaping profits. This has, however, not reduced the number of wired internet subscribers of the country. Given below is a graphical representation of the service provider market share of broadband service providers, including both wired and wireless services in India.

Fig 5: Service Providers' Market Share for Broadband (Wired + Wireless) Service

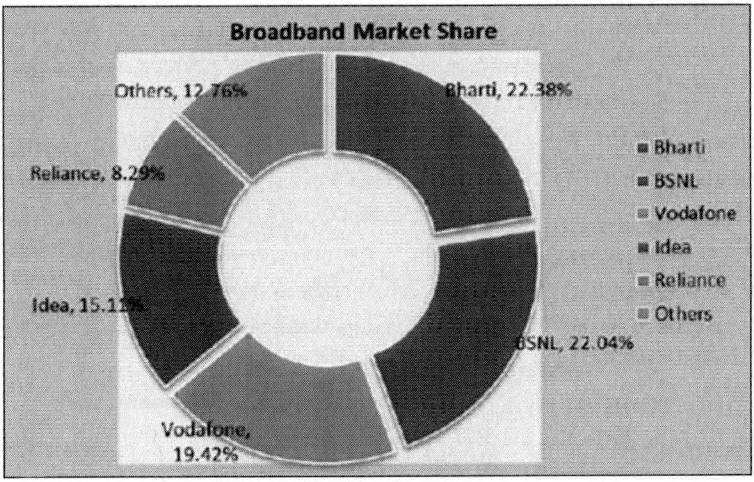

Source: Press release on "Highlights on Telecom Subscription Data as on December 31, 2014", Telecom Regulatory Authority of India, Press Release No 11/2015, February 6, 2015.

The Government of India has taken the necessary steps in making the ICT technology available to all parts of the country. Moreover, the Indian IT industry is a huge contributor to the economy of the country, amounting to more than Rs 108 billion during the financial year 2013.[33] The country houses some of the leading IT companies like Wipro, Tata Consultancy Services, Infosys, etc which are world leaders of the industry. Every year, the country produces large numbers of IT professionals who either work in India or abroad. However, the real number of IT experts in the country remains low or to put in other words, they are yet to be identified and their expertise tapped. Moreover, the country offers a number of e-government services which are growing in number from time to time. And almost all the banks in the country offer online banking and also mobile banking services to their customers.

The ICT sector of the country is governed by the central government through the Ministry of Communications and Information Technology. The ministry has three departments, namely:

- Department of Telecommunications (DoT).
- Department of Electronics and Information Technology (DeitY).
- Department of Posts.

DoT operates with the vision to provide secure, reliable, affordable and high quality converged telecommunication services anytime, anywhere for an accelerated inclusive socio-economic development.[34] And DeitY operates towards the mission to promote e-governance for empowering citizens, promoting the inclusive and sustainable growth of the electronics, IT & ITES industries, enhancing India's role in internet governance, adopting a multi-pronged approach that includes development of human resources, promoting R&D and innovation, enhancing efficiency through digital services and ensuring a secure cyber space.[35]

On the policy front, in terms of legal aspects, India has made deep inroads in order to regulate, manage and ably secure the ICT environment. A few highlighting policies and legal mechanisms by India in the ICT sector are as follows:

- With the entry of the private sector coming into the telecom industry in the country in the late 20th century, India framed its Telecom Regulatory Act 1997 to regulate telecom services, including fixation/revision of tariffs for telecom services.
- Starting from day one, the ICT sector in India progressed at a fast pace. In order to guide the country's growing sector, the Government of India formulated its first Information Technology Act 2000, and amended certain aspects of the law through the IT (Amendment) Act 2008. Thus, India was able to legally manage a rapidly developing sector since its beginning.
- The National Cyber Security Policy (NCSP), 2013, was released on July 2, 2013, with a vision to build a secure and resilient cyber space for citizens, businesses and government activities and also to integrate the various events taking places in the highly dynamic cyber arena of the country. This policy is an overview of the government's approach and strategy for protection of cyber space in the country.[36]
- On July 19, 2013, the National Technical Research Organisation (NTRO), which is the technical intelligence agency operating under the supervision of the Prime Minister's Office (PMO), released the Guidelines for Securing the National Critical Information Infrastructures (NCII) of the country. Having identified 14 critical information infrastructures like energy, transportation, banking/ finance, telecommunication, defence, space, etc, the NTRO guidelines created a framework for securing these infrastructures all over the country.[37]

- Also, in September 2013, India achieved another milestone in the field of cyber security by becoming an 'authorising nation' for IT products from its previous status of a mere 'consuming nation'. In less academic terms, it can be stated that all those IT products that are certified in India can be authorised to be used in the 26 member countries of the Common Criteria Recognition Arrangements (CCRA) without having them retested.[38]

India has set up various agencies responsible for developing and safeguarding the ICT infrastructures and services of the government. The following agencies function under the Department of Electronics and Information Technology:

- **National Informatics Centre:** This is responsible for the government's e-governance programmes and for providing institutional linkages with all the ministries / departments of the central government, 35 state governments/ union territories, and about 625 district administrations of India.[39]
- **Standardisation Testing and Quality Certification Directorate:** This provides quality assurance services in the area of electronics and IT through a countrywide network of laboratories and centres. The services include testing, calibration, IT and e-governance, training and certification to public and private organisations. Apart from this, the agency also provides training programmes.[40]
- **Controller of Certifying Authorities:** This is the agency for authorising and regulating electronic transactions and digital signatures.
- **CERT-IN**: This is the Computer Emergency Response Team-India, which is the nodal agency responsible for prevention, detection, and recovery, for computer related incidents.

The Indian Army is also setting up a Cyber Command for the armed forces of the country in order to deal with the growing threat of cyber warfare and to provide a robust network security for the country's sensitive defence networks.

Despite the various initiatives taken by the Government of India, the cyber threat landscape of the country remains volatile. The country's cyber infrastructures and the domain itself face a host of threats which pose a great challenge for the nation. The various threats affecting India's cyber security include data theft, malwares, hacking, web defacements, identity thefts, online financial frauds, e-mail spoofing, social engineering scams, DOS and DDOS attacks, unauthorised access to critical infrastructures of the country, online surveillance and digital espionage. For instance, CERT-IN handled 71,780 incidents in 2013 caused by various cyber threats related to the cyber security of the country.[41] While many web defacements are emanating from Pakistan, unauthorised intrusions into sensitive Indian networks also emanate from countries like China, the USA and a few others. It was identified that India was the fifth most snooped country by the USA through its digital surveillance programme that was revealed in mid-2013. Various fatal malwares like Stuxnet, Duqu, flame, etc which have the capability to deflate the critical infrastructures of the country, have also been indentified from different Indian networks.

The abovementioned threat landscape clearly describes the vulnerability of cyber space in India. Despite the various government initiatives, India is unable to reduce the threats due to lack of awareness related to cyber security among the general public. Effectively addressing this issue would help reduce the threat level to the cyber security of the country by many degrees. The country also lacks in implementing stringent policies. It was identified in the National Cyber Security Policy 2013 that India would need 500,000 cyber security experts by 2018. While the government claims to have created a National Security Database, which consists of a verified list of credible and trustworthy 'ethical' hackers who would respond during distress, the country does not have a mechanism to identify new talent in this field.[42] Although the country produces a large number of IT professionals every year, it remains an unanswered question as to how many of these professionals would qualify to be an expert in the field. Also, there is overlapping of functionality by different agencies. It is opined by many legal experts that the country's cyber laws are obsolete, with some being vague in nature. Addressing these issues would help India achieve a robust cyber security environment in the longer run.

Maldives

Maldives, a country which comprises 1,192 islands, is facing slow extinction from the face of the earth due to the rise in sea level as a result of the global climate change. Ironically, this country is one of the most popular tourist destinations—tourism is the largest contributor to the country's Gross Domestic Product (GDP). In order to provide comprehensive tourism services, the country has made serious efforts and ICT developments form a part of it. Starting in 2001, under the Telecommunication Policy 2001-2005, the government aimed to address the digital divide within the country. Through this policy, the country gained basic infrastructure of, and awareness about, the ICT sector. Later, under the Telecommunication Policy 2006-2010, the facilities started spreading to different parts of the country, now reaching more islands, without any discriminatory charges.

Until 2005, Maldives relied on satellite technology (VSAT) for its internet. In 2005, the government revisited its policy and gave approval to connect the country to the international optical fibre cable network. As a result, in 2006, Maldives got its internet with the Dial-up connection through Dhiraagu, a telecommunication company created as a joint venture between the Government of Maldives and a private company. Since then, the internet has advanced rapidly in the country especially in the capital, Malé, and other populous islands. Two forms of broadband internet service are available in the capital and in many islands. They are (i) ADSL based broadband services through fixed-line telephone; and (ii) broadband through Cable TV (CATV) networks. Recently, the introduction of GPRS and EDGE based services in the mobile communications technology has enhanced the number of mobile internet users in Maldives, creating a nomadic communication culture in the country.[43]

All the inhabited islands are connected to one another through some sort of network. The government initiated project "Government Network of Maldives" (GNM) consists of the physical and logical infrastructure enabling data exchange between government and government related organisations and the e-government service platform in a secure and reliable way. The long list of e-government services offered by the Maldives government include services like registration of births, driving licence renewals, attestation of certificates, ambulance services, senior citizens allowances, housing registrations, police reports, import/ export declaration processes, appeal for court cases, registration of tourist resorts, etc. Maldives has now become the leading country in the South Asian region with the highest rate of e-government readiness. Apart from the above mentioned services, the Bank of Maldives, the national bank of the country, since August 2007, offers its customers internet banking services along with other credit card and debit card services. Additionally, the Maldives Monetary Authority (MAA), the central bank of Maldives, has encouraged mobile banking facility since 2008.[44]

As a new entrant into the ICT sector, Maldives has taken steps to develop its ICT resources in terms of software developing and enhancing its human resources. It was for this purpose that the National Centre for Information Technology (NCIT) was set up on March 25, 2003, with a mission to lead the nation in developing an IT culture and to proactively harness IT for the socio-economic development of the country.[45] Under this programme, an IT incubator facility was established for enabling an environment for start-ups and entrepreneurs in the field of ICT.

However, Maldives does not have any sort of cyber security agency or cyber threat detection and mitigation centre. As a result, the country is vulnerable to almost all sorts of cyber crimes, ranging from credit/debit card frauds, phishing, hacking and defacement of websites, unauthorised access into the country's cyber networks, social engineering frauds, cyber stalking, and other cyber related crimes. The Maldivian government websites are often prone to hacking and defacement by various hackers due to the lack of effective security mechanisms. For instance, the website of the Maldivian National Defence Forces (MNDF) was hacked and defaced by unknown hackers on October 5, 2014.[46] This is evidence of the fact that not even the military networks of Maldives are secure. However, the Department of Defence and the Maldives Police Service have initiated a cyber crime project in 2008, reportedly with assistance from the US Federal Bureau of Investigation (FBI). Although this unusual assistance from the FBI to this miniscule country to combat cyber crime raises a few questions about its intentions and real agenda behind the project, it is unclear as to how much ground this project has really covered.

On the legal front, the country does not have any cyber laws but is keen on developing them. When situations arise, the cases related to cyber crime are dealt with by the ordinary penal code of the country. The country also lacks cyber security expertise—the existing expertise is limited to a very few people. The fact that the country does not provide high-tech cyber related courses in its universities to its students is also responsible for the dearth of expertise in the country.

Maldives is fast growing in the cyber world in terms of usage but is lagging behind in terms of security in this domain. The government initiatives are aimed more towards spreading the usage of the technology which would help in increasing the revenue rather than securing the networks. The government's attitude is understandable as the country itself is facing a severe threat to its very existence, and is in dire need of revenues for its dream project of buying new lands for resettlement. However, the Maldivian government should also take cognisance of the fact that a highly sophisticated cyber attack can be as devastating as a natural disaster like a tsunami.

Nepal

Nepal is again a landlocked country like Bhutan in South Asia, sandwiched between China and India. Like Bhutan, this country also rejected its traditional monarchical form of government and turned to the parliamentary system in 2007. Since the untimely death of King Birendra, the country's political environment has been unstable. Unlike Bhutan, Nepal is not only dependent on India, but also influenced by China. The same reflects in the two optical fibre cables which form the backbone of internet connectivity in the country.

The country successfully established an 'East-West Optical Fibre Link' connecting from Bhadrapur in the east to Mahendranagar in the west which runs along the East-West National Highway. Telecommunications Consultant India Limited, an Indian agency, assisted Nepal in this project since 2002, both technically and financially. Other important cities in Nepal including Birtamod, Kakarbhitta, Butwal, Kaligandaki, Pokhara, Damauli and Kathmandu were also connected through the second phase of the above mentioned project. Nepal got its first international optical link connectivity when its 'East West Optical Fibre Link' was connected to India's international optical link gateway. Realising the need for having more international connectivity, Nepal extended its optical fibre cable to China through Tatopani, along the Araniko highway connecting Bhaktapur, Banepa and Dhulikhel. This project was assisted by the Chinese government.[47]

With the successful completion of these infrastructural developments, especially on the cable front, the number of broadband internet subscribers began to increase in the country which reached 208,773 total subscriptions by the end of 2013. Apart from broadband, other methods like dial-up, leased line, VSAT, GPRS and wireless hotspots are also provided by more than 44 Internet Service Providers (ISPs) across the country for their subscribers to connect to the internet. However, in recent years, use of mobile phones has been increasing in Nepal with the advent of the internet and other services inbuilt with this technology. Mobile companies in Nepal offer services like fund transfers and bill payments. Mobile banking service has also been introduced in Nepal by Laxmi Bank. Other leading banks of the country offer internet banking services to their customers.

Nevertheless, Nepal's government has not been able to harness the ICT sector for e-government services to the people. Low literacy rate, low per capita income, poor ICT infrastructure, insufficient human resources, lack of political will and commitment by the leadership, and insufficient financial resources are thought to be the constraints that have stopped the Government of Nepal from implementing e-governance in Nepal.[48]

Therefore, the internet and mobile technology are used by the general public of Nepal only for day-to-day communication, general browsing and other social media activities. Although, there is an upward trend in the private sector's participation in the IT sector, it is limited to a few small scale software companies, Business Process Outsourcing (BPO) and call centres owned by Nepali citizens. There is lack of foreign investment or joint ventures in the IT industry of the country.

The cyber threat perception of Nepal comprises a host of malwares distributed through spam mails and other infested plug and play devices, electronic fraud, website hacking and defacement, online accounts hacking, phishing, etc. Government and business websites are the most targeted by hackers and defacers. Social engineering scams like the infamous 'Nigerian 419 scam' are common, resulting in financial losses to the victims. There is a lack of awareness related to cyber security among the public and the government also has no mechanism to curb the prevailing and growing cyber crime in the country. The country also lacks in technically qualified human resource as a result of lack of education and proper means of training in the field of cyber technology.[49] The only exception is the Kathmandu Metropolitan Police Department, which has set up a separate cyber cell to deal with criminal cases involving cyber technology. However, their expertise to deal with such cases is still questionable.

On the policy front, the country's information technology and communications are primarily based on the Telecommunications Act 1997 followed by the Telecommunications Regulations 1997 and Telecommunications Policy 2004. In December 2006, Nepal released its Electronic Transaction Act which is also domestically known as Nepal's Cyber Law. Apart from defining, authorising and legalising electronic records and digital signatures, this Act also deals with computer offences/ cyber crimes like online piracy, hacking, physical and virtual damage to cyber infrastructures and also delineates punishments for such offences. Though the Act is considered to be in its nascent stage, it is a welcome move toward formulating guiding principles from the initial stages of growth of cyber space in the country.

Due to lack of an agency for dealing with cyber security in the country, in 2014, a group of IT experts of Nepal created an organisation called the Information Technology Security Emergency Response Team-Nepal (ITSERT-NP) with the aim of providing immediate assistance in case of a cyber mishap and also to increase awareness among the stakeholders regarding the challenges in cyber security. The organisation also aims to bring all cyber security experts of the country under one roof.[50]

In short, Nepal's cyber environment and cyber security environment is in a chaotic condition due to lack of proper government mechanisms. Although internet usage is increasing, lack of proper regulations creates favourable conditions for anti-social elements to misuse the technology. It is time for Nepal's government to initiate appropriate steps to regulate the country's cyber space on the right track in order to have a secured cyber space in the future.

Pakistan

The Islamic Republic of Pakistan, another country from the Asian region, is infamous for its frequent military coups, hostility and wars with India, and its support to, and harbouring of, terrorist operations and terrorists, including Osama Bin Laden. Being the sixth largest populated country in the world, Pakistan's telecommunication network is expanding rapidly every year. The "Pakistan Telecommunication Authority" (PTA) is the nodal agency overseeing the internet and telecommunication of the country as a whole. This agency was formed as a result of the "Telecommunication Reorganisation Act 1996" and is responsible for monitoring telecommunication traffic, blocking and filtering content on the internet, and providing licences to internet service providers in the country.

Pakistan's internet network is connected to rest of the world through landing points of international submarine cable systems – SEA-ME-WE-3 and SEA-ME-WE-4, 3 Intelsat satellite earth stations, three international gateway exchanges (two in Karachi and one in Islamabad) and microwave radio relay to neighbouring countries.[51] Beginning with e-mail services in 1992-93, the internet in Pakistan has expanded over the years, and the subscriber base is of over two million. Fast expanding mobile phone technology is to be credited for the increase in internet usage in the country as most people access the internet through their mobile phones. In fact, Pakistan has one of the highest penetration rates of mobile phones in the South Asian region. Out of the six mobile network providers, Mobilink leads the market, amounting to 28 percent of the total subscribers of the country. Several banks in Pakistan provide online and mobile banking facilities and Telenor, the mobile network service provider also offers a mobile wallet service called "Easypaisa". However, the e-government services in Pakistan are yet to gain momentum owing to lack of awareness and poor usage rate in the rural regions. At present, e-government services are limited to application processing, salary distribution through ATMs, IT related services between ministries and government offices in different provinces, and submission of documents, etc.

While an overall developing ICT environment in Pakistan is a welcome factor, it comes with its own disadvantages, causing issues for the cyber security, not only of the country but of the whole cyber world. Pakistan faces a host of cyber security threats which include:

- hacking and web defacement;
- online financial frauds (credit/ debit card frauds, online money laundering);
- cyber stalking;
- cyber bullying;
- DOS and DDOS attacks;
- unauthorised intrusion into critical information infrastructure networks;
- malwares;
- social engineering threats;
- digital surveillance and espionage, etc.

However, Pakistan is not only a vulnerable state in terms of cyber threats but is also one of the most prolific perpetrators of cyber threats. The world cyber community is well aware of the hostile situation between the hackers of Pakistan and India who at times create panic in each other's cyber space.

The Government of Pakistan has not shown adequate interest in providing capable legal and policy initiatives to support the operations of the cyber security related agencies in the country. Two existing laws that have reference to cyber crime are the Pakistan Telecommunication Reorganisation Act 1996 and Electronic Transaction Ordinance 2002.[52]

The Prevention of Electronic Crime Ordinance 2009 was another ordinance which elapsed in November 2009, due to the lethargic nature of the government. This lapse has limited the activities of Pakistan's cyber security agency, the National Response Centre for Cyber Crime (NR3C), which is currently based on the Electronic Transaction Ordinance 2002.[53] In 2014, the "National Cyber Security Council Bill" was introduced in the Pakistani Senate in order to establish a National Cyber Security Council to develop and draft policies, guidelines and governance models related to cyber security of the country in the future. However, this Bill failed to see the light of the day as the Ministry of Information Technology did not approve of it, terming it as "anti-state" and "against national security". Thus, it can be said that Pakistan does not have an adequate legal framework to support cyber security in the country.

The NR3C is the law enforcement agency under the Federal Investigating Agency of Pakistan that is responsible for fighting against cyber crime in the country. This agency is touted to have expertise in digital forensics, technical investigation, information system security audits, penetration testing and training. The agency provides a 24x7 support helpdesk for cyber crime reporting and it is the leading agency in Pakistan related to cyber security.[54] Pakistan also has a Computer Emergency Response Team (CERT) known as 'PakCERT' which helps in prevention, detection and recovery from computer emergency situations. It also provides coordination, cooperation and information sharing related to computer security information, tools and techniques, to various government and private sector organisations. The agency is also a member of the Asia-Pacific Security Incident Response Coordination Working Group (APSIRC-WG), a multinational organisation working towards cyber security of the region.[55] However, the operational expertise of PakCERT remains unproven. Pakistan has also established a cyber warfare unit in its air force.[56]

Nevertheless, Pakistan's cyber environment is strictly monitored by its government agencies under the pretext of national security and religion. As mentioned earlier, PTA is the nodal agency in Pakistan that monitors, blocks and filters internet and mobile networks whenever the government feels the need for it. According to a few reports, more than 40,000 websites are blocked in Pakistan, including the most famous video hosting website YouTube. The has been blocked since September 18, 2012, following the posting of a video "The Innocence of Muslims," a film deemed to be blasphemous and against Islam. In order to determine what online content should be blocked, the "Inter-Ministerial Committee for the Evaluation of Websites" was created within the framework of the Information Technology Ministry in 2006. Mass blocking of mobile phone services has also become a norm in Pakistan during important religious or political events under the excuse of national security.[57]

On the whole, Pakistan's cyber environment is expanding in terms of usage but the lack of government initiatives to secure the cyber space has left the domain vulnerable to serious threats from various sources. Also, uncontrolled and unprotected cyber space in Pakistan is a threat to the cyber security of the world because of the number of threats emanating from the country. Terrorist and other anti-social elements present in Pakistan are ably exploiting the situation for their operational needs, thereby worsening the scenario. While an unstable Pakistan is considered to be a serious threat to the region, the same epithet applies to cyber space as this domain also has similar capacity to damage the lives of people. Therefore, it is high time for Pakistan to think about framing legal and policy initiatives for securing its cyber space and enhancing the capabilities of its agencies working in this realm.

Sri Lanka

Sri Lanka, the island nation situated south of India in the Indian Ocean Region had a disturbed history in the recent past, marred by a civil war between the government forces and the rebel-LTTE (Liberation Tigers of Tamil Eelam) forces. Despite a war-torn situation, the country has surprisingly made good advances in the ICT sector, especially through measures undertaken by the government.

Internet and e-mail services were first introduced in Sri Lanka in 1996 by Sri Lanka Telecom. By 2000, 15 cities were connected by optical link cable and this infrastructural development kept expanding with time. In 2006, Sri Lanka started its local operations of the landmark SEA ME WE 4 submarine cable system and in the same year, two submarine cables were operational between Sri Lanka and India and Sri Lanka and Maldives. In 2010, a year after the end of the civil war, the optical fibre link cable infrastructure was expanded to the northern peninsula too which was earlier the breeding ground of the rebellion.[58] However, fixed line broadband usage is limited to the urban areas and the penetration of this service in the rural areas is poor.

Nevertheless, the mobile phone usage rate is high in the country—as high as 95.50 subscriptions for every 100 people, largely used for internet connectivity. Dialog, Mobitel, Etisalat, Airtel and Hutch are the mobile network service providers in the country. Dialog, the leading mobile network service provider, with a subscriber base of over seven million also offers a mobile wallet service called EZ cash.[59] Many Sri Lankan banks offer online banking facilities to their customers.

In 2002, the government launched the "e-Sri Lanka" project, tasked with the mission of developing an ICT roadmap for the country. This roadmap led to the implementation of the Information and Communication Technology Act 2003 (ICTA). Under this Act, the Information and Communication Technology Agency of Sri Lanka was established to lead the country's cyber initiatives.

Fig 6: Design of e-Sri Lanka Project

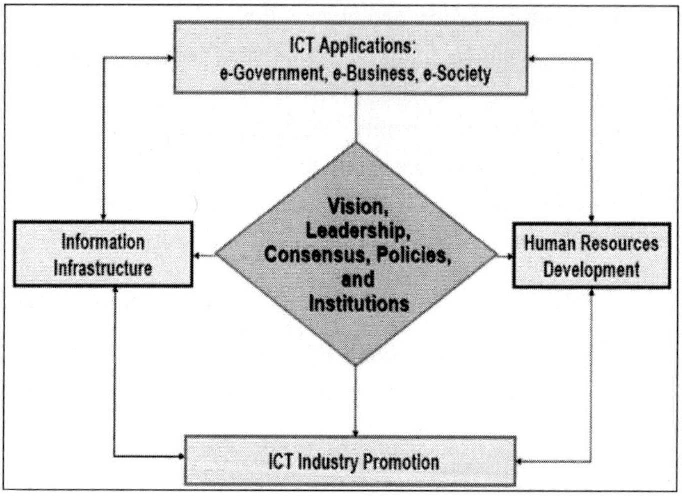

Source: ICTA

As follow-ups for ICTA, a few more Acts like the Intellectual Property Act (No 36 of 2003), Payment and Settlement Systems Act (No 28 of 2005), Electronic Transactions Act (No 19 of 2006), Payment Devices Frauds Act (No 30 of 2006) and Computer Crimes Act (No 24 of 2007) were implemented by the Sri Lankan government. The Computer Crimes Act 2007 provides identification methods for computer crimes and also provides procedures and prevention mechanisms for such crimes in the country. This Act primarily focusses on computer-related crimes and hacking and defacing offences, and other content related crimes are addressed using the penal code and other provisions.[60]

Other government initiatives include the setting up of the Telecommunication Regulatory Commission Sri Lanka (TRCSL) with the aim of providing advanced and high quality telecommunication service throughout the country at an affordable price. The Information and Communication Technology Agency of Sri Lanka is closely working with TRCSL on various infrastructural development projects, various policies implementations and providing ICT training at various levels with the aim of making Sri Lanka a tech-savvy nation. The government is also encouraging the domestic IT based industry to produce software and other products for export which can boost the economy. Sri Lanka's profile as one of the 'outsourcing' destinations for IT related jobs has been moving in a positive trend in recent years.

However, the cyber landscape of Sri Lanka, like in other countries, faces various threats from different sources. Some common offences that threaten the cyber security of the country are malwares, phishing, hacking, defacement of both government and other non-government websites, DOS/ DDoS attacks, hate/ threat mails, identity and information thefts, etc. There have also been cases of credit/ debit card frauds and social engineering scams.

With realisation of the need for a secure cyber space and to protect its cyber users from the existing threats, Sri Lanka has established the "Sri Lanka Computer Emergency Readiness Team | Coordination Centre" (SLCERT | CC). The SLCERT | CC offers its services with the objectives of responsiveness, awareness and consultancy. The SLCERT | CC conducts incident responsive services in case of a cyber emergency, conducts awareness through workshops, seminars and by organising cyber security weeks, and provides consultancy related to cyber security for both government and private sectors on a request basis. The SLCERT | CC is also a member of the Asia-Pacific Computer Emergency Response Team (APCERT), which is a collective organisation that includes CERTs from different countries in the Asia-Pacific region and works for the cyber security of this region.[61]

Irrespective of its advancements in the ICT sector, Sri Lanka's cyber security environment needs to develop more in terms of public awareness, widespread usage of IT resources, especially in the rural areas, human resource development in the IT sector, IT industry development and, most importantly, e-government. Although, the e-Sri Lanka ICT Roadmap was drafted more than a decade ago, the country has not been able to provide proper e-government services to its people. Moreover, there is a dearth of expertise in the cyber security field due to lack of cyber security related courses and training mechanisms in the country. Addressing these issues and working towards comprehensive cyber laws might help Sri Lanka become a tech-savvy country in the future.

Conclusion

Overall, looking at the cyber environment of South Asia, it is obvious that connectivity and usage are increasing day by day and the countries are active in enhancing their respective

ICT sector for economic gains. However, as connectivity grows, so does the need for cyber-focussed policies, legislation and regulatory frameworks. The governments of the South Asian countries have realised this and are taking up initiatives to address the shortfalls in their domestic arrangements, but some states like Afghanistan, Nepal and even Pakistan, lag behind in either the formation or implementation of cyber-centric mechanisms, frameworks and policies. Moreover, a major widespread deficit in the region is lack of awareness related to cyber security. Therefore, there is an urgent need for all the South Asian countries to expand their cyber awareness programmes beyond organising seminars and workshops, and to conduct widespread public awareness programmes for the common public to understand cyber security. Also, the countries should start producing and identifying cyber experts in their respective countries and formulate a mechanism to inculcate these experts into the system to support the operations in their respective country's cyber space to ensure a secure future.

Comprehensive cyber security is an elusive concept for any one country to achieve due to the universal nature of the cyber domain. Therefore, mutual trust and cooperation, universal coordination, information sharing, equal universal regulations and neutral governance are the essential factors to be achieved in the cyber domain by all its stakeholders, across borders, in order to achieve comprehensive cyber security.

Notes

1. "Individuals Internet 2000-2013", International Telecommunication Union, Statistics, 2014.
2. "Fixed Broadband 2000-2013", International Telecommunication Union, Statistics, 2014.
3. **Ibid.**
4. "Mobile Cellular 2000-2013", International Telecommunication Union, Statistics, 2014.
5. **Ibid.**
6. Calculations were made based on population data collected from the World Bank database. According to this source, the population of Maldives by the end of 2013 was 345,023 and that of Afghanistan was 30,551,674. "Total Population", World Bank, in www.data.worldbank.org/indicator/SP.POP.TOTL. **Accessed on January 20, 2015.**
7. Calculations were made based on population data collected from the World Bank database. According to this source, the population of India by the end of 2013 was 1,252,139,596. "Total Population", World Bank, in www.data.worldbank.org/indicator/SP.POP.TOTL. **Accessed on January 20, 2015.**
8. "Web Defacement Statistics", CERT-in, in **http://www.cert-in.org.in. Accessed on January 21, 2015.**
9. Although the terms CERT (Computer Emergency Response Team) and CIRT (Computer Incident Response Team) are often interchanged synonymously, there exists a distinct difference between the two. A CERT typically encompasses numerous facets of the security spectrum and is not solely dedicated to incident response. It incorporates various information assurance disciplines within the team that may or may not be found within a limited CIRT - such as intrusion detection, vulnerability analysis, policy formulation, and enterprise oversight. On the other hand, a CIRT can be a formalised team or an ad hoc team. A formalised team

performs incident response work as its major job function. An ad hoc team is called together during an ongoing computer security incident or to respond to an incident when the need arises. While a CERT is typically a distinguished and unified team within a sizeable organisation, a CIRT does not always operate on such a grandiose scale.

10. "Telecom Sector's Recent Achievements", Ministry of Communication & Information Technology, Islamic Republic of Afghanistan, in http://mcit.gov.af/en/page/4876/6005. Accessed on January 22, 2015.
11. Ibid.
12. "Afghanistan National Defence Centre", Ministry of Communication and Information Technology, Islamic Republic of Afghanistan, in http://andc.gov.af/en/page/3001. Accessed on January 23, 2015.
13. "Afghanistan Network Information Centre", in http://www.nic.af/aboutus.htm. Accessed on January 23, 2015.
14. "Cyber Wellness Profile- Afghanistan", ITU, 2014.
15. "Cyber Defence Training for Afghan Professionals", North Atlantic Treaty Organisation, June 1, 2012, in http://www.nato.int/cps/en/natolive/news_88116.htm?selectedLocale=en. Accessed on January 24, 2015.
16. Warner Gregory, "Afghans fall Prey to Pyramid Scheme", *Marketplace*, February 28, 2008, in http://www.marketplace.org/topics/life/afghans-fall-prey-pyramid-scheme. Accessed on January 24, 2015.
17. https://www.facebook.com/AfgCyberArmy/timeline?ref=page_internal. Accessed on January 24, 2015.
18. https://www.youtube.com/user/AfgCyberArmy. Accessed on January 24, 2015.
19. "Readiness Assessment for Establishing National CIRT (Afghanistan, Bangladesh, Bhutan, Maldives and Nepal)", ITU Report, January 2012.
20. Ibid.
21. "National Cyber Security Strategy", Bangladesh Government Press, Government of the People's Republic of Bangladesh, 2014.
22. "Government Websites Hacked", bdnews2.com, March 20, 2010, in http://bdnews24.com/bangladesh/2010/03/20/govt-websites-hacked. Accessed on January 24, 2015.
23. n. 21.
24. "Bhutan, Telecoms, Mobile and Internet", Budde Comm, at http://www.budde.com.au/Research/Bhutan-Telecoms-Mobile-and-Internet.html?r=51. Accessed on January 26, 2015.
25. "Bhutan E-Government Master Plan", Department of Information Technology & Telecom, Ministry of Information & Communications, Royal Government of Bhutan, January 3, 2014.
26. "About US", Thimpu Tech Park, http://www.thimphutechpark.com/about. Accessed on January 27, 2015.
27. n. 25.
28. "Bhutan Computer Incidence Response Team", Bhutanomics: The Bhutan Analytics, September 22, 2012, in http://bhutanomics.com/2012/bhutan-computer-incidence-response-team/. Accessed on January 28, 2015.
29. "A Cyber Unit to Specialise in Cyber Crime", Security-Risks.com, August 31, 2014, in http://www.security-risks.com/security-issues-south-asia/iw-cyber-security/bhutan-cyber-unit-to-specialise-in-cyber-crime-3388.html. Accessed on January 29, 2015.
30. http://www.internetworldstats.com/top20.htm. Accessed on February 12, 2015.
31. Press release on "Highlights on Telecom Subscription Data as on December 31, 2014", Telecom Regulatory Authority of India, Press Release No 11/2015, February 6, 2015.
32. Ibid.
33. http://www.ibef.org/industry/information-technology-india.aspx. Accessed on February 13,

2015.

34. http://www.dot.gov.in/about-us/vision-mission. Accessed on February 13, 2015.
35. http://deity.gov.in/content/vision-mission. Accessed on February 13, 2015.
36. Dilipraj E, "India's Cyber Security 2013: A Review", *CAPS Issue Brief,* 97/14, January 27, 2014.
37. Ibid.
38. Ibid.
39. http://www.nic.in/about-us. Accessed on February 15, 2015.
40. http://www.stqc.gov.in/content/about-stqc. Accessed on February 15, 2015.
41. "Annual Report 2013", Indian Computer Emergency Response Team, Ministry of Communications & Information Technology, Government of India, March 31, 2014.
42. Joji Thomas Philip and Harsimran Julka, "India Goes on Offensive Against Cyber Rogues", *The Economic Times*, December 3, 2011.
43. n. 19.
44. Ibid.
45. "About US", National Centre for Information Technology, in http://www.ncit.gov.mv/index.php/en/aboutus. Accessed on January 30, 2015.
46. "MNDF Website Hacked", *Minivan News*, October 05, 2014, in http://minivannews.com/news-in-brief/mndf-website-hacked-90368. Accessed on February 1, 2015.
47. "Optical Fibre Projects & its Impacts", 9th anniversary Souvenir, Nepal Telecom, 2013.
48. Purusottam Kharel, Subarna Shakya, "E-Government Implementation in Nepal: A Challenges", *International Journal of Advanced Research in Computer Science and Software Engineering*, vol. 02, issue 01, January 2012.
49. n.19, p. 46.
50. http://www.itsert-np.org/index.php?about_us. Accessed on February 5, 2015.
51. http://en.wikipedia.org/wiki/Telecommunications_in_Pakistan. Accessed on February 10, 2015.
52. Muhammad Amir Malik, "Capacity Building in Cyberspace Security", Ministry of Information Technology, Government of Pakistan, 2013.
53. "Cyber Crimes", *Dawn*, May 17, 2014, http://www.dawn.com/news/1106784. Accessed on February 10, 2015.
54. http://www.nr3c.gov.pk/about_us.html. Accessed on February 11, 2015.
55. http://www.pakcert.org/aboutus.html. Accessed on February 11, 2015.
56. n. 19.
57. "Pakistan: Upgraded Cencorship", Enemies of Internet, http://12mars.rsf.org/2014-en/2014/03/10/pakistan-upgraded-censorship/#more-58. Accessed on February 11, 2015.
58. "Profile – Milestones", Sri Lanka Telecom, http://www.slt.lk/about-us/milestones. Accessed on February 6, 2015.
59. "Mobile Phones – Networks and Prices in Sri Lanka", Just Landed, https://www.justlanded.com/english/Sri-Lanka/Sri-Lanka-Guide/Telephone-Internet/Mobile-phones. Accessed on February 6, 2015.
60. Gen Sir John Kotelawala, "Cyber Terrorism; Is Sri Lanka Ready?", Defence University, Sri Lanka.
61. http://www.slcert.gov.lk/aboutUs.php. Accessed on February 7, 2015.

9

Environmental Degradation and Associated Security Challenges in South Asia

Nishant Gupta

History is replete with examples of climatic shifts or extreme weather incidences triggering conflicts and, in extreme cases, even contributing to the rise and fall of civilisations. During the 4th and 5th centuries, growing aridity and frigid temperatures from a prolonged cold snap caused the Huns and German tribes to surge across the Volga and Rhine rivers into the Roman Empire, eventually leading to the overthrow of the Romans. Muslim expansion into the Mediterranean and southern Europe in the 8th century was to some extent driven by a persistent drought in the Middle East. The Viking community in Greenland died out in the 15th century partly because of a sudden cooling of temperatures across northern Europe known as the "Little Ice Age". A changing climate may have been responsible for the collapse of China's Tang dynasty and the disappearance of the Mayan world in Central America a thousand years ago.[1] Jawaharlal Nehru, in his seminal work *The Discovery of India*, also flagged that climate change was the probable cause of the end of the mighty Indus Valley Civilisation.[2] Climate change continues to be a cause of concern and now it is being termed as a threat multiplier having the potential to exacerbate many of the challenges we already confront today and to produce new challenges in the future.[3]

This chapter is a study of environmental stresses in South Asia and their likely impact on the national security. Water being the elixir of life and the primary vehicle of climate change effects, will be covered in greater detail. Phenomena like glacial melt, sea level rise and changing pattern of the monsoon will also be studied. The impact on agriculture, which continues to be the primary profession of people in South Asia, as well as a vehicle of their survivability/well-being, will be touched upon. South Asia has many rivers which are flowing across international borders, and water disputes continue to be a sore point in international relations. The Kashmir issue, which is one of the most contentious issues in the region, will be studied through the prism of the water dispute. Cross-border migration and the water-food-energy nexus will also be deliberated upon. In the last section, linkages will be drawn between environmental stresses and militaries.

Environmental Stresses

South Asia's vulnerability to environmental change has been observed in many ways. As per the South Asian Centre for Environmental Protection (SACEP), land degradation, desertification, deforestation, loss of biodiversity, fresh water depletion and degradation, degradation of air quality, solid waste management, degradation and depletion of the marine and coastal ecosystem, rise in temperature, rise in sea level, environmental health issues, natural disasters and their consequences are amongst the most significant environmental problems in South Asia.[4]

Western literature also repeatedly highlights South Asia's vulnerability to environmental change. A 2014 CNA Military Advisory Board report entitled "National Security and the Accelerating Risks of Climate Change" underscores that Asia, among other regions, is already witnessing the impacts of sea level rise and extreme weather incidences such as prolonged drought and flooding. Resulting food shortages, desertification, population dislocation and mass migration are posing security challenges to these regions. And these trends are growing and accelerating. As the sea level rises, storm surges will become more invasive, more destructive, costlier, and deadlier. Densely populated areas, including many large cities along coasts or major waterways are particularly vulnerable to monsoon and storm surge flooding. Low-lying nations, such as Bangladesh, and entire island countries, such as the Maldives, particularly face existential threats in the near term from sea level rise and devastating storm flooding. Projected sea level rise will also put critical regions at risk, including eastern India, and Bangladesh, which combined produce the bulk of the region's primary food staple, rice.[5] This report also brings out that the major projected impacts from climate change in Asia were associated with water. A 2012 National Intelligence Council assessment held that water challenges are likely to increase the risk of instability and state failure, exacerbating regional tensions.[6]

Back home, Jaswant Singh, a well known parliamentarian, a former cavalry officer of the Indian Army and an accomplished politician who served at many important government positions, including as deputy chairman of the Planning Commission of India and finance minister of India, in his book *Defending India,* published in 1999, highlighted the environmental aspects of security. He stated:

> Global warming, and the consequences of that warming upon nations in India's neighbourhood, indeed even its own coastal areas, is the environmental aspect of security. Just as access to food and water or their denial can result in tension, so also the consequence of environmental degradation, deforestation, excessive siltation result in national problems. There exists in India, at present, neither any focused study in this regard nor any proper thought. ... a battered environment can cause violence upheavals and migration.[7]

Water Crisis

Water, despite being renewable, is indeed a scarce resource, without any substitute. Early civilisations were essentially inhabited around rivers. Water, being a basic requirement for domestic purposes as well as for growing food, impelled people to settle close to fresh water resources, particularly rivers. Gradually, these communities grew into cities, and cities, in turn, grew into nations. With a rising population, the advent of industrialisation, rapid urbanisation and ever changing lifestyle, the demand for water continued to grow. Fresh water, thus, continues to be a crucial resource and its importance in the calculus of peace and security dynamics is bound to increase.

Globally, access to clean drinking water as well as water tables continue to decline. Worldwide, an estimated 768 million people remain without access to an improved source of water. By some estimates, the number of people whose right to water is not satisfied could be as high as 3.5 billion.[8] As per the UN World Water Development Report, society is close to approaching the global limit of sustainable availability of water. Reportedly, the Indus basin, in India as well as Pakistan, has also crossed its sustainable water extraction limit. [9] In India, gross per capita water availability is projected to decline further from about 1,820 cubic metres to as low as around 1,140 cubic metres a year by 2050.[10] It is estimated that in India, one million new tubewells become operational every year.[11] In the Water Poverty Index, India is the lowest amongst the South Asian nations, though the whole region is similarly placed at a level which is not encouraging by any standards.

Table 1: Water Poverty Index (WPI)[12]

Nation	Water Poverty Index
Bangladesh	54
Bhutan	56
India	53
Nepal	54
Pakistan	58
Sri Lanka	56

Units: Index Numbers 0-100; lower scores indicate water scarcity and poor water provision.

Besides limited availability, there are several other water related stresses/ challenges in the region. Heavy rainfall and high silt load on water bodies cause recurrent floods over large areas. The "break monsoon"[13] is another feature that affects the hills during the rainy season. Rains during the "break monsoon" are the cause of flooding in the foothills as well as contiguous areas in the plains. The 1954 and 1968 floods in the Kosi river were caused by the "break monsoon" occurring over the eastern hills of Nepal. In 1993, 540 mm of rain occurred in just 15 hours, causing floods over central Nepal.[14]

On the other hand, large areas face droughts due to scanty rainfall which results in depleting ground water levels. Long coastlines and island territories are threatened by cyclones, storm surges and sea level rise. The slow but steady Himalayan meltdown is considered as one of the greatest environmental security threats in South Asia.

Climate Change and Water

The increasing salience of climate change is highlighted in the following statements:

> Climate Change is a Global Emergency. The world is in danger of going into cardiac arrest, yet we behave as if we've caught a common cold.
>
> — Mohammad Nasheed, president of Maldives, March 15, 2009[15]

> ...this is going to be more serious threat to international order than Islamic radicalism or piracy or resource sharing.
>
> — Mohammad Nasheed, president of Maldives, at a seminar in New Delhi on 'Environment and Conflict Resolution' on October 23, 2009[16]

> Global warming is a weapon of mass destruction and at least as dangerous as international terrorism.[17]
>
> — Sir John Houghton, chief climate change adviser to the British prime minister

Water is typically the primary medium through which climate change influences the earth's ecosystem and, thus, the livelihood and well-being of societies. Higher temperatures and changes in extreme weather conditions are projected to affect availability and distribution of rainfall, snow melt, river flows and ground water, which would lead to deterioration in water quality. Climate change is also known to be the primary cause of sea level rise.

The projected decrease in the winter precipitation over the Indian subcontinent would reduce the total seasonal precipitation during December, January and February, implying less storage and greater water stress during the lean monsoon period. On the other hand, expected increase in intense rainfall occurrences over fewer days, would imply increased frequency of floods during the monsoon and loss of the rain water as direct runoff leading to reduction in ground water recharging potential. Therefore, expansion of areas under severe water stress will be one of the most pressing environmental problems in South Asia.

Table 2: Summary of Key Observed Past and Present Climate Trends and Variability In South Asia[18]

Country	Change in Temperatures	Impacts
Bangladesh	An increasing trend of about 1^0 C in May and 0.5^0 C in November during the 14-year period from 1985 to 1998	Decadal rain anomalies above long-term averages since the 1960s
India	The updated 100 year linear trend for 1906-2005 is 0.74^0 C	Increase in extreme rains in the northwest during the summer monsoon in recent decades, lower number of rainy days along the east coast
Nepal	0.09^0 C per year in the Himalayas and 0.04^0 C in the Terai region, more in winter	No distinct long-term trends in precipitation records for the period 1948 to 1994
Pakistan	0.6 to 1.0^0 C rise in mean temperature in the coastal areas since the early 1900s	No distinct long-term trends in precipitation records for the period 1948 to 1994
Sri Lanka	0.016^0 C increase per year between 1961 to 1990 over the entire country	Increased trend in February and decreased trend in June

The Himalaya-Hindukush, the youngest, the largest and seismically the most active mountain system of the world, has the largest non-polar glacial deposits. Statistically, these glaciers contain 40 percent of the world's fresh water, and feed 40 percent of humanity via seven great Asian rivers. About 15,000 glaciers form a unique reservoir that supports perennial rivers such as the Indus, Ganges and Brahmaputra, which, in turn, are the lifeline of millions of people in the South Asian countries (Bangladesh, Bhutan, India, Nepal, and Pakistan).

Due to the effects of climate change and global warming, these glacial deposits are increasingly melting. As per the World Welfare Fund (WWF) 2005, glaciers in the Himalayas are receding faster than in any other part of the world. The large glaciers of Gangotari, Yamnotari and Go-Mukh, feeding the rivers Ganga and Yamuna, have started to melt at an alarming pace. If the present rate continues, the likelihood of their disappearing by the year 2035, or perhaps sooner, is very high. By the year 2035, total area under these glaciers is likely to shrink from the present figure of 5,00,000 km^2 to 1,00,000 km^2. [19]

Glacial Lake Outburst Floods: Studies suggest that glacial melt will have an adverse impact on hydropower, biodiversity, industries, agriculture and may even make the region dangerous to live in. Disappearance of glaciers means a reduction in the mountains' natural water storage capacity, making water flows more erratic. Additionally, excessive melting would also lead to formation of lakes at the base of the glaciers that can subsequently burst at their banks as temperatures continue to rise. This phenomenon, termed as the Glacial Lake Outburst Floods (GLOFs), will have devastating effects downstream. Even during small earthquakes, water rushes down, picking up debris on the way and creates havoc for downstream areas. Some of these floods have produced discharge rates of up to 30,000 m^3/sec and can run for distances of 200 km.[20] In the recent past, 21 GLOF events have adversely affected Nepalese territory; and to date over 200 potentially dangerous glacial lakes have been documented across the Himalayan region.[21] The Tibetan plateau glaciers, that are 4 km in length, are projected to disappear with a 3^0C temperature rise and no change in precipitation.

In addition, limited opportunities for safe and sustainable livelihoods in the mountains mean that population densities are growing within the river valleys where their vulnerability to GLOFs increases. The population growth means that there are now more people exposed to GLOFs and other climate-related disasters, and this is compounded by the expansion of infrastructure and settlements in the vulnerable areas.

These facts underline the urgent need to enhance scientific knowledge of glacier environments by continuously monitoring glaciers and glacial lakes, carrying out vulnerability assessments, implementing mitigation and adaptation mechanisms, and developing a GLOF early warning system. Regional cooperation to develop a coordinated strategy to deal with trans-boundary issues related to the impacts which can occur as a result of climate change is also essential.

Sea Level Rise: Reportedly, sea level rise started accelerating in the early 20th century. Satellite altimeter measurements reflect that since the early 1990s, the sea level has risen at the rate of 3 mm per year. Thermal expansion is producing about half of this annual increase in global sea levels.[22] In the coastal areas of Asia, the current rate of sea level rise, according to the Inter-governmental Panel on Climate Change (IPCC) Fourth Assessment Report, is reported to be between 1 to 3 mm/year. A rate of sea level rise of 3.1 mm/year has been reported over the past decade compared to 1.7 to 2.4 mm/year over the 12th century as a whole, suggesting that the rate of sea level rise has accelerated vis-a-vis the long-term average. Progressive inundation of the coastal village of Satabahya in Orissa's Kendrapa district is a live example of sea level rise in the Bay of Bengal. In the last two decades, the villagers have been forced to move inwards thrice. Two decades ago, the sea was a scenic 2 km walk from the village, whereas today, the original village site is somewhere 1 km inside the sea.[23]

Projected sea level rise is very likely to result in significant losses of coastal ecosystems and a million or so people along the coasts of South Asia are likely to be at risk from flooding. A rise in temperature of between 3° and 4°C will result in hundreds of people being flooded each year. This involves serious risks and increasing pressures on coastal regions, small islands (like Maldives) and large coastal cities (like Kolkata and Mumbai). Even under the most conservative scenarios, sea level will be about 40 cm higher than today by the end of the 21st century.

The rise in sea level is bound to complicate maritime boundary disputes. Maritime boundaries are determined by the baseline or low water mark. Any shift in baseline points would alter maritime boundaries significantly which could become a source of contention. The outer boundaries of oceanic zones being claimed by coastal states will also be shifted. Submergence of small atolls, rocks, low lying islands may also have implications on maritime claims. Thus, sea level rise may further complicate already contested maritime issues.

Sea level rise would also lead to reduction of the gradient of rivers at the point of discharge into the sea, resulting in slower drainage and probable flooding upstream. It will also lead to saline intrusion further upstream in the river system.

Coastal Areas Inundation

The projections indicate that coastal populations that are flooded annually may increase from 13 million to 94 million globally. Almost 60 per cent of this increase will occur in South Asia along the coasts of Pakistan, India, Sri Lanka and Bangladesh. Maldives, being a very low-lying nation, has an increased risk. Certain parts of India like Andaman and Nicobar and Lakshadweep Islands also face a similar threat. Bangladesh has already been facing the effects of this increase. Large fertile tracts of the land have now been submerged in the Bay of Bengal.

Salt water ingress is making the ground water unfit for most uses while reducing the soil fertility. Areas dependent on coastal fishery and agriculture are also likely to be affected adversely. Large-scale migration from coastal zones is expected due to submergence of coastlines and other adverse effects caused by sea level rise. This will create large numbers of environmental refugees, especially from low-lying delta regions. Additionally, likely increase in cyclones will threaten human settlements and environmental refugees would cause disruption across national borders.[24]

Changing Ecosystems: The changing climate is also adversely affecting ecosystems, being particularly vulnerable to climate change. A study estimates that with 2°C of warming, between 15 to 40 per cent of species would face extinction.[25] The impact of climate change would be adverse on the forests, wetlands and coastal regions. Consequent to climate change, large decreases in the natural capital of grasslands and savannas are likely in South Asia. Warmer climate in recent decades are increasingly threatening wetlands. The precipitation decline and droughts in delta regions of Bangladesh, India and Pakistan have resulted in drying up of the wetlands and severe degradation of ecosystems.

Table 3: Shared Ecosystems of South Asia

- Terrai ecosystems (e.g. Shiwalik range) between India and Nepal.
- Sundarbans mangrove forest between India and Bangladesh.
- Manas sub-tropical forest between India and Bhutan.
- Gulf of Mannar between India and Sri Lanka.
- Rann of Kuchch between India and Pakistan.
- Coral atoll ecosystems between India (Lakshwadeep) and Maldives.

The **Maldives** essentially has a fragile, low-lying small ecosystem, highly vulnerable to climate change. Its particular concerns are sea level rise and adverse impact on the availability of ground water. It has been estimated that a two metre rise in the sea level will submerge virtually all the coral islands scattered over 850 km across the equator, forcing 3,00,000 people to evacuate.

In the islands, generally rain water lenses lie atop salt water. As the sea level rises, the thicknesses of the fresh water lens decreases, reducing the fresh water holding. The sea level rise would also increase the likelihood of storms over the islands, causing increased incidence of salt water contamination of the fresh water lenses. As the nation does not have any river, its fresh water requirements are largely met through a desalination plant. Recently, in December 2014, a major fire in Male's only desalination plant had put about 1,00,000 people in a crisis situation. The Indian Air Force (IAF) and Indian Navy came to their rescue in terms of airlifting potable water as well as conveying RO plants through the sea route.

The islands of Maldives are reef-based, and coral reefs serve as natural breakwaters. An increase in temperature can very easily bring the reef growth and reef ecosystems to an alarmingly poor status. The corals, already growing at the highest tolerable temperatures (approximately 30°C), have a very grim possibility of survival, given the predicted rises in temperature of 1.4° to 5.8°C for the period of 1990 to 2100.[26] Therefore, with damage to the coral reefs comes the bigger danger of losing the natural protection of the islands from the sea waves and currents. An island with a degraded reef is more open to coastal damage such as beach erosion and more susceptible to inundation by uncontrolled waves reaching the shore. Although almost all the reefs have recovered from the coral bleaching event of 1997, the impacts of bleaching were felt on around 90 per cent of the reefs of Maldives, either totally or partially.[27] Its tourism industry, being heavily dependent on the marine ecosystems, is also under threat from the impacts of climate change.[28]

India, being the nearest neighbour, having long time cultural and political proximities, would be expected to help the nation in rehabilitation and resettlement of environmental refugees. The Maldives is also strategically important to India as any foreign military presence in the area may jeopardise India's national security in terms of safeguarding its maritime interests.

Impact on Agriculture

In South Asia, the agriculture sector is the major source of employment and this will continue to remain so in the coming decades.[29] Agricultural productivity in South Asia is likely to suffer severe losses because of climate change and its various manifestations, be it high temperature, severe drought, flood conditions, soil degradation or sea level rise. Production of rice, maize and wheat in the past few decades has declined in many parts of Asia due to increasing water stress arising partly from increasing temperature, increasing frequency of El Niño and reduction in the number of rainy days. In a study conducted at the International Rice Research Institute, the yield of rice was observed to decrease by 10 per cent for every 1°C increase in the growing-season minimum temperature.[30] As per certain forecasts, increasing temperatures may lead to grain yield reduction in Asia by 15 to 20 percent by 2050.[31]

Studies show that decreased winter snowfall on glaciers does indeed decrease the spring/summer runoff. This phenomenon has already caused severe droughts in Pakistan, particularly in areas that depend on water from mountain sources. A similar pattern would severely affect irrigation and farming livelihoods in Nepal. The land that can be cultivated varies by location and season, since the vast majority of surface water irrigation systems in Nepal depend on the water flowing at its source.[32] In some cases, the winter cropping area is only 20 per cent of the summer cultivable area. In Bangladesh, under a severe climate change scenario (a 4^0 C temperature rise and increased evaporation of 22 per cent), the potential shortfall in rice production could exceed 30 per cent, while for wheat and potato, it could be as high as 50 and 70 per cent, respectively.[33]

Food supply and ability to purchase food are functions of purchasing power and price of the product. The global cereal prices have been projected to increase more than three-fold by the 2080s, as a consequence of decline in net productivity due to projected climate change.[34] The anticipated drop in agricultural production, when coupled with losses in other sectors, will threaten food security. It will also badly affect the developmental agenda of the region, including poverty reduction and improving access to safe drinking water, two of the important Millennium Development Goals.

On the contrary, there are also studies/predictions suggesting that climate change and its causes, such as increased temperatures and higher carbon dioxide levels, would have a positive bearing on agriculture. While there may be a positive impact on crop yields, this will be applicable only to areas where moisture is not a constraint. For example, in Bangladesh, the apparent increase in the Boro yield, as a result of increased carbon dioxide, would be constrained by moisture stress. A 60 per cent moisture stress, apart from other effects, might cause a decline of as high as 32 percent in the Boro yield, instead of an overall 20 per cent net increase.[35] It is feared that moisture stress would be more intense during the dry season, which might force Bangladeshi farmers to reduce the area for Boro cultivation. Warmer temperatures may also increase the occurrence of extreme events or pests, offsetting any potential benefits. Both crops and livestock would be affected by the increase in disease or alien/invasive pests. Increase in temperature, despite reduction in humidity, can also hamper the farmers' ability to work.

As a result, low-income rural populations that depend on traditional agricultural systems or on marginal lands are particularly vulnerable to climate change and their livelihoods will be at risk.

Fishery is also expected to suffer from the impacts of climate change. Climate change induced changes in the strength and seasonality of ocean currents are likely to cause some of the fish species to migrate and may also disrupt their breeding grounds.

The movement of deep water fish may become unpredictable, causing livelihood problems and also the problems of overfishing. This may lead to increase in unlawful activities. For example, tuna, the main fishery in Maldives, is a migratory species and there is a strong possibility that change in temperatures would drive tuna stock out of the area to more favourable temperatures. This may lead to a decline in the fisheries industry as the fishermen would lose their fishing grounds. Tuna fishery is based on the pole and line method using bait fish. Any changes to the availability of bait fish caused by damage to the reefs would also affect the tuna fishery. Additionally, increased frequency of El Niño events is likely to lead to measurable declines in fish larvae abundance in coastal waters. These phenomena are expected to contribute to a general decline in fishery production in the coastal waters of South Asia. A recent report suggests that in 2014, marine catch in India reduced by 5 percent when compared to the previous year.[36]

Natural Disasters

Two-thirds of the disasters that South Asia experiences are considered to be climate related and there has been a phenomenal increase in their frequency, severity and unpredictability in the recent times.[37] It is estimated that the South Asian countries lose between 2 to 12 per cent of the Gross Domestic Product (GDP) annually on account of natural disasters.[38] The Indian subcontinent is highly prone to droughts, floods and other natural calamities. As many as 22 states are said to be multi-disaster-prone regions. Among all the natural disasters that occur in India, floods are the most devastating. Over 40 million hectares of land has been identified as flood prone. An average of 18.6 million hectares of land is flooded annually. Another killer is the earthquake—the most dangerous and disastrous. About 57 per cent of the total area in India is vulnerable to seismic activity of varying intensities. Generally, areas located in the Himalayan and sub-Himalayan regions and Andaman and Nicobar Islands are vulnerable to earthquakes. Drought is also an eternal feature of Indian livelihood—18 per cent of the country's total area is drought prone. Approximately half of the Indian population is affected by drought annually and 68 per cent of the total cultivated area is estimated to be drought prone.

India has a long coastline, of about 8,040 km. This is exposed to tropical cyclones in the Bay of Bengal and Arabian Sea in the ratio of 4:1. The Indian Ocean is one among the six key cyclone prone regions of the world. The Coromandel coastal line is more prone—about 80 percent of the total cyclones generated in the region hit here.[39] In South Asia, an increase of 10 to 20 per cent in tropical cyclone intensity is projected for a rise in sea-surface temperature of between 2^0 and 4^0C, relative to the current threshold temperature.[40]

The intensity of cyclones originating from the Bay of Bengal and Arabian Sea has also been noted to increase since 1970.[41] Amplification in storm-surge heights could result from the occurrence of stronger winds, with increase in sea-surface temperatures and low pressures, associated with tropical storms, resulting in enhanced risk of coastal disasters along the coastal regions of countries.

Increasing trends in climate-induced disasters in South Asia have added to the overall damage potential in the region. In South Asia, after earthquakes and floods, windstorms affect the largest number of people. Cold and heat waves are also emerging as severe risks for certain areas/social groups in South Asia. Elaborating on the relationship between climate change and disasters, a report by the International Institute of Sustainable Development (IISD) states:

> The poor are already vulnerable to climate risks. Settlement on marginal or unstable lands such as steep slopes or floodplains heightens their exposure to the impacts of climate hazards. Heavy dependence on ecosystem services can place their welfare and survival at the mercy of environmental conditions. As the availability and quality of natural resources decline due to natural and human-induced pressures, so does the viability and security of their livelihoods. With limited capacities and resources at their disposal to respond to stresses such as droughts and floods, their ability to meet basic needs and move out of poverty is constrained. Climate change, therefore, threatens to exacerbate existing vulnerabilities and further entrench development disparities. Those with the least, stand to suffer the most. Thus, with regional changes and impacts already being observed, the need for adaptive response measures is imperative. For the poor and other vulnerable people, the need is urgent.[42]

Impact on Well-being

Poverty is one of the major concerns in facing environmental stresses. The Human Development Index (HDI) 2014 report reemphasises that poor people are more vulnerable than others in society because for the most part, the risk of adverse shocks is greater for the poor than for others.[43] The report also underlines that poor people are more likely to live in areas vulnerable to the impacts of climate change, whether in low-lying coastal regions which are at greatest risk of inundation from rising sea levels or on marginal land subject to increasing dryness and drought due to climate change.[44]

In South Asia, governance and poverty are amongst the major concerns. About 40 percent of the world's poor (500 million), live in this region and half of the malnourished children also belong to South Asia. Illiteracy is also a significant handicap: 46 percent of the world's illiterates belong to South Asia. This region has the lowest sex ratio reflecting deeply rooted gender discrimination in society. Unplanned urban areas, growing at a fast rate of 4.5 percent per annum, are further creating layers of urban vulnerabilities.

In South Asia, climate change poses substantial risks to human health. The global burden (mortality and morbidity) of climate change attributable to diarrhoea and malnutrition was already the largest in Bangladesh, Bhutan, India, Maldives and Nepal in 2000, and the relative risks for these conditions for 2030 are expected to be the largest.[45] A large number of deaths due to heat waves – mainly among the poor, elderly and labourers such as rural daily wage earners, agricultural workers and rickshaw pullers – have been reported in India, especially in Andhra Pradesh and Orissa.[46] Increase in coastal water temperatures would exacerbate this problem. Additionally, increase in temperature in South Asia will also increase abundance and/or toxicity of water-borne diseases like cholera and vector-borne (like dengue fever and malaria).

The poor, particularly in the urban and urbanising cities of South Asia, are highly vulnerable to climate change because of their limited access to profitable livelihood opportunities and to areas that are fit for safe and healthy habitation. Consequently, the poor sector is likely to be exposed to more risks from floods and other climate-related hazards in areas they are forced to stay in. Decrease in water availability and resulting reduction in food production, especially if there is a shortage of water for irrigation, would heighten the problem of poor nutrition.

As per IPCC 2014 Report (Summary for Policy Makers), until mid-century, projected climate change will impact human health mainly by exacerbating health problems that already exist. Throughout the 21st century, climate change is expected to result in increase in ill-health in many regions across the globe, especially in the developing countries with low incomes. Examples include:

- Greater likelihood of injury, disease and/or death due to more intense heat waves and fires.
- Increased likelihood of under-nutrition resulting from diminished food production in poor regions.
- Risks from lost work capacity and reduced labour productivity in vulnerable populations.
- Increased risks from food, and water-borne and vector-borne diseases.

On the other hand, a few positive effects are also expected, like modest reductions in cold related mortality and morbidity in some areas due to fewer cold extremes, geographical shifts in food production and reduced capacity of vectors to transmit some diseases. However, in South Asia, over the 21st century, the magnitude and severity of the negative impacts are projected to increasingly outweigh the positive impacts.

Himalayan River Systems and Water Disputes

Internationally, there is a substantial source interdependence on water. About 40 percent of humanity gets water from sources controlled by two or more countries. The South Asian countries are no different. About 20 major rivers run through this region, and the three largest basins (the Indus, the Ganges, and the Brahmaputra) affect not only Bangladesh, Bhutan, India, Nepal, and Pakistan, but China as well.[47]

According to some climate change scenarios, following an initial period of high flows caused by accelerated glacial melt, the amount of water flowing into the Indus river system may decrease by as much as 30 to 40 percent within the next two decades. Additionally, the effects of climate change and siltation may reduce already-low reservoir capacity in the basin by 30 percent. The overall reduction in water availability may potentially have a serious impact on irrigation. This, in turn, may affect food security. There are concerns about forecasts that increasing temperatures may reduce grain yields in Asia by 15 to 20 percent by 2050.[48]

Diminishing availability of fresh water calls for a critical appreciation of the river systems in the region. Sharp seasonal variations in the water flow due to climatic phenomena, including monsoons and droughts, occurring in some countries, add to the difficulty of finding equitable and durable water-sharing arrangements. Due to spatial and seasonal variations, water has heightened both conflict and cooperation over a large number of international rivers. According to the 2002 United Nations World Water Development Report, during the previous 50 years, there were 507 conflictive events over water. Amongst these, 37 involved violence, of which 21 consisted of military acts.[49]

The Kashmir issue, the core dispute between India and Pakistan, also has its roots in water distribution and environmental survivability. As per some experts, Pakistan wanted Kashmir to be its integral part essentially to strengthen its survivability as all the rivers providing canal irrigation to west Punjab flowed through Kashmir. However, religion is another dimension and face of the issue. The Kashmir Valley depends largely upon the glaciers for its water supply as the rivers feeding the valley draw water from the Himalayan glaciers and climate change induced drying up of the glaciers will turn Kashmir from a *water surplus* state to a *water deficit* one.[50]

In 1990, Gen Parvez Musharraf had argued as a young brigadier, that the Kashmir dispute was dependent on the distribution of the Indus river water between Pakistan and

India, and if one were resolved, the other would not exist. He contended that from the Pakistani perspective, fair distribution of water is a prerequisite for resolving the Jammu and Kashmir (J&K) conflict.[51] Later, Gen Musharraf played a key role in conceptualising, strategising and executing the Kargil War in 1999.

In the recent years, Pakistan has been giving greater salience to water issues in international relations. Until recently, there had been criticism of particular Indian projects on the western rivers as not being compliant with the 1960 Indo-Pakistan, Indus Water Treaty (IWT) but there was no accusation of "water theft" by India. But now the perception of "India is stealing Pakistan's water" has become a familiar cry.

In 2010, Gen Kayani, successor of Gen Musharraf, also highlighted the water issue as one of the important disputes between India and Pakistan. Asif Ali Zardari, president of Pakistan (2008-13) also raised the water issue several times and wrote in an op-ed article in the *Washington Post* (January 28, 2009) that the water crisis in Pakistan was directly linked to relations with India and if this was not resolved, it could fuel extremism and terrorism.[52] Some of the media reports in this regard are flagged below.[53]

- *Dawn* quoted the former Foreign Minister Sardar Asif Ali as saying that "if India continues to deny Pakistan its due share, it can lead to a war between the two countries" (January 18, 2010).
- In a similar vein, Pakistan Muslime League (Quaid-e Azam) Chief Chaudhary Shujat Hussain said that the water crisis between Pakistan and India could become more serious than terrorism and result in a war (*Dawn*, January 18, 2010).
- Majid Nizami, chief editor of the *Nawi Waqt* group of newspapers, said that "Pakistan can become a desert within the next 10 to 15 years. We should show upright posture or otherwise prepare for a nuclear war" (*Dawn*, January 18, 2010).
- Politicians are ratcheting up the rhetoric. Members of the Punjab Assembly passed a resolution to deny India trade transit facility until the resolution of the Kashmir dispute and issues related to water distribution (*Dawn*, January 27, 2010).
- Member of the Punjab Assembly Warris Khalo said that India would "remain an enemy" until the Kashmir dispute and water issues are resolved (*Dawn,* January 27, 2010).
- Palwasha Khan, member of the National Assembly, accused India of perpetrating "water terrorism" against Pakistan and said that "experts foresee war over the water issue in the future and any war in this region would be no less than a nuclear war" (*Daily Times,* February 17, 2010).
- In a recent debate in Pakistan's National Assembly, several members urged the government to impress on New Delhi "not to use" Pakistan's share of water (*Daily Times*, February 25, 2010).

- Dr. Manzur Ejaz, a commentator, writing in the *Daily Times* (March 3, 2010) warned that "unless Pakistan was assured on the supply of water, it will never abandon the proxies that can keep India on its toes by destabilizing Kashmir." He further added: "For Pakistan, the territory of Kashmir may not be as important as the water issue."

The concerns/issues brought out by Pakistan can be summarised as follows:

- Pakistanis often say that in 1947 India got the headworks of their canals as India wanted to green its deserts. Pakistan was a new state, with meagre resources and could not afford a war. So it accepted the 1960 Indus Water Treaty (IWT), though unwillingly. It was not a happy marriage.[54]
- Dams and hydro projects constructed/conceived by India are seen as strategic moves of gating the rivers/canals flowing into Pakistan as an ability to cut off water to Pakistan, even temporarily.
- India is often blamed for polluting the water that is reaching Pakistan and pushing the limits of the IWT against the spirit of the agreement. Indian promises to not manipulate the water are viewed sceptically.
- Pakistan is apprehensive that even while maintaining strict compliance with the provisions of the IWT in each case, India might, considering all the projects together, reach a high degree of control over the waters of the western rivers and acquire the potential to inflict harm on Pakistan. In other words, with the assistance of such structures, India will be able to use water as a weapon of war.
- The issue of managing the prevailing water crisis through better management is largely an internal matter for the people of Pakistan. But this crisis tends to be attributed to Indian wrongdoings and this is echoed in the media and picked up by the *jihadists*. At times, it is affirmed at the official and expert levels through silence or even aggravated by official statements.

Perceptions highlighting Indian wrongdoing on water have become so widespread in Pakistan that it is affecting India–Pakistan relations even at the people-to-people level. This highly jingoistic and uninformed approach is a disturbing development against the regional cooperative spirit and it needs to be responded to appropriately. The fact that the treaty apportioned 80 per cent of the water of the Indus river basin to Pakistan and only 20 per cent to India is never highlighted in the Pakistani discourse on the Indus Water Treaty. Pakistan also ignores the fact that the treaty gives India the right to construct river dams on the western rivers (Indus, Chenab and Jhelum) as well as 3.6 Million Acre Feet (MAF) of storage facilities. India is yet to construct any storage dam on these rivers despite the fact that the treaty permits it to do so. Moreover, India is yet to exploit the full potential of irrigation from the western rivers as provisioned under the treaty. Pakistan conveniently overlooks the fact that even though the treaty gives India the right to use the waters of the eastern rivers (Ravi, Beas, Sutlej), Pakistan is getting 2 MAF of water free through these rivers because India has not been able to fully utilise the waters of these rivers.[55] The poor state of the water structure on the Indian side has allowed this water to flow into Pakistan.

There is a need to bring the focus of the water debate on these provisions of the treaty, while highlighting the fact, that despite three wars and numerous conflicts/skirmishes with Pakistan over the last five decades, India has been abiding the treaty. The Tulbul navigation project and the Baglihar, Kishanganga, and Salal hydroelectric power projects continue to be contentious issues revolving around the treaty. During Op Parakram, to end the stalemate and to pressurise Pakistan, in the summer of 2002, the Cabinet Committee on Security (CCS) had deliberated upon the possibility of preventing water supply to the Pakistani deployments,[56] but India finally decided in favour of abidance by the treaty and, thus, maintained the tradition of holding the high moral ground.

A study on the water supply-demand balance in rapidly growing countries and regions, including China and India, reflects that by 2030, current trajectories and unchanged policies would lead to growth projections incompatible with water endowments. In India, by 2030, there is expected to be a 50 percent gap between water demand and supply. Increasing water scarcity would make cross-border water sharing a more sensitive issue, and that may further exacerbate strained Indo-Pak relations. Any crisis between India and Pakistan is bound to draw in China,[57] Pakistan's "all weather friend", and the United States, a longstanding ally of Pakistani regimes, but now increasingly getting close to India. Thus, environmental stress in terms of a water crisis in South Asia, poses security challenges not only for India and Pakistan but the US and China may also get involved—and all the four states are nuclear armed.

Cross-Border Migration

The primary causes of migration can be classified as: political, economic, ethnic/religious and environmental. State sponsored repression in the then East Pakistan, now Bangladesh, in 1971, resulting in 10 million people migrating to the neighbouring states of India, particularly Assam, Tripura and West Bengal, is a classic case of political migration due to the state unleashing violence against its own people. Poverty, indebtedness and pauperisation process may force the poor section of a community to migrate. This form of migration is categorised as economic migration. Religious/ethnic migrations are often the result of failure of the dominant racial and religious groups to allay the fears of the ethnic and religious minority, leading to a feeling of insecurity that results in migration to places where that feeling is assuaged. The large scale migration of Hindus to India and Muslims to Pakistan and the exodus of 65,000 Chakmas from the Chittagong Hill Tracts to Tripura in the face of counter-insurgency measures by the Bangladesh security forces, are two prominent examples.

Globally, as per the "Stern Review: The Economics of Climate Change", a well-known report on the economics of climate change, 200 million people may become permanently displaced due to rising sea levels, heavier floods, and more intense droughts.[58] Environmental migrations could be slow or sudden. Cyclones, tidal surges, floods and earthquakes cause sudden migration, whereas suffering due to the slow onset of soil erosion, inundation, water-logging and salinity contributes to slow migration. Moreover, migration may be attributed to more than one cause.

Cross-border migration from neighbouring countries is a grave challenge for India. As per a 2013 report of the UN Department of Social and Economic Affairs (UN-DESA), 3.2 million Bangladeshis are living in India and it is termed as "the single largest bilateral stock of international migrants".[59] India is also reported to have 2.2 million Nepalese, 70,000 Sri Lankan Tamils and about 100,000 Tibetans.[60] Bangladesh, a country with scarcity of land, rapid population growth, declining cultivable land and unequal distribution of land resources, has induced large-scale migration and will continue to do so in the predictable future. The combined influx of Hindu minorities (due to repression) and Muslims (in search of space) has changed the demographic profile of northeast India. Initially, movement of people from Bangladesh was confined to the neighbouring Indian states of Assam, Tripura and West Bengal. Now the migrants are moving further afield to states including Tamil Nadu, Maharashtra, Gujarat and Delhi.

Several studies have suggested that migration may lead to conflict in host communities and the case of Bengali immigration from the plains into the Chittagong Hills and Assam has been a commonly cited example.[61] The emergence of insurgencies in Tripura and Assam is also known to be directly related to uncontrolled illegal immigration combined with the marginalisation of the indigenous communities. In Tripura, the indigenous population has fallen from a high of 70 per cent in 1947 to a mere 27 per cent partly because of the influx of Chakma refugees. The primary causes of this migration were: a series of natural disasters between 1970-91, landlessness, soil erosion and resource competition with lowland migrants, and inadequate policy response. This resulted in negative socio-economic ramifications which led to an increase in revolutionary activities against both the government and local administration. The tribals accuse the federal government of neglecting the local economy and doing little to stop outsiders from exploiting the region's rich timber and mineral wealth.

Migrants coming from conflict areas retain a direct stake in the outcome of fighting in their country of origin. Therefore, it is easy for the insurgent groups to mobilise migrants for (or against) one side or the other, thereby increasing the probability of organised armed conflict and spread of armed violence. However, purely environmental refugees would not carry any political agenda nor would they have experience in organising armed insurgencies. While competition for resources or jobs in the host country and inter-ethnic fears, may lead to violence in various forms, from murder to riots, organised armed conflict is less likely. For example, large numbers of economic migrants are attracted to Western Europe and North America every year because of the employment opportunities. While such immigration is not without friction, it generally does not lead to armed insurgency. On the other hand, migrants may also be instrumental in value addition to cultural variability through their skills and other contributions.

Therefore, the host nation needs to look at different categories of migrants from different perspectives. The solution lies in assessing the gravity of the situation in the correct perspective and then formulating appropriate policies depending upon the prevailing circumstances and nature/type/magnitude of the migrants. Given the political, social, economic, ethnic and communal tensions associated with migration, this will mean considerable effort on the part of, as well as a challenge for, India, to manage its borders, requiring coordination and concerted action by the political leadership. The administrative, diplomatic, security, intelligence, legal, regulatory and economic agencies of the country are expected to secure our frontiers and sub-serve the best interests of the country.

Environmental Stresses/Changes: Implications for the Indian Military

Environmental stresses/changes have a direct bearing on the military in many ways. The Himalayas (and the Tibetan plateau), having large-scale military presence, are among the areas which are most susceptible to the effects of climate change, as brought out earlier. The rapidly melting glaciers in the region would call for a change in infrastructure parameters, training philosophy, deployment plans as well as operational considerations, especially at the Siachen Glacier, the highest battlefield in the world. For example, artillery gun platforms, which are presently in the form of hardened snow, would melt rapidly and would necessitate redeployment. Unexpected meltdowns would make troop movements extremely dangerous, and nearly impossible in some of the affected areas. Melting of glaciers would also affect air-dropping zones and helipads, which are the lifeline for air-maintenance of troops deployed in remotely located forward posts.

Likely change in snowfall and weather patterns will also have a varied impact on troop deployment and mobility. For example, during winters, the militaries of India and Pakistan used to withdraw from some of the pre-designated forward posts, as these posts were considered to be extremely difficult to man during this season. In this context, there was a tacit understanding between the two militaries to respect and abide by the prevailing arrangement. However, in 1999, Pakistan violated the tradition, and made clandestine intrusions into the Kargil area and occupied the army outposts that were abandoned by the Indian military during the winter season. This might have become feasible because of lesser degree of weather severity during that year. On the other hand, due to reduced snowfall during the winter season of 1998-99, the Zojila axis could be opened up in early May 1999, well ahead of the annual schedule of road opening in June 1999.[62] This allowed rapid induction of Indian troops from Srinagar to Zojila by road. Had there been normal snowfall in that particular year, this rapid induction would have not been possible. Continued increase in temperature and reduction in snowfall may make these outposts more manageable during winter, as compared to the present circumstances. However, this will be countered by the glacial melting, leading to flash floods, and severing of lines of communication.

Vector diseases comprise another cause of concern for army deployments as, generally, army combat/war zones are in natural surroundings which normally support biodiversity, including disease vectors like mosquitoes. For example, during World War II, in the Burma theatre, malaria was one of the biggest enemies. With climatic and weather changes, there is a possibility of spread of vector diseases even in the higher reaches which were until recently known for not having the same. A case in point is Leh: malarial cases in this region comprise a recent phenomenon.

Unexpected floods in generally dry regions are forcing the military to review its infrastructure policies in these regions. For example, flash floods in Leh have mandated operational and infrastructural changes at the military bases. Till recently, the military was managing with mud bunkers which are easy to build and are cost-effective. But in view of the flash floods, these bunkers are being replaced by concrete ones. Leh was known to be a rain shadow area and an effective airfield drainage system was not considered an operational necessity. But in view of the changing rain patterns, a special drainage system has been introduced at the Leh airfield to avoid flooding.[63] Similarly, having learnt lessons from calamities like the 2014 J&K floods, more redundant communication systems are being instituted.

Most weapons are required to be stored within specified temperature and humidity ranges for which temperature controlled weapon storage areas are created. Increase in temperature would require more such storage areas, even at cold places, which up till now are considered to have ambient temperature suitable for storing weapons without a temperature control facility. Tactical deception methods may also be required to be refined due to deforestation, increasing desertification and change in foliage patterns.

Logistics requirements, including those of energy, water and appropriate equipment are dependent on weather conditions and ambient temperature. Performance of men and machine also depends upon temperature. Therefore, logistics plans are required to be suitably amended to cater for increase in temperature/extreme weather conditions. In mountain warfare, measures against GLOF, flash floods and vector diseases are required to be factored in.

As of now, the militaries of the South Asian countries largely continue to be out of the ambit of mandatory energy audits. However, the increasing global focus on climate change will certainly enhance the salience of audits/regulatory mechanisms in the militaries with regard to energy consumption during peace-time training as well as during operations in war/crisis. To strengthen the image of the military and to remain aligned with the global community, these militaries would be required to go 'green'. Militaries need sensitisation to the fact that availability of fossil fuel and drinking water is likely to decrease in the coming decades and they have to plan and train in such a manner that their infrastructure, training philosophy and organisational culture accord due attention to energy and water efficiency while adopting eco-friendly equipment and practices. Renewable energy, nuclear energy, hybrid fuel equipment and electric vehicles are to be preferred over fossil fuel equipment. The procurement procedures need to factor in the lifetime energy consumption/cost of a system. Simulator-based training is to be augmented to the extent possible.

International treaties and mandates on climate change may have a direct bearing on military operations. It is important for the militaries to be aligned with national mandates and the targets a country is subjected to under various international regimes/multilateral/bilateral agreements. Management of Ozone Depleting Substances (ODS) under the Montreal Protocol of 1987 is a classic example. Under this protocol, ODS like halons and chlorofluorocarbons (CFC) were being phased out. Militaries had to realign their approach towards the use of ODS like halons and CFCs.[64] In order to preserve and use the available halons judicially, a halon bank was created by the Indian Air Force since there was no provision for the supply of additional stocks.

The increasing number and intensity of extreme weather incidences and disasters is increasing the deployment of military forces in Humanitarian Assistance and Disaster Relief (HADR) operations within the country as well as across the border. Increasing participation in such operations calls for realignment of operating procedures and training principles. The militaries need to enhance the component of HADR training in the training doctrines/patterns, while maintaining focus on conventional war-fighting training. This is one of the biggest challenges for the militaries of South Asia, essentially because of limited resources. As per an Indian Navy officer, training and exercises in the Indian Navy (IN) are focussed largely on conventional naval warfare, with humanitarian aspects being covered in classroom instructions only. He further recommends that training naval personnel to operate effectively in humanitarian missions would require integration of such missions in full-scale functional exercises.[65] Same stands good for the Army and the Air Force.

Impact on Indian Navy: In order to carry out relief missions at short notice, the navy needs to have the capability to rapidly move large volumes of supplies. Sea level rise may affect the availability of amphibious landing sites. The IN may be required to acquire more shallow draught ships capable of landing in disaster areas. The use of cushion vehicles and hovercraft could be a more practical option. The IN may be required to replace a number of brown water ships with multi-role expeditionary capability ships. Sea level rise will have a significant impact on naval operations. Rapid deployment in HADR operations would require ship designs with greater role adaptability for the crew and the hull.[66]

Operational oceanography has a direct bearing on naval operations and tactics. Ocean data in terms of temperature, salinity, pressure profiles and ocean circulation patterns, govern submarine operations and performance of underwater sensors, including sonars, underwater telephones and firing of weapons. Changing climate could alter the ocean circulation pattern. At the tactical level, this would imply the need for more predictive data on ocean currents, surface temperature and evaporation ducts in operational areas. The requirement of strengthening predictive data would call for greater meteorological equipment and effort offshore as well as in vessels/ships, especially those operating closer to the coast and in environmentally threatened areas. Naval bases like INS *Kadamba*, INS *Karwar*, and INS *Angre* at Mumbai are particularly at threat from the predicted increase in storm surges and cyclones in the west coast.[67] The location of bases and other shore/offshore assets would be required to be reassessed on the basis of weather risks and operational necessities.

Many naval activities, especially weapon firing, have sea-state restrictions and weather restrictions. Extreme weather conditions would restrict the operational capability of the navy. Additionally, operating under adverse conditions would degrade efficiency levels of the crew, necessitating frequent turnarounds and revising manning policies.

Climate change induced alteration in marine resources, especially marine fisheries, may occur across international boundaries. As a result, the affected countries may call for revision of maritime zones, fishing zones and coastal navigation routes as mentioned earlier. Ocean acidification has already resulted in fish stock migration. This may have repercussions like increased illegal fishing. Hence, strengthening of efforts towards protection of maritime resources would lead to an increase in the tasking of the Indian Navy as well as the Indian Coast Guard.

India is yet to conclude delimitation of the maritime boundary with Pakistan and Bangladesh. The zone of contention between India and Pakistan is the Sir Creek and the delimitation of maritime boundaries. Similarly, issues with Bangladesh include New Moore Island and the maritime boundary dispute. Any shift in the baseline point will further alter the maritime boundaries and complicate the issue.

The Indian Navy is known for adhering to environmental norms, most notably the controlled discharge of sewage overboard and pumping of fuel bilges. This tradition of being concerned about environmental issues needs to be taken to a higher level through further adoption of green technology and environmental friendly practices.

Impact on Air Operations: Indian strategists opine that India's strategic area of interest stretches from the Persian Gulf in the west to the Strait of Malacca in the east, and from the Central Asian Republics in the north to near the equator in the south. Hence, the IAF needs to be ready to operate in this vast area which requires weather monitoring of this region. Weather is always factored into flying activities at all stages, ranging from planning to the execution stage, because climatic as well as weather conditions have a direct bearing on military aviation. Unfavourable weather conditions put restrictions on the air operations as it affects aircraft, sensors, equipment/systems, weapon delivery as well as pilots are affected by them. Therefore, increasing variability in weather conditions is required to be looked into in a systematic and comprehensive manner.

Increase in temperature will have a direct bearing on air operations, especially at high altitudes, since the lift capability is inversely proportional to the ambient temperature and the altitude of operations. As the temperature/altitude increases, the lift capability of the aircraft reduces. Additionally, any change in temperature would call for calibrations in fire tables/parameters. Therefore, the military focus on weather forecast is bound to increase.

Comprehensive Vulnerability Assessment: In the wake of the above, the Indian military needs to undertake a comprehensive vulnerability assessment of its bases, installations, equipment, training doctrine and operational philosophy against environmental stresses and challenges, including climate change.

Conclusion

Nations and regions with political instability, weak governance structures, and low economic performance are expected to be more vulnerable to climate change/environmental degradation amplified conflicts. Limited resources, lack of mitigation and adaptation capabilities, and non-availability of effective public institutions reduce the national capability to address environmental challenges. And this increases the dissatisfaction amongst the masses as well as the rift between the government and the governed. Crisis and conflict management in such areas is certainly more challenging. There is always a risk of the spilling over of the climate change/environmentally induced crisis to the neighbouring countries, transcending borders.

In South Asia, the mutual trust deficit and territorial disputes continue to be a stark reality. Creation of two states—Pakistan in 1947 and Bangladesh in 1971—is a typical reflection of the prevailing atmosphere of doubt, suspicion and scepticism. Continued distrust between India and Pakistan, terrorism and insurgencies, home grown as well as sponsored from across the border, do not appear to be adequately addressed despite numerous political and civil society initiatives. This distrust is consuming a phenomenal amount of national resources—human, material as well as intellectual—which otherwise could have been harnessed towards regional growth and development had there been an atmosphere of peace and trust.

Environmental stresses/challenges should be viewed as an opportunity to bring the regional leadership onto a common platform for working towards the common good. Somehow, the environmental leadership needs to bring home the point that the biggest weapon of mass destruction is climate change and the only possible way to address this threat is to take initiatives that are consensual and mutually beneficial. The trust and understanding developed through these initiatives is then to be extrapolated to other spheres of international relations that are challenging to handle. There is a need to convince the policy makers that addressing environmental challenges is a positive sum game (and not a zero sum game) in the arena of regional international relations. Overlooking environmental issues is a highly self-destructive proposition.

Notes

1. Alan Dupont, "The Strategic Implications of Climate Change", *Survival: Global Politics and Strategy,* June–July 2008, vol. 50, pp. 29-54.
2. Jawaharlal Nehru, *The Discovery of India* (New Delhi: Penguin Books, 2004), p. 68.
3. Speech by Secretary of Defence Chuck Hagel, Arequipa, Peru, Monday, October 13, 2014. Accessed at http://www.defense.gov/Speeches/Speech.aspx?SpeechID=1893 on February 8, 2015.

4. SACEP official website www.sacep.org. Accessed on April 13, 2015.
5. CNA Military Advisory Board, *National Security and the Accelerating Risks of Climate Change* (Alexandria, VA: CNA Corporation, 2014), p. 2. Accessed at www.cna.org/reports/accelerating-risks on January 4, 2015.
6. National Intelligence Council, *Global Water Security* (Washington, DC: Office of the Director of National Intelligence, 2012). Accessed at http://www.dni.gov/index.php/newsroom/press-releases/96-press-releases-2012/529-odnireleases-global-water-security-ica. on January 5, 2015.
7. Jaswant Singh, *Defending India* (New Delhi: Macmillan India Ltd, 1999), pp. 284-285.
8. The United Nations World Water Development Report 2014.
9. Nishant Gupta, "Environmental Stresses and Regional Cooperation: A Perspective", *Defence and Diplomacy*, vol. 2, no. 4, 2013, pp. 23-32.
10. *South Asian Environment Outlook 2009* (UNEP, SAARC, Development Alternatives, 2008), p. 25.
11. n. 8.
12. "Centre for Ecology and Hydrology 2002", as mentioned in n. 10, p. 25.
13. During these events, rainfall is exceptionally high in the hills while there is no rainfall in the plains.
14. Ajaya Mani Dixit and Diak Gyawali, "Environmental and Energy Dimensions of Cooperative Security in South Asia: A Perspective from Nepal" in D.D. Khanna, ed., *Sustainable Development: Environmental Security, Disarmament and Development Interface in South Asia* (Delhi: Macmillan, 1997), pp. 432-455.
15. Duncan Clark, "Maldives First to Go Carbon Neutral", *The Observer,* March 15, 2009. Accessed at www.guardian.co.uk/environment/2009/mar/15/maldives-president-nasheed-carbon-neutral on May 4, 2015.
16. "Maldives President says Melting Glaciers can Result in Serious Conflicts". Accessed on May 4, 2015, at http://www.thaindian.com/newsportal/india-news/maldives-president-says-melting-glaciers-can-result-in-serious-conflicts_100264777.html
17. Dupont, n. 1, pp. 29-54
18. *IPCC 2007,* as mentioned in n. 10.
19. *An Overview of Glaciers, Glacier Retreat, and Subsequent Impacts in Nepal, India and China,* WWF Nepal Program, March, 2005.
20. S Richardson and J Reynolds, "An Overview of Glacial Hazards in the Himalayas" in *Quaternary International* 65/66 (2000).
21. A similar pattern was observed during the Uttarakhand 2014 flash floods which were caused by bursting of a glacial lake that was formed due to excessive rain over a very short period of time. Though the lake was formed due to accumulation of rain water, and not because of glacial melting, glacial melting would result in similar occurrences.
22. Neil Gadihoke, "Climate Change: Implications for the Indian Navy", *Maritime Affairs*, vol. 6, no. 1, Summer 2010, p. 119.
23. Ibid., pp. 116-131.
24. The mass exodus of 10 million refugees from East Pakistan to the neighbouring states of India was essentially one of the causes of the 1971 Bangladesh War.
25. n. 10, p. 48.
26. IPCC Third Assessment Report, Climate Change 2001.
27. I Naeem, A Rasheed, M Zuhair and M Riyaz, "Coral Bleaching in the Maldives –1998", Survey carried out in North and South Malé, *Climate Change and Human Health*, WHO/WMO/UNEP.
28. The Lakshadweep group of islands in India has similar problems as those of the Maldives, insofar as terrain and vulnerabilities are concerned. The consequences of climate change in the

Maldives would be replicated in these islands.

29. In Pakistan, agriculture presently contributes 25 per cent to its national income; provides employment to 50 per cent of the labour force; and 60 per cent of the country's exports are directly or indirectly based on agriculture. Nepal also has a high dependency on agriculture and over 80 per cent of water in the country is used for irrigation. Higher temperatures, increased evapo-transpiration and decreased winter precipitation may result in more droughts.
30. S Peng, J Huang, JE Sheehy, RE Laza, RM Visperas, X Zhong, GS Centeno, GS Khush and KG Cassman, *Rice Yields Decline with Higher Night Temperature from Global Warming* (USA: National Academy of Science, 2004).
31. "The United Nations World Water Development Report 4" (Paris: UNESCO, 2012), Chapter 44, p. 822.
32. US Country Studies Program (USCP), 1997.
33. Z Karim, "Agricultural Vulnerability and Poverty Alleviation in Bangladesh", in TE Downing ed., *Climate Change and World Food Security* (Berlin: NATO ASI Series, 137 Springer, 1996).
34. ML Parry, C Rosenzweig, Iglesias, M Livermore and G Fischer, "Effects of Climate Change on Global Food Production under SRES Emissions and Socio-Economic Scenarios", *Global Environmental. Change* 14, (2004), pp. 53-67.
35. M Habibullah, AU Ahmed, and Z Karim, "Assessment of Food Grain Production Loss due to Climate Induced Soil Salinity: A Case Study", in S Huq, Z Karim, M. Asaduzzaman and F. Mahtab, eds., *Vulnerability and Adaptation to Climate Change for Bangladesh*, (Netherlands: Kluwer Academic Publishers1999).
36. Sudha Nambudiri, "Fish Catch Across India Drops by 5%" , *The Times of India,* May 3, 2015.
37. SAARC Workshop on Climate Change and Disasters: Emerging Trends and Future Strategies, Kathmandu, Nepal August 21-22, 2008 *Regional Cooperation on Climate Change Adaptation and Disaster Risk Reduction in South Asia: Road Map*. Accessed at http://saarc-sadkn.org/downloads/road_map%20CCA&DRR.pdf on October 4, 2014.
38. PG Dhar Chakrabarti, director, SAARC Disaster Management Centre and executive director, National Institute of Disaster Management, *Regional Cooperation for Disaster Management in South Asia: Challenges and Opportunities for Regional Early Warning System for Natural Disasters*. Accessed at www.dmb.gov.bd
39. The official website of "Indian Red Cross Society", accessed at http://www.indianredcross.org/program.htm on August 21, 2014.
40. TR Knutson and RE Tuleya, "Impacts of CO2 Induced Warming on Simulated Hurricane Intensities and Precipitation: Sensitivity to the Choice of Climate Model and Convective Parameterization", in *J. Climate* 17, 2004, pp. 3477-3495.
41. M Lal, "Tropical Cyclones in a Warmer World", in *Current Science,* India 80, 2001, pp. 1103-1104.
42. n. 10, pp. 52-53.
43. Human Development Index Report 2014, p. 71.
44. Ibid., p. 71.
45. AJ McMichael, Campbell-Lendrum, S Kovats, S Edwards, P Wilkinson, T Wilson, R Nicholls and Co-authors, "Global Climate Change: Comparative Quantification of Health Risks: Global and Regional Burden of Disease due to Selected Major Risk Factors" (edited by M Ezzati, A Lopez, A Rodgers and C Murray), World Health Organisation 2004, Geneva, pp, 1543-1649.
46. M Lal, "Global Climate Change: India's Monsoon and its Variability", in *Final Report under Country Studies Vulnerability and Adaptation.* Work Assignment with Stratus Consulting's Contract of the U.S. Environmental Protection Agency, 2002.
47. River systems of the Himalayan region can be divided into different sub-regions. The Western Himalayan sub-region includes the Indus system comprising the Chenab, Jhelum, Beas, Ravi,

and Sutlej rivers. The Indus river system is the largest, contiguous irrigation system in the world with a command area of 20 million hectares and an annual irrigation capacity of over 12 million hectares. This system is shared by India and Pakistan (as well as China and Afghanistan). The Central Himalayan sub-region includes the Ganges system consisting of the Yamuna, Mahakali, Ramganga, Gandaki, Kamali, and Kosi rivers. The Mahakali river flows along the Nepal-India western border. The river was fixed as the western boundary between Nepal and British India, in 1816. The Ganges basin is shared by India, China, Bangladesh and Nepal. The Eastern Himalayan sub-region includes the Brahmaputra system to which the Teesta, Manas and Raidak rivers belong. The Brahmaputra system is shared by India, Bangladesh, Bhutan as well as China. There are several other tributaries of these rivers which also flow into more than one country. The Ganges-Brahmaputra-Meghna system, which carries 60 percent of the nation's total river flow, is second only to the Amazon with an annual discharge of 1,350 billion cubic metres and a total drainage area of 1.75 million sq km. With a population of over 600 million people living in the region, which is growing at an annual rate of 2 percent, there is considerable anthropogenic pressure on the region's resources.

48. The United Nations World Water Development Report 4 (Paris: UNESCO, 2012), Chapter 44, p. 822.
49. Nishant Gupta, "Mainstreaming Environmental Security and Cooperation in South Asia" in Vinod Patney, ed., *Asian Defence Review 2013* (New Delhi: KW Publishers, 2014), pp. 109-131.
50. "How Green was my Valley?: Climate Change will only Intensify Problems in Kashmir", *The Economist*, Asia Edition October 23, 2008. Accessed at http://www.economist.com/node/12480378 on March 18, 2013
51. Sundeep Waslekar, *The Final Settlement: Resurrecting India-Pakistan Relations* (Mumbai: International Centre for Peace Initiatives, 2005), pp. 47-48. And Nitin Pai, "Climate Change and National Security: Preparing India for New Conflict Scenarios", *The Indian National Interest Policy Brief*, no 1, April 2008.
52. Asif Ali Zardari, "Partnering With Pakistan", *Washington Post,* January 28, 2009.
53. Arvind Gupta, "Vicious anti-India Propaganda in Pakistan on Water Issues", March 29, 2010. Accessed at http://www.idsa.in/idsacomments/Viciousanti-IndiapropagandainPakistanonWaterissues_agupta_290310c16f.html?q=print/5207
54. Under the World Bank mediated 1960 'Indus Water Treaty' (IWT) the eastern rivers—Sutlej, Beas and Ravi—were allocated to India while the western rivers—Jhelum, Chenab and Indus—were allotted to Pakistan (barring their use by India under specified conditions in Jammu and Kashmir), with limited consumptive rights over these to India.
55. Gupta, n. 53.
56. Aditi Phadnis, "A Water Conflict in Kashmir", *Business Standard,* May 16, 2005. Accessed at http://www.strategicforesight.com/sfgnews_122.htm on May 13, 2013.
57. China is also claiming Arunachal Pradesh - a rare regional area with rich water resources and great potential for hydroelectric power. But Indo-China issues have been kept out of the scope of the scope of this research.
58. "Stern Review: The Economics of Climate Change". Accessed on April 15, 2015, at http://webarchive.nationalarchives.gov.uk/+/http:/www.hm-treasury.gov.uk/media/4/3/executive_summary.pdf
59. "Bangla Migration to India Largest in the Developing World", *The Times of India* (New Delhi) September 13, 2013.
60. Uttam Kumar Sinha, "Environmental Stresses and their Security Implications for South Asia", *Strategic Analysis*, vol. 30, no. 3, Jul-Sep 2006, pp. 599-618.
61. Ragnhild Nordås and Nils Petter Gleditsch, "Climate Change and Conflict," Centre for the

Study of Civil War (CSCW) at the International Peace Research Institute, Oslo (PRIO) & Department of Sociology and Political Science, Norwegian University of Science and Technology, Trondheim.

62. Sunil Chauhan, PK Gautam and Ajey Lele, "Impact on Warfighting capability of the Indian Military" in Report of the IDSA Working Group, *Security Implications of Climate Change for India*, (New Delhi: Academic Foundation, 2009) pp. 144-145.
63. Vijay Mohan, "Leh Airfield Unfit for Fighter Ops: Runway Degradation, Lack of Requisite Lighting System to Blame", *The Tribune* (New Delhi), July 24, 2014.
64. Air Mshl AK Singh, Wg Cdr Manoj Kumar, Atul Bagai, *Ozone Protection and National Security: A Military Perspective* (New Delhi: UNEP, 2009).
65. Neil Gadihoke, "Climate Change: Implications for the Indian Navy," *Maritime Affairs*, vol. 6, no. 1, Summer 2010, p. 127.
66. Chauhan, et. al., n. 62, pp. 147-153.
67. Ibid., pp. 150-151.

10

Network-Centric Operations: The Human Dimension

MondarBandopadhyay

Machines don't fight wars. People do and they use their minds.[1]

When there is a discussion on the theory of Network-Centric Warfare (NCW) and its implementation by way of Network-Centric Operations (NCO), there is always an attempt to understand the need for enhanced networking and the characteristics of the network structure. There is also an attempt to fathom the various milestones that could enable efficient progress towards a network-enabled force. As various nations today move in the much spoken of direction, it may not be incorrect to say that the technology is in place, the willingness to adapt is there, the structure is being made and the integration is taking place. However, it may appear that the tip of the spear, the war-fighter himself, is not so much the focus of attention. In all debates and postulations and theorising, it may be almost natural to miss out on the human element. However, when looked at closely, it is not difficult to realise that the human element is by far the most central to all processes and is also the most fragile, as it is the last bastion of the chain that would execute the mission.

Network-centric operations or warfare is a war-fighting concept that utilises the power of networking to enhance the application of combat power in the process of achieving the commander's intent. In the process, we utilise information superiority through the network, rather than the traditional assets of mass and momentum through platforms and weapons. Major components of NCO are information sharing and collaboration that would lead to greater shared awareness and mission success[2]. To ensure this, quantum improvements would be needed in the fields of communications, sensors and automation. However, while all this is required, it would be critical to understand the interface of technology with the human element. To be more precise, there would be a need to decide how, why and where this technology supports the human function. In the final analysis, all the processes, whether traditional or part of network-centric warfare, must lead to decisions that translate into physical actions. Therefore, as this would be considered part of the command and control net, it is imperative that the human element is intricately woven into all processes in a network-centric environment.

Every decision and every course of action is a product of processes that take place in the mind of the war-fighter and these processes are called **cognitive processes.**[3]There are two sides to this, as cognitive processes can improve own decision-making and at the same time, impair that of the opponent. Better understanding of the cognitive aspects would lead to greater clarity in understanding how and where technology can and must interface with the human element. Operations in the cognitive domain, the impact on the cognitive capability of the war-fighter and self-synchronisation are a few aspects that would be discussed in the paper, with a view to bring out the centrality of the cognitive processes in the concept of network-centric operations. The seminal work has been published under DOD CCRP Publication 2002, titled Effects Based Operations – Applying Network Centric Warfare in Peace, Crisis and War, authored by Edward A Smith.[4] This paper aims to bring out the primacy of the human element while highlighting the impact of a networked environment on the war fighter.

Operations in the Cognitive Domain

Network-centric warfare, when implemented in earnest, must not just improve war-fighting capabilities but must change the way war would be fought. The pay-off must be non-linear for the concept to succeed and this must be derived from the interplay among information superiority, the network itself and the war-fighter. Finally, all this must translate into actions/ events that influence the *behaviour of friends and allies as well as the adversary.* Every action or event that can be observed would elicit a response and so the action could be termed as the stimulus or cause and the response could be termed as the effect. This "cause and effect" link is a concept that could become a useful tool in predicting behaviour, provided we understand not only that a response was a result of a stimulus but also why that particular stimulus resulted in a particular response. Therefore, it would be desirable to know the 'why of it'.

The OODA Loop

The theory of the Observe, Orient, Decide, Act (OODA) loop, as proposed by Boyd, provides a rather simplistic and tactical version of the entire cognitive process. One observes and orients oneself, a process that leads to decision-making and further translates into the desired action. For example, a pilot would observe his opponent's action or presence and then orient himself to respond. In this, he would go through numerous processes in his mind and, at the end, choose a particular course of action or decision. He would then act accordingly. His opponent, on his part, would do precisely the same; from observe to act, as a response to the first pilot's actions. The one acting faster would ideally be the victor. These actions could be applicable to "one on one" situations at tactical levels, but could also be taken up to the operational level. This OODA theory, however, does not clearly amplify the pace of operations required to overwhelm the adversary. It also does not also indicate how the behaviour and will of the opponent can be influenced.[5]As we move up from the tactical level, towards interaction at the operational levels and higher, simple systems morph into a complex system of systems. Interactions at these levels are at the military-strategic as well as geo-strategic dimensions, and the nature of decision-making is different in both.[6] Also, these dimensions operate in different timelines as compared to the interactions at the tactical level. These push us to factor in not only personal behavior but also institutional and organisational behaviour[7] and in this process, as we move away from the OODA loop, we are now coaxed into exploring "operations in the cognitive domain".[8]

Just as the human element is at the heart of warfare, the cognitive domain is central to the human dimension. A better understanding of the domain is essential for war-fighting and is the only manner in which exponential benefits can accrue. In an attempt to obtain clarity, the OODA loop was taken and stretched a bit further, wherein the decision-making process in it was described in terms of three different domains:[9] the physical domain, the information domain and the cognitive domain. These domains would find mention whenever anybody talks of NCO/NCW. However, here the discussion would aim to bring out the relationship among the three domains and the primacy of the cognitive domain. Very simply put, military actions take place in the *physical domain*, actions are detected and reported to the authorities in the *information domain* and the decision making takes place in the *cognitive domain.*[10] It is also understood that these domains are not limited to the military alone but transcend virtual and physical barriers into activities that may be undertaken by other agencies such as the state/ government, non-state players, Non-Governmental Organisations (NGOs) as well as terrorists/ irregular warriors. Secondly, the domains are not water-tight compartments, but overlap each other. These domains provide a general frame within which the various processes of war-fighting can be understood. It becomes simpler to trace the 'cause-effect' and the 'stimulus-response' relations and understand how actions in one domain translate into effects and then into decisions in the others.

The Physical Domain

This domain encompasses all the physical actions or events that serve as stimuli for other domains.[11] This is where there is actual movement of military forces/ actors. In fact, movement is not as essential as the very presence of such forces. A military force becomes an object to be observed and responded to by an adversary. Therefore, even the presence of the force at the right place, at the right time, would be able to produce a response. Secondly, the physical domain should not be restricted to military forces or actions alone. At higher levels of interaction, say the strategic and national levels, physical actions could also mean those that occur in the political or economic spheres and these could equally have an effect on the adversary as well. This would be better understood at the geo-strategic levels. Lastly, the physical domain would encompass effects created by our own actions: direct effects of an action as well as the derived effects that are a result of such actions.[12]

The Information Domain

This is the domain in which information flow takes place. All the means that help us in becoming aware of events or objects or a situation in the environment would ideally be included in this domain. This would then mean a domain that encompasses all the means to collect information about the environment and then managing our own actions to achieve the objectives. In military parlance, it would mean all the sensors that monitor actions and events and collect data, as well as the mechanism to collate this data, analyse it, store it and disseminate it to the required stakeholders. In sum, in the information domain, a stimulus is recognised and conveyed to the human element or the human organisation.[13] However, this is only half the job done. The means of conveying all the decisions and the orders that translate the response into the physical action, as seen in the physical domain, also fall in this domain. This is the domain where there are constant efforts to enhance efficiency and effectiveness by bringing in newer technologies.[14] This domain could be viewed as three separate parts, namely, the surveillance and sensor systems; the characteristics of awareness; and, finally, the human information system.

The Surveillance System

It can be said that the information domain is actually a domain in which data is collected and conveyed to the human element and thereafter the awareness and the decisions are conveyed back to the physical domain. All this data and information is collected by various sensors and sources of information that are employed and, therefore, the entire system could be termed a large surveillance system of sensors.[15] Now, as our observation of the daily world is limited by what our eyes can see or *fail* to see, we are equally limited in the collection and assimilation of the data and information that we derive through all these sensors. This is because sensors and sources can see only what has transpired at any given time, provided the sensor was present in that physical or geographical space to observe the data. Each sensor or source is limited either in its geographical expanse or in the time of its operation. For example, a satellite would be able to provide information on only a particular portion of the earth based on its swath and orbit. Similarly, a radar would be able to monitor only a part of the frequency spectrum that it is designed to observe. The rest would remain unobservable and, hence, that particular data would not be collected. This arrangement would not, however, mean that the system would fail. The success of the system cannot depend on any one 'all encompassing sensor' but it would rather depend on a combination of sensors and how they interact with each other. Just as all the five senses of the human body combine to provide some sort of a complete picture, so does sensor integration attempt to integrate various bits of data in the information domain. It would be highly unlikely for any nation to be able to place sensors to cover the entire environment every time as the number of sensors is limited and would always be so. Hence, there needs to be a balancing act in terms of deployment of the sensors, the nature of the sensors being deployed and what these are tasked to see. This implies that what is observed depends on *what sensor is deployed* and this, in turn, depends on *the specific decision that was taken to deploy the same.* However, this decision-making and reasoning of what sensor is to be placed where and for what, could ideally be termed as cognitive processes and would not form a part of the information domain. This is where there is a blurring of lines between the two domains—the information domain and the cognitive domain.

Characteristics of Awareness

There is enough talk about terms such as awareness, shared awareness and collaborative awareness. Simply put, it could mean knowledge obtained of the entire environment that is available to all relevant players (to the extent desirable), within the constraints of information gathering mechanisms at our disposal, that finally enables decision-making. This knowledge that is obtained, ideally, would translate into awareness through cognitive processes. However, the kind of awareness that is desired must be clearly defined so that it can result into decisions. To get to know the nature of this awareness, we need answers to a few questions. We need to know what we want to do, or rather what the end state of any situation or scenario is. Then we need to decide what level of awareness would enable us to achieve that end state and, finally, we need to ask ourselves what is the information required to get that awareness.[16] Answers to such questions would help in deciding how to balance sensors to achieve the required awareness.

With a definite end state in mind, as articulated through the commander's intent, it may be right to assume that levels of awareness required would depend on, or be dictated by, the availability of a defined quantum of data and information from the specified environment. As an example, in a Tactical Battle Area (TBA), the data/ information could include location and strength/ disposition of own and enemy forces, the activities being undertaken, force capabilities in terms of equipment being carried/ present at site, logistical stocking and command and communication infrastructure, to name a few. Now if the environment were to be enlarged beyond the TBA, the sensors would bring into calculations various factors such as terrain, weather, and phases of the moon and light conditions. These are a few of the so-called indirect factors that add up to the information data base available.[17] The number of factors or variables that influence decision-making would be humungous and it may be reasonable to assume that the number of sensors would always be in short supply – when placed against this task of persistent observation. This brings in an interesting thought: as we would never have enough sensors for the required inputs of data and information, it stands to reason that sensors would be employed at some places and some would be bereft of these. Therefore, while on the one hand, the presence of sensors would directly influence the information available, on the other, the absence of the same would result in a gap in the overall picture. So when the decision is taken to deploy sensors at place A and *not* at place B, it suggests that a balance has been reached – a balance between the data availability and the degree of uncertainty (because of non-availability of sensors).[18] As data availability to a large extent governs situational awareness, the above logic would mean that the availability of sensors would govern a critical decision – a decision concerning what kind of situational awareness is desirable and what can be done without. In other words, the number of sensors would dictate what kind of awareness is being looked at and what the acceptable degree of uncertainty is. This also implies that constraints that are imposed upon situational awareness are a result of conscious decisions taken by the planners themselves. The infantry soldiers or the fighter pilots would be able to see only what the sensors permit them to observe—those sensors that have been either placed or not placed by way of a conscious decision-making process itself.How the tactical situation pans out thereafter would depend much on how the individual war-fighter adapts to the situation, but then that is a different matter in itself. And, finally, awareness is limited not only by numbers but also by space and time. Assuming that the numbers are definite, as we increase the geographical space that needs to be kept under surveillance, the sensors would have to be more and more dispersed. As this happens, the gaps in the coverage or the degree of uncertainty would keep increasing, consequently, lowering the probability of detection.[19] It is imperative to strike a balance between the physical space under surveillance and the time lines of the surveillance.

The Human Information System

So far, the sensors that have been considered earlier have been mechanical and electronic in nature. The picture so conjured is a result of all such sensors employed and deployed in the physical realm and while these provide a large canvas, there are two specific issues that merit attention. One, such sensors focus only on an immediate and unambiguous military battle space that provides a fraction of the total data that could be available. Secondly, the entire data that could be available from the human element is largely ignored as the data from the human information system is not collated by such means. At this stage, it would be prudent to clarify that human information as is being discussed here is not the traditional *Human Intelligence* (HUMINT). It is the range of data on events and objects that is derived from human sources in much the same way as the data drawn from electronic and mechanical sensors.[20] However, there is a difference in the nature of human information that presents a challenge. Information derived through human resources/ sources tends to be subject to uncertainty and ambiguity.[21] This is so because human information is amenable to different points of views, and, hence, subject to differing interpretations. As these processes reside in the cognitive domain and each human (now read sensor) is different, no matter what the extent of education and training may be, each interpretation would be subject to the individual providing the data or the information. Two radars of the same make, design and vintage would provide ideally an identical picture of a target or an event, but *never two humans.* Therefore, while a mechanical or electronic sensor would provide pure data and leave the interpretation part to those that can do so, data from human sources may not be as objective and would, in all likelihood, be coloured with individual perceptions. Also, reporting of data through human sources could be part of deliberate disinformation (deception) or misinformation (degree of clarity). This, though, is equally applicable to data collected through mechanical and electronic means.

Another issue with the nature of human data is the varied levels of information. At tactical levels, this data may comprise locals giving information about movement of infiltrating groups. At a higher level, the information may mean a more conventional form of input, for example, open source data or intelligence exchanges or information through contacts in agencies of the government or through NGOs. And moving even higher, information could be through inter-governmental sources, Foreign Office exchanges, international organisations or allied partners. It is clear that the human element is capable of providing data at levels from the tactical to the geo-strategic, unlike other sensors that are limited to the physical realm. Therefore, each level of information would need to be analysed appropriately and differently.

The two factors discussed in the preceding paragraphs highlight the fact that information available through the human element is subject to varied interpretations and requires analysis differently at different levels. This analysis requires human effort and therefore, interestingly, it may not be far removed from the truth that while automation of processes may be an attempt to take the "*man out of the loop*", as processes get more and more automated, the very requirement of analysis may be getting the *"man back into the loop"!*[22] Also, data received through the human element needs to be processed so that adequate intelligence is created for decision-making. This requires human intervention and, therefore, analysis in this case would also have to deal with what could be believed and what need not. In effect, it would call for drawing on human judgment, a process that resides in the cognitive domain. In sum, it may be true to assume that information acquired through the human element is relatively difficult to automate.[23]

The Cognitive Process

The cognitive domain is the seat of all basic functions loosely associated with mental faculties such as attempting to derive a sense of a situation, assessing alternatives, and deciding on courses of action. Primarily, these functions rely on conscious reasoning, that is, the domain of reason, and also on sub-conscious mental models, that is, the domain of belief.[24] Now reason and belief are both influenced and shaped by culture, education and experiences. Military operations are generally looked at from the point of view of the action-reaction or stimulus–response model. And as it is in the cognitive domain that a stimulus produces the response, this should be the normal focus of any operation.

In the preceding paragraphs, it has been brought out that a lot of decision-making is involved in creating a surveillance system of systems, preparing a data gathering network, employing and deploying sensors, analysing what data is required and what is not, balancing the resources against the constraints, and weighing the imperatives of time and space. The critical question pertains to how the correct decision and course of action is arrived at by weighing time and space logically and balancing the risks against the opportunities. A similar question could be posed with respect to the information that is provided through the information domain. What is important here is how decision-makers deal with such information. It is well known that "only the right information must go to the right man, at the right time." Excess information would lead to overload, and inadequate information would lead to taking decisions in a vacuum. So the right amount of information is as important as the right type of information. All these are, very clearly, human engineering issues and can be solved. The true challenge is to find out how decision-makers respond to the information provided from the physical domain and how they make decisions. That is, how a situation is perceived to be developing, how sense is made of it, how choices are assessed and decisions taken to arrive at a course of action. These are basic questions, answers to which would lie in better understanding of cognitive functions.

Perception: Knowledge and Understanding

This could be the first step in the cognitive process – perception or how we perceive a situation. The Information Superiority Working Group, in the various sessions that it concluded, observed that the decision processes and the ability to deal with information depended on various human dimensions such as physiology, emotions and beliefs.[25] However, this is not all, and influences other than the ones spoken of also matter a great deal. Humans tend to look at problems from a reference frame, that is, there is a tendency to be influenced by factors like prior knowledge, education, training, societal culture, national culture and beliefs.[26] Precedence is always an important part of the reference frame and humans draw from analogy a large percentage of reason. Any circumstance or set of circumstances is balanced against a previous incident or happening, either consciously or sub-consciously. Such a comparison is also made against a generalised or accepted mental model of what the solution *"should be"*. An understanding of the situation now comes out of noting the peculiarities of the current situation at hand. The gaps in the information are sub-consciously or even consciously, filled in by the mental models or the prior knowledge/ experience. This process is true of a particular individual as well as a human organisation, although the organisation would be equipped with far greater knowledge and experience.[27] Here the organisation could be political, corporate or military and as commanders/ leaders act and react with reference to their organisations, it may be prudent to suggest that it should be the organisation's intent or rather the 'command's intent' and not the 'commander's intent' that needs to be understood.Secondly, the culture of the organisation would play an important part in the knowledge and experience levels that it possesses. A culture that encourages different and diverse points of views would definitely be enriched in this organisational knowledge and experience.

Prior knowledge, education, training and the various mental models are strongly influenced by culture, national and organisational. All these have an effect over the decision-making processes of the individual or the organisation. These determine how decision-makers would view the information, how they would comprehend the cause and effect relationship, how they would look at the time dimension and how they would work at the alternatives. Therefore, knowledge, education, training and mental models have an impact on cognitive processes and this is in two dimensions. Firstly, in how the sensors or sources are deployed for information collection and, secondly, how the same information is treated and converted into intelligence or sense. While the first part is relatively simple and difficult to corrupt as it is mostly mechanical, it is the second aspect that is most vulnerable. The translation from raw data/ information to logical sense would be critically impaired should there be false perceptions of either the source of information or of the entire situation. This is more likely if decision-makers have little or inadequate knowledge of the environment on the outside, or they have fixed mental models or perceptions that are more likely to refuse or reject any differing model or point of view.[28] This is a context that would need to be understood in order to comprehend outcomes of given situations.

Making Sense and Taking Decisions

Making 'sense' is an important part of the cognitive process. Various factors such as knowledge, mental models, education and training merge together into comprehension of a particular situation which thereafter provides a base to create sense. This could also be defined as a process of setting the various pieces of information obtained into a virtual canvas to get a somewhat complete picture that would provide a mental appreciation of the entire situation. The information would comprise facts and data obtained from the information realm and the picture would get completed with the help of the many factors discussed above, that is, prior knowledge, education, training and mental models, to name a few. This picture would contain information of changing or dynamic futures/ end states and it would also contain information of a few alternative paths to these different futures/ stated objectives.[29] This process of making sense would then logically provide a platform for decision-making. It would help in identifying the various courses of action available for providing a response. One choice could be to take absolutely 'no action' at all. This would be necessitated by the fact that adequate information may not be available and re-tasking of sensors may have to be undertaken. Another reason could be to not give a reaction immediately. On the other hand, the choice of 'taking some action' may be explored. In such a case, a separate decision-making process would have to be undertaken to decide which of the various available courses of actions would be more viable.[30] Those actions would then have to be assessed in a different process altogether to ensure that the desired end states are achieved.The decision-makers would analyse and assess the actions to lead to the desired objectives/ end states and each of the choices—to wait, to act or to analyse further—would be measured against the same understanding provided in the sense making process.

The Physical Action

Every course of action, when crystallised and decided upon, must result into physical action. This would involve a planning process that would again span the information, physical as well as cognitive domains. The process would entail identifying the actions, carrying out a decongest exercise and communicating the commander's/ command's intent to the agency/ units executing the decision. This communication is one of the most difficult of actions as the factors that need to be taken into the planning consideration comprise a huge number, not limited by the immediate battle space.[31] The problem of perceptions once again plays up in this effort as understanding the intent would be different across the various levels of operations as well as laterally across the different units or individuals involved. With the increasing complexity of the action, the number of levels and lateral coverage that need to be coordinated are greater. Therefore, the greater are the chances of information distortion and misunderstanding the intent. While command and control communications can be improved by improving the infrastructure, the impediment is in conveying understanding of the intent and this involves an interplay between the cognitive and information domains. The planners need to understand what is possible with the assets at hand, and the war-fighter needs to understand the commander's/ command's intent. The human element plays truant once again. As there is a difference in every human's prior knowledge, education, training and mental models, so would there be a difference in their individual understanding of the situation and the intent. Varying backgrounds, different standards of education and training and a more diverse experience base would lead to greater miscommunication and misunderstanding.[32] However, if the backgrounds, the training patterns and the education levels were similar, the understanding would be more or less uniform and, hence, the chances of distortion of the intent would be less. The more uniform the base, the less likely the problems.

The Action-Reaction Cycle

In sum, knowledge and understanding help in creating a frame of reference against which information and events are measured, sense is made of the entire proceeding, courses of action or choices are analysed, the intent is communicated and physical action or inaction is planned, leading to the action-reaction cycle. This would then result in physical actions, the sole aim of which would be to produce an effect on the opponent, thereby affecting his behavior. After all, that is the final aim – producing the desired effect on the opponent. Therefore, all the cognitive processes outlined in the preceding paragraphs, from the data collection, to the making of sense, to the execution and the response from the opponent is half of the entire cycle, the other half being the observation of the response to recalibrate own actions once again.[33] Each side then observes and responds to the actions of the other and, in simple terms, this is no different from the well known OODA loop theory.

The Key Take Aways

Comprehending this cognitive cycle is important because it provides a base to understand the implications of actions on the behaviour of the opponent. Therefore, three critical issues need to be discussed at this point that would reinforce our understanding of the cognitive cycle. First is the 'nature of the actions'[34]. In due course of the cognitive cycle, the effects that are created are a result of the opponent's observations and the perceptions thereof. This means that the behaviour of the adversary can be affected ***only by those actions that can be observed.*** Therefore, the desired end state/ objective as well as the actions that are perceived to enable the attainment of the objective must be looked at from the point of view of what the opponent is likely to observe. And, therefore, it must be understood that the opponent would see not only *what* is being done but also *how* it is being done.

Secondly, the 'impact of the actions' also needs a greater understanding.[35] While it is true that actions would impact the behaviour of the opponent, what is equally true is that the opponent would frame his response based upon the history of responses in similar situations, as observed by him. That is to say, all such previous actions and responses would form a part of the data base of the opponent's education and prior knowledge and would definitely influence his reaction. This history would, in effect, provide the opponent with a mental model of his own against which to measure our own actions. Such a history of previous actions—political, military, economic or otherwise – would lend a deeper understanding of the sense of the situation that the opponent would derive and, logically, this understanding would cast an influence over his actions or reactions. Therefore, it is amply clear that cognitive operations do not begin with actions that have been decided upon in the present—they begin with all those actions that have already been undertaken in the past, well before the present has been conceived. And logically, therefore, if the history of our actions supports the present scenario, this would reinforce and amplify the behaviour and, hence, the action or the reaction of the opponent. Should the history be different, our own efforts would need modification, failing which the desired behavioural pattern may not emerge.

Finally, the third aspect is the 'nature of the observer'.[36] The cognitive cycle brings out clearly that actions and events are observed by different agencies/ human elements with inherent differences in their own experiences, mental models, education and training base, etc. Secondly, such actions/ events would be observed by an entire spectrum of observers, from the state agencies to the military soldier to the economist and also the non-state actor. All these observers would view the same event differently, analyse and understand it differently and draw different conclusions. Therefore, these different observers would *make sense of the same situation differently.* If that be so, then the responses to the same event would be different for different observers and this would need to be factored in the planning and the calculus. How a specific observer would respond to a specific set of events that has been observed is a study in itself. The applicability of such a cognitive construct would, therefore, appear to hinge on the concept of *rationality* of the observers, an aspect which has been a subject of debate. Apparently it can be concluded that decision-makers in a confrontation would logically be rational.[37]At this stage, however, it would suffice to understand the process by which the human mind functions and notwithstanding the varied differences, the functioning is essentially the same.

Impact on the Cognitive Capability of the War-Fighter

Battle Remains the Freest of all Enterprises.[38]

Understanding is the root of success. Cognitive processes and operations, from the point of view of military operations, have been discussed in some detail in the preceding paragraphs. As covered earlier, the basic fabric of NCO rests on sharing of information across various levels of command and control. This is made possible by ensuring that last mile networking is achieved and, hence, networking will allow availability of a humungous amount of information on the battle space displayed typically as icons on an electronic display on a screen.[39] This entire picture consequently would then lead to better shared awareness and understanding, leading to proper choice of courses of action, thereby, reaching the right decisions. It is amply clear that NCO is bringing in newer technology to the battlefield which would confer newer operational capabilities. A few such capabilities that are enabled by technology today have been outlined by Fred Stein and are specific to force employment.[40] 'Proactive planning' is one such ability which implies a proactive approach in the planning process to, firstly, avoid head-on confrontation by choosing alternate approaches, exploiting all opportunities when such a confrontation is inevitable and carrying out predictive planning to rehearse, evaluate and adapt plans rapidly. Next is the ability to bring in "dynamic synchronisation" of resources and thereby the mission(s) in an effort to synchronise distributed force operations. The third operational capability that he talks about is the ability to allow rapid target search, acquisition, selection, handing over to the shooter and engagement of 'time critical targets'.

Another critical operational capability that is enhanced by the networked environment is "self-synchronisation". Very simply put, self-synchronisation is the ability of a group to organise naturally and optimally, without any directions, in the process of achieving a task. This is similar to the behaviour seen in a flock of birds, moving rapidly through space synchronously, avoiding terrain obstacles while maintaining the cohesiveness that makes it a flock. It seems almost uncanny and unnatural that each member of the flock would seem to know exactly where the obstructions appear, evade those, not collide with another member in the process of doing so and yet remain integrated in a closely knit flock. This is self-synchronisation at its basic best! This behaviour can be looked at as a combination of a few distinct criteria such as avoiding crowding the local flock mates, moving towards the average location of the flock, and moving towards the average heading of the flock.[41] Such an analysis has been used to produce algorithms that permit similar physical behaviour among soldiers.[42] However, a similar analogy can also be found to exist in the case of humans. Self-synchronisation of individuals within groups conducting aggressive actions has been an ancient practice.[43] This behaviour draws on all such cognitive attributes as those covered in the preceding paragraphs. In the current context, it implies that with accurate and detailed information available at all levels, small and complex groups of military personnel would be able to organise themselves optimally and execute the command's intent—all this without any direction from the higher levels of authority. Needless to say, this would require near real time accurate and credible information that would enable unhindered sharing of awareness and incredible levels of cognitive cohesion to generate the requisite understanding of the command's intent among the members of the group.

An aspect that merits attention at this stage is that self-synchronisation is *a bottom-up approach*, very unlike the standard military *top-down one.* Traditionally, one of the reasons for the top down command and control chain in military operations was the limitation of line of sight contact. This meant that the operating picture was available only at the higher levels and not distributed fully to the actual units on the ground. Hence, each action and response at the tactical level necessitated directions from the top. However, what networking has achieved is that information can now be made available to the last soldier on the ground, hence, his operating picture is as real time and complete, if not better, as is the picture available at the top. Therefore, the combination of cognitive cohesion and technological ability makes it possible for generation of multiple options at the tactical level itself, without falling back for the command's response or direction from the higher level. This has allowed the soldier in combat to absorb the operating picture, take in the information, assess the situation, weigh the various options, take a decision based on all this and finally execute the plan – all this in consonance *with* the overall command intent but *without* the traditional top down direction. An example may be worth highlighting at this point to elaborate the capability. During the Battle of the 73rd Easting in the Gulf War of 1990-91, a particular armoured regiment was ordered to locate the main enemy forces, defeat the supporting forces if any, determine the extent of the main defences and fix them *in situ* for the main assault by the follow-on echelons. However, the regiment, on making contact with the enemy, determined that waiting for the follow-on echelons would increase the risk incurred to own forces and, therefore, chose to assault immediately, causing heavy attrition on the enemy and claiming a lop-sided victory. Post assault analysis revealed that the regiment had *chosen the most optimal path through the battle space;* anything different would have caused heavy casualties to friendly forces.[44] While this might constitute a disregard of direct orders, it is an indication of the capability that can be provided by a networked force that can achieve cognitive cohesion.

This then reinforces the fact that self-synchronisation is only possible in a bottom-up approach and, therefore, is in absolute contrast to the functioning of the armed forces. Traditionally, military forces have been strictly hierarchical, with clear and defined information and decision flow directions. Military formations have always been characterised by strong centralisation, top-down command and control directives and bottom-up feedback chain. The intent of the commander is transmitted from the top down to the last mile. However, should a force resort to self-synchronisation, it is clear that intense levels of information and awareness sharing would take place laterally, something that may not be possible within appropriate timeframes in a standard chain of command. Would this aspect, among many others, bring in a change[45] in how militaries the world over are organised? Would it change the way they function? These questions would need to be answered on the way to a net enabled force structure. At this stage, it would suffice to understand the implied changes such a technology is likely to bring about and work from ground zero to prepare the forces for the impending requirements.

On the one hand, while it is right to say that self-synchronisation is more a function of the human element armed with cohesive cognitive capabilities built through common training and education patterns, a share of the credit must also go to technology. After all, it is technology that provides an opportunity and permits human capability to extend itself to provide the enhanced combat effectiveness. In this specific case, technology allows for an "*extended line of sight* capability. Hitherto, most combat operations were controlled based on what could be seen visually (unaided line of sight). This has been so for the past few centuries. Commanders atop a hill (high feature) could see greater distances (line of sight) and thereby control operations by various means (visual signals) such as indications by waving flags, blowing trumpets/ bugles, etc. As the battlefield extended (beyond immediate line of sight), the same responsibilities were delegated to those below in the hierarchical chain of command—those in the immediate tactical area. In times much closer to date, technology has permitted images of battlefields, via sensors, to be transmitted to the commanders who are geographically removed from the battle, enabling their planning of operations. However, execution is done by those in the tactical vicinity and is based on information provided by the top. Therefore, there has been an increase in visual ranges, albeit technologically, and this is being touted as the *extended line of sight*. With the kind of technology available today, it is possible to ensure that sensors can provide information from well ahead of troops/ in remote locations such that transparency of the battlefield is at new highs. This means that troops will *always be able to see* the enemy, no matter what the geographical disposition may be. It may be appropriate at this point to say that this extended line of sight and self-synchronisation of the human element/ group could actually be termed as a force multiplier effect in NCO. In fact, while NCW allows for such capabilities and effects to be further enhanced, these capabilities have a symbiotic relationship with the overall concept and would enable a change in war-fighting methodology.

What follows is that the importance and the centrality of the cognitive domain can never be overemphasised. Nevertheless, the question remains: is the networked war-fighter ready cognitively? Deeper insight into such technology would help in greater clarity about the cognitive readiness required to operate in a truly networked environment. In fact, understanding the implications of the technology and its impact on the war-fighter is just the first rung of the steep NCO ladder. There are numerous steps that need to be taken on the way to a truly networked force. Cognitive readiness is one such important aspect and there is a need to understand what effects and what kind of impact the technology would have on the cognitive capability of the war-fighter. Decision-making processes by themselves place a premium on the war-fighter and so it would be correct to presume that operational capabilities like those covered earlier, including self-synchronisation, would place heavy demands on the mental faculties of the networked warrior. However, there are some other factors also and the subsequent paragraphs would elaborate on a few such issues.

While it would be right to surmise that the operational capabilities of proactive planning, dynamic sychronisation, time sensitive targeting and self-synchronisation have been capabilities that were always available, albeit in a rudimentary form, there is no denying the fact that the concept of network-centricity has exponentially enhanced the same capabilities to unimaginable performance levels. Also, the network makes it possible to extend the same capabilities to increasingly larger units and organisations. Now while a networked environment facilitates these operational capabilities, the cognitive functions of situational awareness, anticipation, judgment, initiative and choice of courses of action bridge the gap between availability of the capability and its implementation. Desired military/ operational results depend upon the speed of response and the focus on the command's intent and this depends on the ability to perform complex mental operations – operations involving the pre-frontal cortex of the human brain – the seat of initiative and planning, reason and emotion and synchronisation.[46] This is the part of the brain in which processes such as creating choices for courses of action and forecasting results of actions and events take place. Directly, therefore, these cognitive abilities contribute towards enhancing the three functional capabilities as mentioned by Fred Stein, namely, predictive planning, dynamic synchronisation and time critical mission execution.

However, these are the very capabilities that are exacerbated by the various stressors that a war-fighter is exposed to today. Among others, these stressors include heat and cold, fatigue, loss of sleep, dehydration, etc. Cognitive and mental capabilities outlined earlier do get adversely affected by these environmental stressors and a major impact is clearly seen in the case of *sleep loss.*[47] In today's networked battle space, the enhanced transparency of the battle space that the network provides enables a continuous flow of information that is sifted, analysed, stored, evaluated into intelligence and utilised for creating alternatives and choosing courses of action. For this to happen, sensors are tasked round the clock to provide the data, and the response is consequent only to the decision being reached or a course of action being arrived at. The capability of sensors today permits decision-makers to *see* and *be seen* at all times, irrespective of the time of day, the weather or the type of medium. In sum, the war-fighter of today (and the future) is constantly *"awake"* unlike his counterparts of yesteryears who may have fought in an era limited by the sensor/ equipment and governed by diurnal changes and events. If the requirement is to "remain awake", then it is only logical to assume that lack of sleep would adversely affect the cognitive capabilities of the individual. It has been found that sleep restrictions adversely affect the speed of response to simple tasks as well as complex operations associated with the pre-frontal cortex of the brain, such as the ability to anticipate, generate and execute plans of action, maintain situational awareness and carry out critical reasoning.[48] As a corroboration, there are documented incidents of friendly fire in the 1990-91 Gulf War that were supposedly triggered due to sleep loss induced loss of situational awareness leading to reduced ability to distinguish friend from foe – a basic but complex cognitive ability.[49]

Lack of sleep, fatigue, heat and cold, stress, etc would all lead to reduction in vigilance, response time, logical reasoning and would also result in greater rigidity, task shedding and fewer alternatives being considered.[50] This does not imply that a war-fighter would get more affected if he is in a networked environment as compared to a non-networked environment. Nor does it imply that his operational performance would be more vulnerable. The argument just goes to show that cognitive capabilities are likely to be more prominent when looked at from the operational outcome point of view in a networked environment. Also, there are distinct possibilities that the network itself would be able to offset some of the disadvantages of its own creating.[51] However, it is amply clear that networked environment notwithstanding, a basic factor like loss of sleep could become a critical hindrance in attaining optimum capabilities of the force.[52] The importance of the cognitive domain is being emphasised here and this is a prime requirement. The hardware and software that make up the network may appear to be vulnerable. However, redundancy is built in by providing back-up systems at most stages, providing multiple routes for transmission of information and decentralising the entire architecture. Once the information has been analysed, it must result into decision superiority and this brings into play the cognitive domain, the processes within and the cognitive capability and adaptability of the war-fighter. Available explanations of the entire cognitive process and the decision-making leave no room for doubt that this process of converting a stimulus to a desired response is riddled with uncertainty, and it is chiefly because of the human dimension.

The environmental factors briefly discussed are only a few and the list is by no means exhaustive. Therefore, if the business end of the network could have reduced performance ability due to adverse impact on the cognitive capability of the war-fighter, what is required is to maintain cognitive capabilities that are critical to a network enabled force by predicting the states of cognitive readiness in the troops deployed or otherwise. To do this, there is a need to manage cognitive capabilities for which these need to be measured first. There have been attempts in the past to measure cognitive capabilities in the field but these have not yielded success due to the inability to quantify effective performance. Presently, a lot of work is being done in this field, in terms of considering such physiological factors as items of logistical resupply and preparing models to do the same. This aspect is being addressed in a three-pronged manner, by measuring factors that cause variations in mental performance, by using tests through which to infer operational performance and, lastly, by using a mix of the two.[53] As an example of the first solution, current technology allows measuring the sleep history by simply strapping on an electronic device (sleep watch actigraph), like a watch on the wrist of a war-fighter. This is significant as sleep loss directly reduces operational cognitive abilities and, hence, being able to quantify it is important for the commander. This is worn on the wrist and is a standalone digital device that permits the measurement of an individual's history of being awake or asleep and thereafter prediction of performance.[54] Then there are various tasks that can be conducted, even in the field, which could help in the assessment of cognitive readiness. An example is the Psychomotor Vigilance Task (PVT)[55], which is a simple reaction time task that can be conducted in the field. The PVT is known to be responsive to even slight amounts of sleep restrictions[56] and, hence, has been integrated into the Personal Data Assistant (PDA) of the war-fighter. What this task does is measure the response time or the latency in reaction. In the OODA loop theory, "orient" is by far the most important as it represents the central cognitive function in the decision-making process. And if the entire effort of a decision process is to do it faster than the opponent, that is, stay inside the OODA loop of the opponent, then time and, hence, its reciprocal, speed, become significant.[57] To that extent, the reaction time task would appear to be appropriate to predict simple readiness tasks. A final solution could be a synthesis of both measures discussed so far and would include creating mathematical models, specific to individuals, to predict cognitive readiness. Such a model, the Fatigue Intervention and Recovery Model (FIRM), developed in the Walter Reed Army Institute of Research Sleep Performance Model (WRSPM), is integrated with the Sleep Activity Fatigue and Task Effectiveness (SAFTE) model and provides commanders with a means of quantifying the soldier's operational effectiveness as a measure of his sleep/ wake cycle and the time of day.[58] The model has three primary functions, namely, the *sleep function* that describes restoration of cognitive abilities, the *wake function* that describes the degradation in cognitive capability while awake and the *circadian modulator*that describes the cyclic variations in performance based on the time of the day. While a lot of research is currently being done on similar issues, integrating all the required data and measurements into the War-Fighter Physiological Status Monitor (WPSM) is still a long way off and is work in progress.

Conclusion

Network Centric Operations, by virtue of the architecture, would result in a humungous increase in information from ever increasing information sources – sources increasing as the levels of networking increases. This would consequently result in very high and intense pace of operations while at the same time bringing in greater degrees of ambiguity and uncertainty. While it is clear that the network architecture can manage incomprehensible volumes of data at incredible speeds, it is equally clear that unless all this data can be transformed into information that leads to superior decision-making ability, consequently translating to desired responses on the ground, the entire effort would come to naught. This transformation of information to a decision and, finally, to the response, depends on the critical factor of cognitive capability of the war-fighter. It is in this cognitive domain that the processes of sharing mental models, information and awareness would provide a shared understanding, leading to the war-fighter's advantage. Only then would it translate to achieving the command's intent.

The paper has sought to bring into focus the centrality of the human dimension when placed against the vast canvas of network-centric operations. NCW must exist to finally support human intentions and plans and yet till date, the primary focus of research into this field has been limited to improvements and innovations in technology only. This is with an underlying assumption that advances in automation would naturally lead to better human and system performance. Of late, there has been a realisation that this tremendous potential that is on offer is, however, quite vulnerable, should there be a failure of the human element. Therefore, and rightly so, there has been a shift in focus, with attention being given to the war-fighter and the cognitive processes that he has to undergo in order to optimally derive the advantages provided by the networked environment. Without this dedicated effort, the vision of a networked force operating with shared awareness, increased speed of command, self-synchronisation and operational tempo may morph into a sub-optimal and reactive network that *might result in only automating* the entire process of war-fighting. The advantage of network-centricity is accrued only if it changes war-fighting, not merely improves it.Understanding cognitive processes and attempting to predict the readiness in that domain, is still work in progress. However, the fact that adequate importance is being given to the war-fighter is a positive shift, one that would ensure that network-centric operations and network-centric warfare will remain the flavour of the day and will drive the revolution in military affairs in the times to come.

Notes

1. Franklin Spinney and Genghis John, "Proceedings", July 1997, pp. 42-47.
2. "Network-Centric Warfare: Department of Defense Report to Congress", Office of the Secretary of Defence, US Department of Defence, Washington DC, 2001.
3. "The Implementation of Network-Centric Warfare", Office of Force Transformation, Office of the Secretary of Defence, Department of Defence, Washington DC, p. 20.
4. Edward A Smith. *Effects Based Operations: Applying Network Centric Warfare in Peace, Crisis and War* (CCRP Publication, 2002), p. 158.
5. Alberts et al. "Understanding Information Age Warfare" CCRP Publication, 2001,.pp. 131 -133.
6. Ibid., n. 4, p. 158.
7. Miller James Grier, *Living Systems* (Denver: McGraw-Hill, 1995), p.9.
8. Ibid., n. 4. p. 159.
9. "Report of the Workshop on Sense Making,",*DODCCRP/ Evidence Based Research*, Tysons Corner, March 2001.
10. Ibid., n. 4, p. 161.
11. Ibid., n. 4, p. 162.
12. Ibid,, n. 5, p. 16.
13. Ibid., n. 4, p. 164.
14. Ibid., n. 5, pp. 16-17.
15. Ibid., n. 4, p. 166.
16. Ibid., n. 4, p. 167.
17. Ibid., n. 5, p. 16.
18. Ibid., n. 4, p. 169.
19. Ibid., n. 4, p. 170.
20. Ibid., n. 4, p. 171.
21. Ibid., n. 5, p. 17.
22. Ibid., n. 4, pp. 172-174.
23. Ibid.
24. Ibid.
25. Ibid.
26. Ibid., n. 5, p. 18.
27. Ibid., n. 4, p. 176.
28. Ibid., n. 4, p. 177.
29. Ibid.
30. Ibid., n. 4, pp. 179-182.
31. Ibid.
32. Ibid.
33. Ibid.
34. Ibid., n. 4, p. 184.
35. Ibid.
36. Ibid., n 4, p. 186.
37. Office of the Secretary of Defence, Office of Net Assessment Summer Study, Authors Notes, 1995.
38. SLA Marshall, *The Soldier's Land and the Mobility of a Nation* (Quantico, Va: Marine Corps Association, , 1980), p. 75.
39. Arthur K Cebrowski and John Gartska, "Network-Centric Warfare: Its Origin and Future," *Proceedings*, January 1998, p. 28.
40. Fred Stein, "Observations on the Emergence of Network Centric-Warfare," DoD Command and Control Research Programme, 1998, http://www.dodccrp.org/research/ncw/stein_

observations/steinncw.htm. Accessed March 20, 2015.

41. **http://www.red3d.com/cwr/boids/. Accessed March 23, 2015.**
42. A Hachinski, "Irreducible Semi-Autonomous Adaptive Combat (ISAAC): An Artificial Life Approach to Land Combat", Centre for Naval Analyses Research Memorandum CRM 97-61.10 (Alexandria, Va: Centre for Naval Analyses, 1997).
43. Nancy J Wesensten, Gregory Belensky and Thomas J Balkin, *Cognitive Readiness in Network Centric Operations, (*2005), p. 96.
44. Stephen Biddle, "Victory Misunderstood: What the Gulf War Tells us About the Future of Conflict", *International Security*, 1996, pp. 139-141
45. Wesensten, et al., "By enabling more extended self-synchronisation, netwok centric operations are likely to change the balance between bottom-up initiative and top-down directive in favour of bottom-up initiative – an initial shift in balance that is already evidenced by the Army's decision to eliminate divisions in favour of a brigade based organization,". Ibid., n. 43, p. 95
46. Ibid., p. 99.
47. Ibid.
48. Yvonne Harrison and James A Horne, "One Night of Sleep Loss Impairs Innovative Thinking and Flexible Decision Making," *OrganisationalBehaviour and Human Decision Processes,* May 1999, pp. 128-145.

    Ibid., n. 43, p. 99.
49. Gregory Belenky, James A Martin and Scott C Marcy, "Debriefings and Battle Reconstructions Following Combat," *The Gulf War and Mental Health: A Comprehensive Guide* (Westport 1996), pp. 105-114.

    Ibid., n. 43, p.100.
50. Mark A Staal, *Stress, Cognition andHuman Performance: A Literature Revision* (Moffett Field, California: NASA Ames Research Centre, August 2004), pp. 43, 77.
51. Ibid., n. 43, pp. 99-100.
52. **Ibid.**
53. **Ibid., n. 43, p 101.**
54. **Ibid.**
55. David F Dinges and John W Powell, "Microcomputer Analyses of Performance on a Portable, Simple Visual RT Task During Sustained Operations," *Behavioural Research Methods, Instruments and Computers,* 17, 1985, pp. 652-655.
56. GiegoryBelensky, Nancy J Wesensten, Thorne, et al: "Comparative Utility of Instruments for Monitoring Sleepiness-Related Performance Decrements in the Operational Environment," *Journal of Sleep Research,* 13, 2004, pp. 219-227.
57. Ibid., n. 43, p. 102.
58. SR Hursh, DP Redmond, ML Johnson, "Fatigue Models for Applied Research in Warfighting", *Aviat Space Environ Med2004,* 75, no. 3, pp. 44 –53.